AS/A-LEVEL
AQA (A) Psychology

Paul Humphreys
Roger Cocks
Colin Crampton
Eamon Fulcher
Berenice Mahoney
Steve Ward

Exam
Revision
Notes

WITHDRAWN

Philip Allan Updates
Market Place
Deddington
Oxfordshire
OX15 0SE

tel: 01869 338652
fax: 01869 337590
e-mail: sales@philipallan.co.uk
www.philipallan.co.uk

ISBN 0 86003 431 3

Cover illustration by John Spencer
Printed by Raithby, Lawrence & Co. Ltd, Leicester

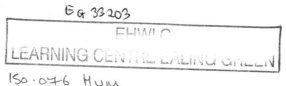

Contents

Introduction

About this book

This book should provide you with all the guidance and focus that you need to do well in AQA(A) AS and A-level examinations.

As you will have noted from the title of the book, these are *exam revision notes*. It is worth considering the implications of this. The fact that it is concerned with *exam* preparation is important. It is likely that you will be making the most use of the book in your build-up to the exams themselves (rather than as you write your class essays or do your mock exams, for example). However, many students take modular rather than terminal exam courses. This book will serve the needs of both groups of students. However, the groups will almost certainly use the book in different ways: modular students will be using it throughout most of their course, whereas the terminal exam students will probably only really get involved with it in the last couple of terms.

The word *revision* triggers one of the key assumptions we make about you, the reader. The word literally means to see again. In other words the topics, concepts, theories and studies should already be familiar to you from the textbooks you have used, your school/college classes, and your wider reading (e.g. articles from publications such as *Psychology Review* and internet searches). Clearly this book serves a very different function from a textbook and we can only point you in the right directions. So if we say that in order to really understand topic X you will need to be familiar with theory Y and study Z, you will need to make sure you are familiar with these and know them in detail. We can only give thumbnail sketches and summarise main points and findings (otherwise, this would turn into a textbook itself!). This is also reflected in the final word in the title, *notes*; the bullet-point approach, free of dense text, should help you see through to the bare bones of what you need to know. It is then for you to be able to elaborate on this.

> What you will find in this book is a list of the things which you need to know and the things you need to be able to do.

Any book can only do so much. It is for you to make it 'come alive'. By this we mean you should endeavour to make it interactive: innumerable psychological studies have shown that active learning is far superior to passive learning. Carefully think about the specimen questions. It will be time well spent. Look up things with which you are unfamiliar. Make your own notes and always read critically (ask yourself *why* a particular finding is important, *why* a particular study is relevant to answering a specific question and so on) — never just let the words drift past your eyes!

Please don't turn the pages expecting to see a set of the 'right' answers to questions. Most examiners get very alarmed if they hear that students are trying to rote learn model answers. There are at least two very good reasons for this. Firstly, psychology isn't the kind of discipline where there is just one right answer to a question — it's not like mathematics. Secondly, an answer will only earn marks insofar as it answers the exact question set on the exam paper. Just a slight change of wording requires a change in the balance and content of the answer.

Throughout the book you will find there is extensive reference to 'names and dates', e.g. 'Bartlett (1932) believed that...'. This is a standard academic convention which gives authority to what you are writing in your answers (rather than 'I think that...'), and shows that you give a source for an experiment, a definition, etc. Don't worry about having to remember them all, just do the best you can. If you can include some it will impress the examiner, but he or she won't 'knock marks off' if you can't remember them. So think of them as a way of possibly gaining credit, but the credit which you will have earned with them won't be taken away. We have included them as it is the recognised way of writing in psychology (there will be many more in your textbook!), and to give you the opportunity to use them where you can and to be able find the studies, theories, etc. in your textbooks.

The book is specifically written to the AQA(A) specification. Although students taking other examinations will find much of interest and help here, we have chosen to focus specifically on the one examination so that students taking it will not have to wade through volumes of material which has no relevance or use to them, and have uncertainties about which sections are relevant and which are not. If you are taking the AQA(A) AS and/or A-level exams, *everything* in this book is relevant to you.

We have to assume that you want to succeed in your exams. This presumably is why you have bought the book. We're talking attitude here, and attitude is half the battle. As one fitness instructor said, 'No pain, no gain'. For our part, we have tried to make the book as easy to read and as enjoyable as any revision guide can be, but the rest is down to you. Roll those sleeves up and let's get going!

The AS exam

Before we begin in earnest, we need to define three key terms. As we have already mentioned, the syllabus (the content of your course) is now called the **specification**; the sub-parts of the specification (e.g. Cognitive and Developmental Psychology) are called **modules**; and the exams are now called **unit tests** — these can be taken in January and June of each year. Enough of the jargon!

Exam preparation and performance

As you prepare for the examination you need to have covered the material listed in the specification (your teacher will have a copy of this and will provide you with one — but you may need to ask). The questions set in the unit tests (doesn't have quite the same ring as 'exams', does it?) will sample the whole range of the content, so you must ensure that you have covered everything and left nothing out. Don't worry if this sounds daunting, there isn't actually a lot of content in the specification. Cognitive Psychology, for example, is made up of short-term and long-term memory, forgetting, and eyewitness testimony. If the specification names a particular theory or work carried out by a particular psychologist (for example, 'the multi-store model of memory [Atkinson and Shiffrin] and alternatives to this, including working memory [Baddeley and Hitch] and levels of processing [Craik and Lockhart]' in Cognitive Psychology), you *must* cover these as they can be specified in the question. If, however, the specification uses the term 'e.g.' (for example, 'explanations of forgetting in long-term memory [e.g., retrieval failure and interference]'), this is only for guidance and you cannot be asked a question directly on the examples given.

The item test skills

Modules 1–3 (Cognitive and Developmental Psychology; Physiological Psychology and Individual Differences; Social Psychology and Research Methods) are assessed through two skills. These are called Assessment Objective 1 (AO1 for short) and Assessment Objective 2 (AO2). Quite simply, AO1 requires a clear and effective communication of your *knowledge and understanding* of a particular topic; AO2 requires *evaluation and analysis*. Knowledge and understanding are essentially descriptive; for example, a demonstration that you know the main features of Atkinson and Shiffrin's multi-store model of memory. This is rather like retelling the story line of a film you have seen. Evaluation and analysis is like adding commentary (that part of the film worked well because...). We can think of analysis as taking things (such as a theory) apart and looking at the constituent elements, and evaluation as an appraisal of their worth (what are the good features of the theory and what are its weaknesses?).

The structure of the questions

All of the questions assessing Modules 1 and 2, and also the Social Psychology part of Module 3 (we will deal with the special case of Research Methods later), are set to a particular formula. Unit Test 1 will contain four questions: two on Cognitive Psychology, two on Developmental Psychology. You will be required to answer one of the Cognitive Psychology ones and one of the Developmental Psychology ones. The same arrangement holds for Unit Test 2 on Physiological Psychology and Individual Differences (four questions, answer one on each section). The first half of Unit Test 3 will contain two Social Psychology questions, of which you will need to answer one.

The good news is that all of these questions must follow a particular format. In each of them 30 marks are up for grabs; 18 of these are AO1 marks, 12 are AO2. Furthermore, the 12 AO2 marks are always contained in the last part of the question. Make sure you remember that.

AO1 questions will deal with:

- giving **definitions** or identifying **differences** between psychological factors or concepts (either 2 marks each or 3 marks each). For example, 'What do we mean by short-term memory? Give three differences between short-term and long-term memory'

- identifying **factors** which contribute to our understanding of something (3 marks each). For example, 'Describe factors which have been found to be associated with secure attachment'

- describing a **theory** (6 marks each). For example, 'Describe the model of working memory developed by Baddeley and Hitch'

- describing a **study** (6 marks each). For example, 'Describe the procedures and findings of any one study into conformity'. In these questions it will be specified that you will need to address two of the following: **aims**; **procedures**; **findings**; **conclusions**. Any two from the four can be asked for. Aims refers to why the study was carried out; procedures to what the researchers actually did; findings to their results; and conclusions to how they interpreted their results. **It is vital that you have something to write on all of these, so bear this in mind when you are doing your revision.** Questions can only ask you to focus on aims, procedures, findings or conclusions, or give criticisms if the word 'research' is explicitly used in the specification. Check carefully **now** with a highlighter pen to hand

- giving **criticisms** (3 marks each). For example, 'Give two criticisms of the multi-store model of memory'

AO2 questions require you to:

- evaluate (you can be positive or negative)

- be analytical (reduce ideas to their constituent elements)

We will consider examples of the sorts of questions you can expect as we work our way through the specification. Make sure you practise answering as many of them as you can before you take your unit tests.

How much should I aim to write?

As we have already noted, in Unit Tests 1 and 2 you have to answer two questions in one hour. Allowing essential time for reading the questions, making your choices, planning your answers and checking them through for mistakes at the end, you will probably have no more than 25 minutes writing time for each question. The average candidate can write about 500 words in 25 minutes (try it!). This means that each 6 marks 'block' should take about 5 minutes of writing time and be about 100 words in length. We cannot over-emphasise how important it is that you allocate your time appropriately. Just think through what a disaster it would be if you spent 10 minutes on question parts carrying 3 marks, and spent only 5 minutes on the last part of the question which carries 18 marks.

What about Research Methods?

Research Methods is assessed in the second half of Unit Test 3. This is the only time that you will have no question choice — there is just one question. This question assesses your ability to design a psychological investigation (experiment, etc.), know how it could be carried out appropriately and know how to interpret the results from the investigation.

The Research Methods part of the unit test contains two different kinds of questions.

The first question will give you a brief description of a fictitious study and will then ask you a series of questions about it (for example, 'What was the independent variable in this study?' 'What would be an appropriate null hypothesis for this study?'). As part of the overall question, you will also be asked more open-ended questions, e.g. 'There are several shortcomings of the study. Describe one and say how it could have been dealt with'.

How will my work be marked?

This is an easy one. In the AO3 (Research Methods) questions, the general rule is that full marks are given for accurate answers, e.g. (3/3; 2/2); answers which are partially accurate but may be muddled or brief will get 1–2/3 or 1/2; and inaccurate answers will get zero.

For the remainder of the questions, the marking scheme is as follows.

AO1 questions:

Marks for 3 mark questions	Marks for 6 mark questions	Criteria
3	6–5	Accurate and detailed (*well* detailed for 6 mark questions)
2	4–3	Generally accurate but less detailed; limited
1	2–1	Basic; lacking in detail; muddled; flawed
0	0	Inaccurate or irrelevant

AO2 questions:

Marks	Commentary (e.g. evaluation)	Analysis	Use of material
12–11	Informed	Thorough	Highly effective
10–9	Informed	Reasonably thorough	Effective
8–7	Reasonable	Slightly limited	Effective
6–5	Reasonable	Limited	Reasonably effective
4–3	Superficial	Rudimentary	Minimal interpretation
2–1	Just discernible	Weak and muddled	Mainly irrelevant
0	Wholly irrelevant	Wholly irrelevant	Wholly irrelevant

The A2 exam

The A2 is the second half of the new A-level qualification. One important thing to remember is that although it has stand-alone status (i.e. is separate from the AS in both content and having different unit tests), it is not a separate qualification. You don't get an A2 in psychology; success at A2 — following success at AS — gives you the A-level.

Your final grade will be determined by simply adding together your AS and A2 scores. So it is possible, though not advisable(!), to fail the AS but still pass the A-level (e.g. fail the AS by 5 marks but pass the A2 by 6). So never give up! Let's consider just what the AS and the A2 have in common and in what ways they are different.

Similarities between the AS and A2 courses
- Most of the subject areas are the same. Cognitive, Developmental, Physiological and Social Psychology are common to both, as is Individual Differences. Research Methods, however, is only in the AS course; Comparative Psychology, Perspectives, and Approaches to Psychology are only in the A2 course.
- Parts of the modules which you learned for the AS course may still be useful to you in the A2 course. For example, you will have covered ethics in Module 3 of the AS course; this is also one of the topic areas in Module 5 in the A2 course. You will have covered different psychological models/approaches (e.g. psychodynamics and bio-psychology) and different methods used by psychologists (e.g. experiments and interviews) in the AS course; these are again relevant to Module 5 in the A2 course. Finally, in the Perspectives part of Module 5 are a number of issues and debates (gender bias; culture bias; ethical issues; the use of non-human animals in psychology; free will/determinism; reductionism; psychology as a science; the nature–nurture debate). You can use studies and theories you learned about in your AS course to help you write Module 5 essays on these issues and debates. Some examples are:

Useful for	AS topic
Gender bias	Stress and gender
Cultural bias	Attachment; social influence
Ethical issues	Ethical issues in social influence
Use of non-human animals in psychology	Harlow's research into attachment; Brady's research into stress
Free will/determinism	Genetic explanations of abnormality; situational determinism in obedience
Reductionism	Learning theory
Psychology as a science	Laboratory experiments (e.g. those in memory research)
The nature–nurture debate	Biological vs psychological explanations of abnormality

- Both AS and A2 measure the same skill clusters: AO1 (knowledge and understanding), AO2 (analysis and evaluation) and AO3 (the ability to design, carry out research and analyse results). In the AS course, however, the AO3 skill is measured by Research Methods (Unit 3), whereas it is assessed by coursework in A2.
- The amount of time you have per question — 30 minutes — is the same in Unit 4 (A2) as in the AS unit tests. Unit 5 questions in the A2 course, however, each have a 40 minute allowance.

Differences between the AS and A2 courses
- Different topics within areas of psychology are studied. For example, the AS Developmental Psychology covers the development and variety of attachments, deprivation and privation, and day care; in the A2 course, cognitive development, social and personality development, and adulthood are covered.

- There is more psychological content in the A2 part of the specification than the AS.
- Whereas you have to cover everything in the AS specification, you can be *very* selective in the A2. There is a guarantee of a question being set on every sub-section of the A2 course (e.g. adulthood in the Developmental Psychology section). *You must ensure that you cover a minimum of three sub-sections of the A2 specification, of which a maximum of two may be taken from the same section. In the case of Developmental Psychology, for example, you would not be allowed to answer questions on all three sub-sections. So you might do two from Developmental Psychology and one from Physiological Psychology, for example. Do bear in mind, though, that covering just three sub-sections gives you no choice in the unit test, so try to cover, say, a couple more if possible.*
- You will need to be familiar with the following terms which are used in A2 unit test questions. This was unnecessary in AS.
  - AO1 only terms: **Define**; **Describe**; **Explain**; **Outline**. (Outline requires a concise, short description only.)
  - AO2 only terms: **Analyse**; **Assess**; **Evaluate**; **To what extent**.
  - AO1 and AO2 terms: **Compare and contrast**; **Critically consider**; **Discuss**.

  You will also need to know what the following terms, used in A2 questions, mean:
  - **Applications**: actual or possible ways of using psychological knowledge in an applied/practical setting.
  - **Evidence**: material from studies or theories that may be used in support or contradiction of an argument or theory.
  - **Findings**: the outcome or product of research.
  - **Model**: an explanation which is less complex/elaborate than a theory.
  - **Research**: the process of gaining knowledge through the examination of data derived empirically or theoretically.
  - **Study**: an investigation providing evidence which may be empirical or non-empirical (such as meta-analysis).
  - **Theory**: a (usually) complex set of interrelated ideas/assumptions/principles intended to explain or account for certain observed phenomena.

  These 'examiner speak' definitions do sound a little formal, but try to remember them.
- Although both AS and A2 measure the same skill clusters, the marking schemes are different. In AS questions the mark-a-minute rule applies, so you may be asked to describe a theory for 6 marks and have around 5 or 6 minutes worth of writing time to do this. The basic building block of the AS unit test questions is 6 marks (reduced down to 2s and 3s for basic questions and doubled up to 12 for the AO2 parts of the questions at the end).
  - The basic building block of the A2 Unit 4 questions is 24 marks, although this may be halved (or even quartered) for more basic questions. To put it in examiner jargon, the A2 questions give you far more opportunity for extended writing. To put it in common English, it's about writing essays!
  - The basic building block of the A2 Unit 5 questions is 30 marks, although again this may be reduced down (e.g. 15 + 15). In case you are wondering why the Unit 5 questions carry 30 marks each and the Unit 4 ones 24, there are two reasons: (i) you have longer to answer them (40 minutes instead of 30); and (ii) Unit 5 is more heavily weighted (40% of the A2 marks, instead of 30% for Unit 4; coursework carries the remaining 30%).
- In the AS you will only ever be asked to describe one study or one theory concerning a particular topic. In the A2, however, you can be asked to address more than one. If you are asked to describe and evaluate two explanations for depression, for example, and you only offer one, you will be judged to have displayed partial performance, by

which we mean only partially satisfying the requirements of the question; the marks you can earn will be capped. Don't say you haven't been warned.

- The final part of AS questions *may* be led by a vignette, or short quotation. However, there is no requirement for the student to make any direct reference to the quotation. Some A2 questions also make use of quotations, but here you will generally be required to specifically address the quotation itself. The wording of the question will make this clear, for example 'With reference to the quotation above, discuss issues that it raises'. The quotation should be regarded as a mini-piece of stimulus material which you need to interact with. A failure to do so will again result in a pegging of the maximum mark you can earn.
- In the A2 paper there is a very different style of question, in the Approaches to Psychology section in Unit 5. See Topic 12 for a detailed discussion.

Unit 4

There are three AO1 criteria: the **accuracy of the psychological content**; **breadth and depth**; and **construction and organisation**. The last criterion reinforces the point about this module being concerned with essay writing. Answers which have a high content of relevant psychological knowledge but are just 'dumped' on the page by the student will score poorly on the construction and organisation criterion. The breadth and depth will usually be determined by the wording of the question. For example, 'Outline and evaluate two theories of attribution' is specific, but 'Discuss research about stereotyping' is not. With the second question, try to discuss two or three theories or studies in detail and several others as background.

There are also three AO2 criteria for Unit 4. From the grid above you will see that they are **commentary**, **elaboration** and **use of material**.

By 'commentary' we are referring to that which goes beyond a descriptive account (of theories, studies, etc.). The best way to think about this is the difference between a football match covered live by radio and television. On the radio, because there are no pictures, there has to be a literal description of what is happening. This is what is called ball-by-ball commentary in the trade. On television, however, because the viewer has visual access to what is happening on the field, the commentator's job is a different one. He or she interprets and analyses the game, rather than just saying X passes to Y who centres to Z who scores. AO1 is descriptive, it is a re-telling of what the psychologist did and what he or she found. AO2 is the commentary — what it means, what it tells us, how good or flawed it is, and so on.

'Elaboration' means that to earn decent marks you need to avoid one-liners for your evaluation and analysis. Saying that Freud is sexist would earn a little credit, but you really need to elaborate the point. For instance, an example of Freud's sexism would be his notion that women suffer from penis envy, but one might also add that Freud was writing a hundred years ago and by today's standards most people were sexist!

'Use of material' means that you need to show the examiner not only that you know a decent amount of psychology but also that you can use it to answer a specific question. An example would be the difference between just discussing a number of studies on television and violence, and what these studies actually tell us about whether television viewing is associated with violence, for instance in children. Once again, don't just dump your psychology onto the page, make it work and use it to answer the specific question on the paper.

Unit 5

Unit 5 is unlike all the rest of the unit tests in that it is concerned with synopticity, and as such has a fourth criterion under both AO1 and AO2. The example of the top band for AO1 is given below.

Band	Mark allocation	
Band 6	Psychological content in relation to the approach which could explain the topic in question is cited which is **accurate** and **well detailed** at the level of knowledge, description and understanding. The organisation and structure are **presented coherently**. There is substantial evidence of breadth and depth and an **appropriate balance** between these is achieved. There is clear evidence of a range of synoptic possibilities relating to the issues raised by the question.	6 marks

Unit 5 is a synoptic paper. What do we mean by synopticity? The examining board define it as 'affording a general view of the whole'. It addresses psychology-wide matters and concerns. In short, it's an overview. For example, in Social Psychology in Module 4 you might study 'nature and causes of aggression'. Some studies will be specific to this part of the specification, but you will also learn about psychological models, for example behaviourism and bio-psychological alternatives (as a critique of behaviourism). You will also see examples of different psychological methodologies being used (e.g. the laboratory experiment). These are psychology-wide issues. Synopticity, in practice, is measured by demonstrating any of the following criteria:

- different explanations or perspectives (e.g. behaviourism; psychoanalysis)
- different methods used in psychological research (e.g. laboratory experiment; interview)
- relating material to overarching issues and debates. This includes those in Perspectives (Module 5)
- making links with other areas of the specification (e.g. your AS material, as discussed earlier)

The Perspectives and Approaches to Psychology questions in Unit 5 will clearly identify how you address the synoptic requirement (see Topic 12 of these Revision Notes), but in Individual Differences you will need to ensure that you add the synopticity yourself. Let's take an example. Look again at the list of four ways of delivering synopticity given above. The Individual Differences question 'Compare and contrast biological and psychological explanations of schizophrenia' is synoptic in itself according to the first criterion (two explanations), but the question 'Critically consider whether Multiple Personality Disorder is iatrogenic or spontaneous' is not as it does not fit any of the four criteria.

In the Individual Differences part of Unit 5, always remember to infuse synopticity into your answer.

Topics 1–6 cover what you need to know for AS, topics 7–10 for Unit 4 and 11–12 for Unit 5.

1 Short-term and long-term memory, and alternative models

1.1 SHORT-TERM AND LONG-TERM MEMORY

Essential definitions

- **Encoding** occurs where information is processed in a manner that allows it to become internally represented; in other words, external sensory information or stimuli become units of memory held in **storage**.
- **Capacity** refers to the volume or amount of information that can be stored in memory.
- **Duration** can mean the length of time that the memory is held, or the length of time taken for retrieval of a memory.

Explain the main features of encoding, capacity and duration of short-term memory. (2+2+2 marks)

The distinction between short-term and long-term memory

William James (1890) suggested that humans have not one, but two memory systems (hence 'Two-Process Theory'): **primary memory**, which is a current system associated with the state of consciousness; and **secondary memory**, which allows storage of past experiences. These two systems can be seen as precursors of **STM** (short-term memory) and **LTM** (long-term memory). Donald Hebb (1949) produced physiological evidence for two such distinctive memory systems, from laboratory studies of nerve cells. Studies of amnesia patients (people suffering from memory loss) supported Hebb's ideas.

Short-term memory is characterised by limited capacity and duration. New information is believed to enter STM, where it is temporarily stored (unless through rehearsal or other active memorisation processes it becomes stored in long-term memory).

> ### Research into short-term memory capacity
>
> George Miller (1956) confirmed the capacity of STM to be, on average, *seven 'bits'* of information (in *most* people within two 'bits' either side of seven).
>
> Miller also found that more information could be stored in STM through a process known as **chunking**. Essentially, single units of information (such as numbers) are grouped together, through meaning. The numbers 2, 0, 0, 1 can be remembered as a single meaningful number, the date 2001 (as in Arthur C. Clarke's *2001 — A Space Odyssey*). Chunking takes up less STM space, leaving more space for other data.

Data stored in STM is vulnerable to loss, through either a rapid '**decay**' of the memory trace (believed to occur after around 30 seconds according to Atkinson and Shiffrin, 1971), or **displacement** by new data entering STM. Information that has entered into STM will, if rehearsed or encoded in a meaningful fashion, become stored in LTM. Essentially, LTM is considered to have almost unlimited capacity, and data that make the transfer from STM to LTM are believed to be stored permanently (this doesn't imply it is easily or permanently accessible, however).

LTM is occasionally divided into subsystems according to purpose. Subdivisions described by Cohen and Squire (1980) are **procedural memory** ('*knowing how*' — memories for procedures, such as riding a bicycle) and **declarative memory** ('*knowing that*' — you may know that you can ride a bicycle).

Tulving (1972) further divides declarative memory into two types: **episodic** and **semantic** memory. Episodic memory refers to an individual's unique set of memories of personal events: their 'autobiographical record of past experience'. Semantic memory refers to memories relating to more general knowledge of the world (such as vocabulary and grammar).

Q Give three differences between long-term memory and short-term memory. (2+2+2 marks)

Evaluation

- Amongst modern researchers there is debate as to the usefulness and validity of the distinction between STM and LTM. There is some evidence of a distinction from early studies of some brain-damaged patients who have shown reduced memory skills *in one system but not the other*.

- However, different models of memory are not consistent in their adoption of the distinction between STM and LTM. Atkinson and Shiffrin's (1968) *Multi-Store Model* of memory makes use of the distinction, whereas Craik and Lockhart's (1972) *Levels of Processing* theory has no need to (both are described in more detail later).

- In terms of the subdivisions of LTM proposed by psychologists such as Cohen and Squire (1980) and Tulving (1972), there seems to be ample evidence from studies of amnesic patients which verifies that distinct memory systems exist. For example, patients with one form of amnesia have been able to verbally describe how a task *should* be done (semantic memory) but when faced with the task, cannot remember how to physically *do* it (procedural memory); while other amnesics can do the task but not describe how it should be done.

Q Explain what is meant by long-term memory and short-term memory and give one difference (other than duration) between them. (2+2+2 marks)

1.2 MODELS OF MEMORY

The Multi-Store Model (Atkinson and Shiffrin, 1968)

The sensory store

This is a short duration store of sensory information. It consists of separate storage for different forms of sensory input, for example an iconic store for visual stimuli, and an echoic store for auditory stimuli. Trace decay results in information being quickly 'lost' from this store. Input that needs attending to by the individual (1/20th of sensory input according to Lloyd, 1984) is translated into a more lasting representation in the short-term store.

$\downarrow$

The short-term store

This store is most analogous to popular understanding of true STM (with space for 7 bits, plus or minus 2). Since it has very limited capacity, data is lost from this store as it is replaced by new material filtered in from the sensory store. In order to become transferred into a more long-term representation in the long-term store, deliberate rehearsal or meaningful encoding is required.

$\downarrow$

The long-term store

The long-term store is thought to possess almost unlimited capacity and duration of trace retention (and is fundamentally the same as other conceptions of LTM). Forgetting can occur here due to problems in retrieving the memory trace amongst numerous similar memories.

Figure 1.1 Multi-Store Model

The model was developed from the ideas of William James (1890), specifically, his 'Two-Process Theory' of memory. It was called the Multi-Store Model since Atkinson and Shiffrin regarded memory as consisting of *three distinct stores*, as shown in Figure 1.1.

Working Memory Model (Baddeley and Hitch, 1974; Hitch and Baddeley, 1976)
Baddeley and Hitch argued that the way the Multi-Store Model operationalised STM was too simplistic and limited in explanatory value. They divided STM into *three components* based on the form of processing each carried out (see Figure 1.2). A fourth component was added later by Baddeley and Lewis (1982) — see research box.

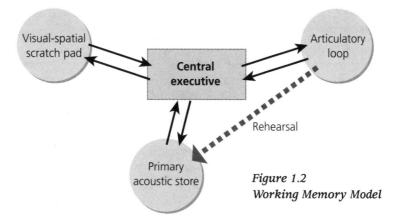

Figure 1.2
Working Memory Model

The **central executive** is the filter ('gatekeeper') that determines what information is and is not attended to. It can process information in any sensory form, and directs information to the other systems and gathers their responses. The executive is limited in its capacity, and research (e.g. Hunt, 1980) suggests that it can only effectively deal with one 'strand' of information at a time.

The articulatory loop is akin to the rehearsal system of Atkinson and Shiffrin's model. Baddeley et al. (1975) suggest that its capacity is limited to what you can say out loud in roughly two seconds.

While the articulatory loop is able to deal with the rehearsal of phonological material (e.g. spoken or 'thought' words), other material is not phonological, such as visual and spatial information. Such is rehearsed and encoded through the visuo-spatial scratchpad. This system forms 'mental pictures'.

> **Research indicating a fourth component of working memory**
> The primary acoustic store was added to the model by Baddeley and Lewis (1981) after discovering that memory of nonsense words was not disrupted by articulatory suppression (where people are not allowed to repeat learned words out loud). They concluded that memory for nonsense words was therefore not reliant upon the articulatory loop, but must use some other memory component. This they called the primary acoustic store, which is believed to be involved in storing recently heard speech or sound.

Levels of Processing Theory (Craik and Lockhart, 1972)
Craik and Lockhart criticised the Multi-Store Model for its oversimplification of rehearsal and how memory traces initially enter into LTM. Their model does not rely upon a distinction between STM and LTM, and regards the duration of memory as dependent upon the depth at which incoming data is processed and analysed. Hence the model *doesn't propose separate structures*.

They distinguished between *two forms of rehearsal*, **maintenance rehearsal** (simple repetition of information) and **elaborative rehearsal** (deeper processing involving *meaningful associations*). The deeper information is processed, the longer the memory trace lasts.

Deeper processing can occur through deliberate choice (i.e. where a person *needs* to learn some information), but also occurs according to the personal relevance of the information.

In terms of processing depth, semantic processing is deepest, followed by acoustic processing, and finally visual processing. The more varied the forms of processing that occur for a bit of information, the more permanent the memory trace.

Describe one model of memory.	(6 marks)
Describe Craik and Lockhart's Levels of Processing model of memory.	(6 marks)

Evaluation

Critical perspective on the Multi-Store Model of memory
- Research has found that memories are held in different capacities and durations, in line with the STM and LTM distinction adopted by this model.
- However, critics argue that Atkinson and Shiffrin offer an oversimplified view of rehearsal (e.g. Craik and Lockhart, 1972).
- Research into amnesia appears to support the STM/LTM distinction (Milner et al., 1978). However, the same findings can be interpreted in a way that doesn't provide any supportive evidence.

> **Research into amnesia relevant to STM/LTM distinction**
> Some different cases of amnesia appear to disrupt one or the other forms of memory (STM/LTM). For example, there is the famous case of HM (Milner et al., 1978). HM's STM was fine, but he appeared to be unable to transfer to his LTM. However, it is possible to interpret the case of HM in a different way: perhaps he *could* transfer to his LTM, but could not *retrieve* from it. If the problem was retrieval, the case does not necessarily suggest an STM/LTM distinction.

Critical perspective on the Working Memory Model
- This model expands the concept of rehearsal to include visual, spatial, and, in the updated model, auditory rehearsal.
- It also has the benefit of being able to explain some selective deficits in brain-damaged patients.
- However, laboratory evidence from neuropsychological studies contradicts the model, and the central executive is not clearly explained.

Critical perspective on the Levels of Processing Theory
- There is an intuitive logic to the central argument of this theory, in that it seems sensible to predict that deeper processing would lead to extended duration of the memory trace.
- However, the argument that deeper processing has occurred where extended duration is observed has been described variously as tautological and circular — the model *describes* what happens but doesn't *explain* it (e.g. Eysenck and Keane, 1990).
- There is some experimental evidence demonstrating that some processing forms (e.g. semantic) are better for recall than others (e.g. visual) (e.g. Craik and Tulving, 1975; Eysenck, 1979). This supports the assumptions behind the Levels of Processing Theory.

Outline one model of memory and give two criticisms of this model.	(6+3+3 marks)

Research into models of memory

Hitch and Baddeley (1976) set out to test their model, which predicts that each component of working memory can work independently (so two tasks using two different components could be processed simultaneously, but two tasks using the same component could not). Twenty-four participants were given a verbal reasoning task. They were presented with sentences such as 'A is not followed by B', then given a pair of letters (e.g. 'AB'). They had to respond by saying true or false (based on whether the sentence was true or false of the letter pair). This task was assumed to be handled by the central executive. At the same time, they were given one of four concurrent tasks, as follows: (1) say 'the' repeatedly; (2) say '1, 2, 3, 4, 5, 6' repeatedly; (3) repeat a different random string of digits out loud every trial; (4) no other task. Tasks 1 and 2 would only use the articulatory loop, while task 3 would involve both the articulatory loop and the central executive. Only task 3 interfered with performance on the main verbal reasoning task. This provided support to the model of working memory, as dual tasks using separate memory components could be processed simultaneously without interference, yet dual tasks that depended upon the same one component created interference.

Craik and Tulving (1975) carried out research to test their Levels of Processing Theory. Participants were shown a word and then asked a question about the word, requiring a 'yes' or 'no' answer. The questions were of three types, one for each of the levels of processing (shallow, phonemic, or semantic). Example questions:

Shallow: 'Is the word in capital letters?'

Phonemic: 'Does the word rhyme with cart?'

Semantic: 'Would the word fit in the sentence "They met a...in the street"?'

After presentation of the words and questions relating to them, participants were given an unexpected recall test — they were asked to recall the words they had seen. Participants who had semantically processed the words recalled the most, followed by phonemic, then shallow. Even if the participants were forewarned about the recall test, differences between the three levels of processing conditions remained. This study demonstrated that the level of processing information received does determine how effectively it is stored, and where it is stored, in memory.

Q **Consider what psychological research has told us about the nature of human memory.**   (18 marks)

---

2 Forgetting

2.1 COGNITIVE EXPLANATIONS OF FORGETTING

Introduction

There are essentially two main types of forgetting: **trace-dependent forgetting** (where the memory trace is actually not present or has been lost from memory); and **cue (or context)-dependent forgetting** (where the memory trace is still held in memory, but it cannot be accessed or retrieved due to unsuitable cues or contexts).

Forgetting can occur in STM and LTM, and during any memory stage (**encoding**, **storage** and **retrieval**).

Explanations of forgetting

There are several theories to explain incidents of forgetting; each accounts for forgetting in different situations, and has different relationships with the aforementioned models of memory. Table 1.1 below describes some of the explanations of forgetting, along with details of the stage(s) when forgetting occurs (STM, LTM, encoding, storage, retrieval) and evaluative comments.

Explanation	Stage	Description	Evaluation
Encoding failure	STM/storage	Data was never stored in memory — usually associated with problems with STM or attentional mechanisms leading to inadequate processing during storage	Has been observed in extreme cases of amnesia. The idea fits well with the levels of processing theory
Trace decay/ decay theory	STM/storage	Memory traces decay over time unless reinforced by retrieval	Supported by Hebb's (1949) 'reverberating nerve cell' idea. Does not account for forgetting followed later by successful retrieval
Displacement	STM/encoding of new information	More recent input overwrites previously held material due to restricted capacity	Fits in with Miller's (1956) assertion that STM can only hold 7 (plus or minus 2) bits of information, and research by Waugh and Norman (1965)
Interference/ interference theory	STM/LTM/retrieval	Information of a similar nature to other stored information is harder to access — similar memories 'interfere' with retrieval of sought memory	McGeogh and McDonald (1931) found that the more similar the information presented was to that already stored, the more interference to recall occurred
Amnesia	Any (depends on type)	Physical damage to brain sites and concussion causes forgetting of memories	Laboratory and case study evidence including brain damage, lesions, concussions, and ECT
Failure in consolidation	LTM/storage	Some suggest that memories need to be integrated with existing knowledge (a process known as 'consolidation'). This is thought to occur during dreaming. Disruptions to consolidation can mean memories are not integrated and become inaccessible	This is a relatively recent idea, but has some evidence from research (Stickgold, 1999). Further investigation into the effects of dream-deprivation on memory consolidation is required to verify the theoretical claims. However, the idea offers an intuitively sensible explanation for the purpose of dreaming
Cue/context-dependent forgetting	LTM/retrieval	Memory trace exists, but cannot be retrieved due to insufficient cues (cues are encoded along with information according to the *encoding specificity principle* of Tulving and Thompson, 1973)	Godden and Baddeley (1975) found that scuba divers recalled information better when immersed in the same environment as the data were learned in. Theory has been criticised for its circularity (Solso, 1974)
Motivated forgetting/ repression	LTM/retrieval	Memories are repressed (repression is one of Freud's 'defence mechanisms'), buried in the unconscious mind. Either the memories are too traumatic or are too closely associated to a traumatic memory, so the mind protects itself by deliberate forgetting	Some experiments have revealed that recall of information during emotionally charged situations is impaired. False feedback has the same effect, and motivated forgetting has not been demonstrated in laboratory conditions in a clear fashion

Table 1.1 Explanations of forgetting

2.2 Emotional factors in forgetting

Repression and state-dependent recall

Many memory researchers have argued that the emotion that we feel during exposure to a stimulus and/or during recall influences the efficiency of the recall.

Freud's **defence mechanism** of **repression** is an example of a theory where emotion has an effect on memory. Memories of *repressed traumatic events* are 'locked away' in the unconscious mind to shield us from the mental pain they could create. Such memories are suggested to include serious ones, such as childhood sexual abuse, and less serious ones, such as conveniently forgetting an appointment with someone that one fears (e.g. a dentist or doctor). According to Myers and Brewin (1994), some people are classed as 'repressors'. These people have low anxiety and high defensiveness, and fail to recall more negative memories than controls. It is suggested that they have lower anxiety *because* they repress such negative or traumatic memories, lending support to Freud's idea behind motivated forgetting through repression.

Recall that Godden and Baddeley (1975) found that scuba divers recalled information better when immersed in the *same environment* as the data were learned in (underwater). Here, immersion in water is known as the **context cue**, since a cue is provided to recall based on the *shared context* that information was learned and retrieved in. Another type of cue is the **state dependent cue**, which is based on our internal physiology and mood. Essentially, if a person attempts recall of information learned while in a particular state or mood, the probability of successful recall is greater when they are recalling in the same state or mood. The state or mood acts as a cue to recall.

Research into state-dependent cues and recall

Some memories encoded while drunk are easier to access when in the same state than when sober — Goodwin et al. (1969) found that alcoholics trying to relocate items they'd put away when drunk were better able to do so when drunk (same state) than when sober.

Bower (1981) conducted a famous experiment where participants learned lists of words while they were either happy or sad. Participants who had learned the lists when happy were better at recalling them when they were again happy than when they were sad; those who had learned while sad were better able to recall when again sad than when happy.

Other research has found similar state-dependent effects when states are induced through tranquillisers and amphetamines.

Flashbulb memories

When an unusual or high impact event occurs, people are often able to recall exactly where they were and what they were doing at the time of the event. Such memory associations are strong and of long duration, and are thought to be due to heightened levels of arousal based on shock and emotionality.

Describe the procedures and findings of one study into flashbulb memory. (6 marks)

Research into flashbulb memory

Brown and Kulik (1977) found evidence for the flashbulb memory phenomenon when they asked people what they'd been doing when they received news of President Kennedy's assassination. Almost all could remember where they had been and what they had been doing, many in great detail.

Conway et al. (1994) tested flashbulb memories associated with the resignation of Margaret Thatcher from her role as Prime Minister. It was found that 11 months after her resignation, 86% of UK participants still had flashbulb memories, compared to 29% in participants from other countries.

Outline two ways in which psychologists have attempted to explain forgetting. (3+3 marks)

Describe one explanation of forgetting in long-term memory.	(6 marks)
Explain the main features of a repression theory of forgetting.	(6 marks)

'Much of forgetting is due to us not being able to retrieve memories because of repression'.
What has psychology told us about the ways in which repression causes forgetting? (18 marks)

3 Critical issue — eyewitness testimony

3.1 INTRODUCTION

Many court cases rely upon evidence submitted in the form of eyewitness testimony. Although eyewitness testimony is generally regarded as less compelling than other 'harder' forms of evidence, such as DNA/material evidence or CCTV, it does frequently provide data for consideration in legal proceedings. The work of forensic psychologists has contributed a great deal to gauging the reliability of such testimony, and this work has also shed light upon our more general understanding of memory.

3.2 RECONSTRUCTIVE MEMORY

Recall the constructionist perspective on memory already described. According to constructionists, memories are not recorded and stored literally like a snapshot of the stimulus, event or situation. Instead, constructionists such as Bartlett (1932) suggest that memories are **reconstructed** over time, influenced by and altered according to active **schemas** (including moods, existing knowledge, contexts, attitudes, feelings and stereotypes). This has implications for the reliability of eyewitness testimony: if people reconstruct events from memory rather than simply regurgitating fixed data, those reconstructions are open to bias from the factors or schemas that are active at the time of reconstruction.

> **Research evidence of unreliability in eyewitness testimony**
> Buckhout (1980) showed a short film of a mugging on prime time television and invited viewers to call in and identify the perpetrator via the telephone. A total of 2000 viewers responded with an identification, but only 14% correctly identified the perpetrator.

> **Research into reconstructive memory in eyewitness testimony**
> Loftus (1975) presented a film of a car accident to two groups of participants. The first group was later asked to estimate the speed of the car as it had passed the Give Way sign. The second group was asked to estimate the speed of the car as it had passed the barn. In fact, the film clip did not include a barn. However, when later asked to recall the events of the film, 17% of the second group included a reference to the car passing a barn, compared to only 3% of the first group. Merely the suggestion that the film had contained a barn had changed the way the events were reconstructed in the memories of the witnesses. This is an example of how information that witnesses receive *after* the event they witness can easily affect the reliability of their account.

Describe one study carried out by Loftus into reconstructive memory. (6 marks)

Leading and misleading witnesses

In court trials, barristers occasionally try to take advantage of the fact that eyewitness memories are reconstructed and subject to change. They do this by asking **'leading'**

questions (which, as you'll have seen from courtroom dramas, often provokes an 'objection' that the barrister is leading the witness).

Research into leading questions in eyewitness testimony

Loftus (1979) presented participants with a film of a car accident. Half of them were asked: 'How fast were the cars going when they hit each other?' while the other half were asked: 'How fast were the cars going when they smashed into each other?' Ratings of the car speeds from the group that were questioned with the term 'smashed into' were significantly faster than from the group who'd been questioned using the term 'hit'. Merely changing the phrasing of the question led them to reconstruct details in a biased fashion, in this case due to the emotive and sensationalising nature of the word 'smashed'.

Explain one approach to studying eyewitness testimony. (6 marks)

'Eyewitness testimony is so unreliable that it should never be used in convicting criminals'.
What has psychological research told us about the accuracy of eyewitness testimony? (18 marks)

Facial recognition in eyewitness testimony

One of the most crucial roles for the eyewitness is to identify the offender, and the best distinguishing feature in most instances is the face. However, like other aspects of memory in eyewitness testimony, facial recognition is subject to error.

In reconstructing the face of an offender, theorists such as Davies (1994) suggest that witnesses incorporate their expectations of what a typical offender's face looks like into their accounts. Though we have moved away from the ideas of Lombroso (1876), who proposed that criminals all have facial features that differentiate them from non-criminals, we still have stereotyped images of offenders. With so much at stake in trials using eyewitness testimony, such evidence of bias and imprecision is a major concern in forensic psychology.

1 *Attachments in development*

1.1 THE DEVELOPMENT AND VARIETY OF ATTACHMENTS

From a developmental psychologist's perspective, one of the most interesting aspects of early human development is that of **attachment**. First appearing in human infancy (generally the first two years of the human life span), attachment lays the foundations of social development, with repercussions extending into adulthood.

Attachment refers to a particularly strong *bond* with a specific person or persons. The bond is emotional and affective, and a person that an infant bonds to in this way is known as an **attachment figure**, usually but not always the biological parent or parents. According to Schaffer (1977), attachment develops through three stages: firstly, the newborn is predisposed to attach to any human; secondly they learn to distinguish **primary** and **secondary caregivers** but accept care from anyone; and finally, they focus attachment on a single specific attachment figure. It is the manner in which the carer interacts with the infant, primarily in times of stress or fear, which shapes the *nature* of the attachment. Accordingly, the infant will develop a degree of **dependence** or **independence** based upon these early, crucial, interactions.

Q | **What is meant by the term 'attachment'?** | (6 marks)

1.2 WHAT LEADS TO ATTACHMENT?

Theorists have proposed a number of factors that are believed to be important in forming attachments.

Earlier theorists, such as Bowlby (1951), tried to explain attachment as a human form of **imprinting**. Imprinting is a natural phenomenon that occurs primarily in certain precocial animals (animals that move freely almost immediately after birth), such as ducks and geese. Ethologists such as Lorenz (1953) observed that such animals have an innate tendency to respond immediately and consistently to specific forms of stimuli (such as visual markings or sounds) which are usually displayed by their parent or parents. They are drawn to the stimuli and therefore instinctively follow their parent (or any other exhibiting the stimuli in the absence of the parent), content when near to them, distressed when separated. This innate 'pre-programming' clearly provides an **evolutionary advantage** — by staying close to their parent(s) and siblings, the newborn animals are less likely to fall foul of predators or environmental dangers than if they strayed.

Bowlby's **Theory of Monotropy** suggests that an infant forms a firm attachment with *one* of their parents or caregivers (usually the mother) in a similar way to the imprinting process observed in animals. Bowlby argues that if such an attachment is broken, through parental death or prolonged separation, the infant, like the duck or goose, is exposed to severe stress and social problems in later life.

Evaluation of Bowlby's theory
- The supporting evidence that Bowlby provided was in the form of clinical observations of, and retrospective data on, those who had and had not been separated from their primary caregiver.
- Bowlby's conceptualisation of attachment as essentially human imprinting implies that it is not important what form of interaction occurs between the caregiver and infant,

and that mere exposure is the only important factor. Much diverse research exists that contradicts this idea (see research box).

Research into factors involved in attachment

- The behaviourist framework of explanation would suggest that an infant would form an attachment with a carer that provides food (in behaviourist terms, food is the primary reinforcer, the provider is secondary). Harlow and Zimmerman (1959) found evidence against this hypothesis using rhesus monkeys. They placed solitary monkeys in cages with two artificial mothers, one soft and made of cloth, the other constructed of wire. Only one 'mother' would provide milk. *Regardless* of which mother provided milk, the monkeys would choose to spend more time with the soft cloth mother than the wire one. When fearful, the monkeys would consistently approach the cloth mother, but sought no comfort from the wire one.

- The amount of physical contact and the amount of time spent together with infants have been explored as explanatory factors in forming attachments. The evidence appears mixed for these factors. Klaus and Kennel (1976) arranged for a group of mothers in hospital to have extra time in contact with their newborn babies during the first weeks of life. The infants in the extra contact group showed stronger attachments compared to those in a control group. However, Fox (1977) studied Israeli children cared for primarily by nurses, and found that their attachments were strongest with their mothers, despite having spent more time with the nurses. This suggests that it is not the *amount* of contact that is important, but the *nature* of the contact.

- Bowlby's idea of monotropy and view of human attachment as a form of imprinting was further contradicted by a set of ethological studies where mothers and babies were observed interacting (Schaffer and Emerson, 1964). Schaffer and Emerson observed that babies did not automatically bond to the mother, but that attachment depended upon complex interactions between a carer (not necessarily the mother) and the infant. They suggest that babies are born with a predisposition to be **sociable** and seek interaction with adults, but that it is the specific and complex nature of the interaction, and not a single factor such as time spent or feeding, that shapes the degree of attachment. Specifically, they noted that babies were more likely to form strong bonds with a carer that was sensitive and responsive to the needs of the baby. They measured a factor they termed '**sensitive responsiveness**' and noted that higher levels were associated with more secure attachments. The ideas and observational methodologies employed by Schaffer and Emerson were developed further and in more detail by Ainsworth in 1978 — see the following section.

Explain one approach to studying attachment. (6 marks)

Describe one explanation of the development of attachments. (6 marks)

1.3 INDIVIDUAL DIFFERENCES IN ATTACHMENT AND THE 'STRANGE SITUATION' (AINSWORTH, 1978)

Much research has focused on how forms of attachment differ between infants. For example, Schaffer and Emerson (1964) discovered what appeared to be innate differences in sociability in babies; some babies preferred cuddling more than others, from very early on, before much interaction had occurred to cause such differences. Such innate differences in **emotionality** are described as '**temperament**'. A temperament is the emotional personality type that we are born with, and is 'hardwired' into us — our temperament influences and is influenced by social interactions. One author defines temperament as consisting of behaviour and emotions that are constitutional, that are relatively stable over time and across situations, that have neurophysiological underpinning, and that have some degree of heritability (Goldsmith, 1993). Temperaments contribute to explanations of individual differences in emotionality.

However, it was probably Ainsworth (1978) who provided the most famous body of research offering explanations of individual differences in emotionality. Her set of observational studies using the '**Strange Situation**' paradigm (see research box) revealed three distinct forms of attachment ('attachment styles'). Caregivers and infant pairs displayed one of the following three attachment styles.

- *Secure attachment*. Just as it sounds! The infant seeks interaction with the caregiver, is temporarily anxious upon separation, but is comforted quickly and easily and is content upon the return of the caregiver. Infants behave as if they are confident that they can depend upon their caregiver.
- *Resistant attachment* (or 'anxious-resistant'). An insecure form of attachment with some degree of tension in the interactive style. The infant stays close to the caregiver before departure, but is overly anxious when they depart, and shows both approach and avoidance behaviours upon their return. They take longer to comfort upon return, and sometimes actively resist the comfort offered by the caregiver. They behave as if they are not certain that they can rely upon the caregiver, and show some resentment to being abandoned.
- *Avoidant attachment* (or 'anxious-avoidant'). A second form of insecure attachment. Such infants are independent to an extreme degree. They do not cry upon the departure of their caregiver, and ignore or avoid them upon return. They tend not to cling or cuddle when handled.

Research into attachment: the 'Strange Situation'

Ainsworth (1978) developed an experimental procedure in order to observe the variety of attachment forms exhibited between caregivers and infants. The procedure, known as the 'Strange Situation', was conducted by observing the behaviour of the caregiver and the infant in a series of seven 3-minute episodes, as follows:

(1) Parent and infant alone.
(2) Stranger joins parent and infant.
(3) Parent leaves infant and stranger alone.
(4) Parent returns and stranger leaves.
(5) Parent leaves; infant left completely alone.
(6) Stranger returns.
(7) Parent returns and stranger leaves.

The pattern of behaviour exhibited, particularly when the parent left and returned, provided the measure of which attachment style was in place (as detailed in the main text).

Explain what is meant by secure attachments. (3 marks)

1.4 CULTURAL VARIATION IN PREVALENT ATTACHMENT STYLES

Ainsworth (1978) found that in the British culture, secure attachments were most prevalent (70%). Insecure attachments were less common, with 20% exhibiting resistant attachment, and 10% exhibiting avoidant attachment. However, other researchers into attachment styles in other cultures have found differing distributions of the attachment styles. For example, one study revealed a high proportion of resistant attachments; a German study revealed that 40% (compared with 10% in the Ainsworth study) of attachments were of the avoidant type; and a Japanese study revealed that 35% (compared with 20% in the Ainsworth study) of attachments were of the resistant type.

Evaluation

Theorists have suggested that such cultural variations reflect the differing values placed upon dependence and independence in different societies, and advise not to make value judgements on our assumptions as to what good parenting should entail. However, there is much evidence indicating the importance of early attachments. The manner in which older children and adults interact with others in relationships and their emotionality appears to be highly influenced by early attachment style. A longitudinal study by Main and Cassidy (1988) illustrates this well, since continuity is observed from 1 year to 6 years. Key findings are summarised in the following table.

Attachment style	Behaviour at 1 year	Behaviour at 6 years
Secure	Seeks interaction, closeness, contact with returning parent. Readily soothed by parent and returns to play	Initiates conversation with returning parent or responds to parent's overture. Remains calm throughout brief separation
Resistant/ 'ambivalent'	Distress over separation; isn't soothed by parent. Child wants contact, but shows overt to subtle signs of anger	Posture and voice exaggerate sense of intimacy and dependency. Shows some resistance, subtle signs of hostility
Avoidant	Actively avoids and ignores returning parent, looks away, remains occupied with toys	Minimises opportunity for interaction with returning parent, looking and speaking only briefly, returns to toys

Table 2.1 Attachment style

Furthermore, as adults, people often adopt the attachment style that they experienced as children. This is illustrated by the findings of Waters et al. (1995), shown in the table below. The table shows the frequencies of three adult attachment styles (secure/ autonomous, preoccupied and dismissing) observed in people who as infants were secure, resistant and avoidant. The table shows continuity in the development of attachment styles.

Adult attachment style (at 20 years)	*Secure* as infant	*Resistant* as infant	*Avoidant* as infant
Secure/autonomous	**20**	3	2
Preoccupied	3	**4**	2
Dismissing	6	2	**8**

Table 2.2 Continuity in attachment style development

'It is tempting to think that the way we bring up children in our own culture is the right way, but there are many alternatives which are just as acceptable.' To what extent has psychological research shown that there are cross-cultural variations in attachment styles?   (18 marks)

2 *Deprivation and privation*

2.1 DEFINITIONS

Deprivation

Deprivation refers to the loss of an attachment or the loss of an attachment figure. This includes short-term and long-term separations.

Examples of short-term separations are:
- Hospitalisation (of infant or attachment figure).
- Working attachment figure (infant cared for by childminder or day-care facility).
- Other short-term separations (holidays, contracts away from home, short-term imprisonment, etc.).

Examples of long-term separations are:
- Death of attachment figure.
- Divorce resulting in separation.
- Adoption by caregivers other than attachment figure.
- Other long-term separations (institutionalisation of infant or attachment figure, long-term imprisonment, etc.).

Privation

Privation is sometimes confused with deprivation, and both are often conflated and used interchangeably as if they mean the same thing (by researchers as well as A and AS-level students!). However, privation refers to a *total lack* of some requirement (for example, a bond with an attachment figure) through development, whereas deprivation refers to a scenario where the requirement was in place but then was removed. Privation means that the attachment *never* formed initially; deprivation means that it was there but was removed.

Q Explain the features of deprivation and privation.   (3+3 marks)

2.2 EFFECTS OF SHORT-TERM AND LONG-TERM LOSS OF ATTACHMENTS

The Maternal Deprivation Hypothesis (Bowlby, 1946, 1956)

Bowlby's Theory of Monotropy led to the formulation of his maternal deprivation hypothesis. Essentially, Bowlby suggested that the nature of monotropy (attachment conceptualised as being a vital and close bond with just one attachment figure, the mother) meant that a failure to initiate, or a breakdown of, the maternal attachment would lead to serious negative consequences, possibly including **affectionless psychopathy** (lack of social conscience associated with separation within first two years of life). His research is detailed in the research box. Note that Bowlby's concept of maternal deprivation conflates deprivation and privation.

> **Research into the maternal deprivation hypothesis (Bowlby, 1946, 1956)**
>
> Bowlby believed that the relationship between the infant and its mother during the first five years of life was most crucial to socialisation. He believed that disruption of this primary relationship could lead to a higher incidence of juvenile delinquency, emotional difficulties and antisocial behaviour. To support his hypothesis, he studied 44 adolescent juvenile delinquents in a child guidance clinic. He found that 17 of the 44 had been separated from their mothers at some point during the first five years of life. In a later paper, he reported that 60 children who had spent time apart from their mothers in a tuberculosis sanatorium before the age of 4 showed lower achievement in school.

Q Describe the aims and findings of one study into the long-term effects of deprivation.   (6 marks)

Evaluation of Bowlby's research into maternal deprivation

While Bowlby's research may appear to demonstrate that maternal separation has negative consequences, his findings have frequently been questioned. Firstly, his research employed a retrospective and correlational methodology. As such, we can only infer an association between maternal deprivation and the observed consequences. Merely because there is a tendency for them to occur together does not provide evidence of a **causal link**. Furthermore, research by Rutter (1976), investigating similar data, led to the conclusion that the antisocial behaviour of the delinquents was more attributable to simultaneous discord in family circumstances than to the simple effect of maternal separation in formative years.

Short-term separation

There is some evidence to suggest that even short-term separation in crucial formative years can lead to problems in sociability and forming relationships in later life. As well as the questionable evidence from Bowlby (1946), Douglas (1975) found that separations of less than a week for children below 4 years of age was correlated with behavioural difficulties. Quinton and Rutter (1976) found that behavioural problems were more widespread in samples of adolescents who had been separated from attachment figures during their first 5 years through hospitalisation, than adolescents without this feature in their backgrounds. Again, this evidence is largely correlational, so a cause and effect process cannot be clearly determined, and other researchers have found no evidence of a direct link between separation and later behavioural and emotional difficulties (e.g. Kagan et al., 1978, 1980).

Long-term separation

It seems logical to assume that separation for longer periods would be more likely to have a negative impact upon the child in later life than short-term separations. Indeed, the research into long-term deprivation and privation is more convincing in presenting a case for such loss or lack of attachments as being harmful to the development of the child. Separation through different causes appears to produce different outcomes, with attachment disruption from divorce leading more to resentment and stress (Richards, 1987), and disruption from the death of an attachment figure more likely to result in depression than delinquency. Tizard and Hodges (1978) conducted a study of institutionalisation which is often recognised as providing valuable insights into maternal separation, and was designed in a methodologically sound manner. The research is discussed in the research box.

Give two criticisms of one study of deprivation or privation. (3+3 marks)

Describe Bowlby's maternal deprivation hypothesis and give two criticisms of this. (6+3+3 marks)

Research into deprivation and privation in institutionalisation (Tizard and Hodges, 1978)

A large sample of children was included in this study; all had been born to unmarried mothers and transferred to institutions for care within 4 months of life. The children were placed in one of four groups, to allow for comparisons to be made in outcome measures:

(1) Children who experienced no home other than the institution.
(2) Children who had been institutionalised and then adopted.
(3) Children who had been institutionalised and then returned to their biological mothers.
(4) A control group of children who were from intact families of matched socio-economic status.

The institutions had staff turnovers high enough to prevent substitute attachments from forming. The study therefore allowed for comparison of children with various degrees of attachment disruption. Children were studied on three occasions in order to monitor longitudinal progress: once as infants, once at 4 years, and finally at 8 years of age.

Results

- At the age of 4: children still in institutions were attention-seeking and clingy towards adults in an indiscriminate fashion. They also exhibited problems in relating to peers, showing argumentative styles of interaction. They did not appear to care very deeply about specific carers, and showed no preference towards individual carers. The children who had been adopted were indiscriminately and excessively friendly towards strangers.

- At the age of 8: children who were returned to their natural mothers exhibited signs of resentment and indifference to their mothers. These mothers, like the caregivers of still institutionalised children, indicated that they had less close bonding and less frequent playing with the children than did caregivers who had adopted at an earlier age and the control group parents. Teachers reported more behavioural problems in those that had been institutionalised (regardless of adoption) than in the control group. Children returned to their natural mothers were reported as having the worst behavioural problems at school, indicating that they may have been resentful, and that they perceived their attachments as artificial.

3 Critical issue — day care

The various findings concerning the effects of deprivation and privation on children have led to much debate (taken up by the media) on day care. The debate has focused on the question of whether mothers who place their children in the care of minders while they work are subjecting their children to potential trauma or attachment difficulties that could impair cognitive and social development. According to Bowlby's early work, separation could lead to such problems.

However, research into the effects of day care has not conclusively established that it has a direct negative impact upon the child. For example, Kagan et al. (1978) found that children attending day care facilities were not different from those cared for at home in terms of their levels of attachment to their mothers, their anxiety at being separated, and their language development. The same was found in a subsequent investigation by Kagan et al. (1980).

Other researchers have concluded that day care can have negative consequences. Belsky (1988) reviewed studies conducted in the USA on children of working mothers and concluded that they were more likely to exhibit insecure attachments than those of mothers who cared for them at home.

On the other hand, some studies have led to suggestions that day care may be beneficial to the development of the child. Rubenstein and Howes (1979) argued that due to greater levels of interaction with peers, such children may receive benefits in development of social skills. Burchinal et al. (1989) found that children who had been in day care scored better on IQ tests upon entry to kindergarten than children cared for at home.

Research into the effects of day care

Andersson (1992) was interested in the effects day care had on subsequent development. Over 100 children were sampled from different social and family backgrounds in Sweden. The children were monitored at various stages from 3 to 4 years old, with notes taken as to whether they attended day care or not. At later stages (8 and 13 years old), their cognitive and social abilities were assessed from IQ tests and teachers' reports. It was found that performance at school was highest amongst those children who had entered day care before the age of 1, and worst amongst those who had not attended day care at all. This suggests day care is not only harmless, but actually provides benefits in later developmental stages. However, critics have pointed out that those entering day care before they were 1 also tended to be from better-off families. Furthermore, day care in Sweden is far superior to that in many other countries due to the funding channelled into it by the government, so generalising to other countries may not be totally reliable.

Other studies have suggested that day care has indirect benefits to the child in that the mother who is free to work experiences reduced levels of stress, frustration and depression (Brown and Harris, 1978). This could have an effect on interactions with the child.

Given the changing economic and political climate, the issue of day care is one that has been frequently under discussion. With such an importan potential impact upon the welfare of children and the adults that they will develop into, and parents and caregivers, further investigation into the effects of day care is vital.

Explain the effects of day care on either children's cognitive development or children's social development. (6 marks)

TOPIC Physiological psychology 1

1 Stress as a bodily response

1.1 HOW THE BODY RESPONDS TO STRESS

Introduction and definitions

While stress is a condition with which everyone is personally familiar (unless *you* have somehow managed to avoid it altogether!), it is necessary before proceeding to be clear on what the term refers to.

Stress is succinctly defined as, '...the effect on a person of being subjected to noxious stimulation, or the threat of such stimulation, particularly when they are unable to avoid or terminate the condition' (Stratton and Hayes, 1993, p. 196). Such definitions refer to 'effects', 'reactions' or 'responses', and many of the more pronounced responses associated with the condition are physiological ones (although there are cognitive and behavioural components). In other words, stress manifests itself as a bodily response — the nature of this bodily response will be discussed below.

Explain what psychologists mean by the term 'stress'. (3 marks)

Stressors are simply the sources of stress — anything that causes stress is a stressor. If you are in a state over a lack of money (aren't we all!), stress is what you feel, while the stressor is the lack of money.

The human nervous system

Stress manifests itself physically through the action of the **nervous system**. Figure 3.1 shows the structure of the human nervous system. Note that for convenience and understanding (and primarily by function) it is divided and subdivided into individual components. While these divisions are justified on their different specific functions or locations, it should be noted that they are not truly separate in the way that your hands and your eyes are.

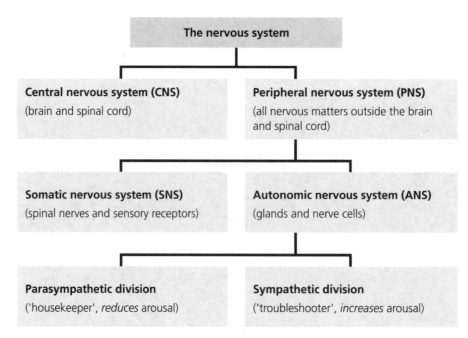

Figure 3.1 The structure of the human nervous system

Changes in the body's physiological state in response to stressors are generally explained in terms of the activity of the **autonomic nervous system**, which comprises two divisions, the **sympathetic** and the **parasympathetic**. The sympathetic division can be thought of as the 'trouble-shooter' — highly responsive to stimuli and, through its activation, responsible for emotional states and elevated arousal. The parasympathetic division can be thought of as the 'housekeeper', stabilising and responsible for maintaining a degree of equilibrium and calming bodily processes. They are essentially opposing forces that interact to produce the bodily state at any given time. The sympathetic division of the autonomic nervous system is the component of the nervous system that is primarily activated by stressors; stress can be measured in terms of consequent changes to various physiological measures, some of which are discussed in the next section.

Physiological effects of stress (short-term)

The short-term bodily response to a stressor is often termed the '**fight or flight response**' or the '**alarm reaction**' (Cannon). The sympathetic division of the autonomic nervous system instigates the response through neural impulses, and the **endocrine system** maintains arousal through release of hormones. The hypothalamus stimulates the **pituitary gland** (known as the 'master' or 'control' gland since it regulates the activities of all other glands) to secrete quantities of **adrenocorticotrophic hormone (ACTH)**. ACTH causes the adrenal gland to release the stress hormone adrenaline, which increases the rate at which energy is converted and released to muscle groups. Short-term physiological symptoms associated with stressful states include: increased heart rate and blood pressure; a faster rate of digestion for sugars (though the digestion rate of foods normally demanding longer digestion times is slowed further); deeper breathing, increased sweating, pupil dilation, and release of endorphins ('endogenous morphines', the body's naturally produced analgesic, or painkiller). Such changes make the body better equipped to deal with physical danger or threat in the short-term (though *not* in the long-term — see the research box below); *immediate* energy production and its distribution to muscle groups are maximised.

Explain the features of stress. (6 marks)

1.2 LONG-TERM EFFECTS OF PROLONGED EXPOSURE TO STRESSORS

General Adaptation Syndrome (Selye, 1956)

The short-term fight or flight response includes changes to both digestion and the immune system. The stressed body is better able to quickly digest sugars (food types that can supply a 'quick fix' of energy), but slower to digest food sources requiring more prolonged digestion (proteins and fats). Essentially, the digestion process during stress favours processing food from which energy can be released most quickly. The activity of the immune system, also a long-term process, is suppressed. The whole fight or flight response is programmed for *immediate* survival — long-term bodily processes (such as digestion of proteins and fats and the activity of the immune system) are temporarily neglected.

The three stages of the General Adaptation Syndrome

- Stage 1, the **alarm stage**, is as described in the previous section on the short-term fight or flight response to stressors. It includes negative consequences of low white blood cell production (essential for the immune system), and sometimes stomach ulcers.
- Stage 2, the **resistance stage**, is characterised by attempts to revert to 'normal' functioning. There are still the high levels of adrenaline in the blood from stage 1, but

the body attempts to cope with the excess and regulate hormone production as it becomes habituated to the stressor.

- Stage 3, the **exhaustion** (or collapse) **stage**, involves a return to what appears to be a normal state, as the body has depleted energy and cannot maintain the fight or flight state. However, there is still an unusually high level of adrenaline in the blood, and in this state, an animal experiencing a new stressor, even a mild one, will react immediately and strongly. The adrenal cortex stops functioning correctly, leaving the body less able to fight infection.

Describe Selye's General Adaptation Syndrome. (6 marks)

Evaluation of Selye's contribution

Selye's work, amongst others, led to the development of **psychoimmunology**, the study of the relationship between psychological factors and the functioning and efficiency of the immune system. Some examples of research into the relationship between stress and physical illness, including cardiovascular disorders and the effects of stress on the immune system, are detailed in the research box below.

Research into the relationship between stress and illness

Various researchers developed the ideas of Selye (1949, 1956) who found that in general the immune system was less effective when exposed (particularly for prolonged periods) to stressors. Jemmot et al. (1985) found that students during examination periods had lower counts of certain antibodies concerned with fighting respiratory infections. Glaser et al. (1987) reported a similar finding in medical students during their examination period. Brady (1958) reported that in stressed individuals, the high levels of adrenaline can lead to stomach ulcers and other somatic illnesses. This is particularly apparent in sufferers of prolonged stress. Schliefer et al. (1979) examined a sample of widowers whose spouses had died from cancer and found that they had less efficient immune systems than controls. Friedman and Rosenman (1974) assessed the personality types of over 3500 healthy middle-aged men as part of a 12 year longitudinal study. Participants were asked questions relating to impatience, competitiveness, motivation for success, frustration at goals being hindered, and their feelings towards being under pressure. High scorers were described as 'Type A' personalities while low scorers were described as 'Type B' personalities. More than twice as many of the Type A personalities went on to develop cardiovascular disorders than did Type B personalities. Further research by Jenkins et al. (1978) examined specific components and behaviours of the Type A personality and found that certain characteristics correlated more or less with specific forms of cardiovascular disorder. For example, angina sufferers tended to be composed of those Type A personalities that were impatient with other people and susceptible to feeling pressure at work, while those with heart failure tended to comprise those Type A personalities that had hasty personal habits and schedules (Hayes, 2000).

What has psychological research told us about the relationship between stress and physical illness? (18 marks)

---

2 Sources of stress

2.1 TYPES OF STRESSOR

Categories of stressors

The research box above details studies that themselves suggest some common sources of stress. Major stressors can essentially be broken down into the following categories: **environmental**, **occupational** and significant **life events**.

- **Environmental** conditions which induce stress include temperature and noise. Baron and Ransberger (1978) correlated weather conditions and the incidence of riot and civil disturbance; they found that the latter were more common when the temperature was moderately hot than when it was cooler or extremely hot (presumably if it is *too* hot, people are more lethargic and less active). Exposure to noise has been found to cause stress and impair cognitive functioning (Glass et al., 1969), but only when the noise is unpredictable (humans become habituated to constant forms of noise and can 'tune out' such predictable distraction).
- **Occupational** stressors encompass deadlines that are unattainable (or perceived as such), prolonged conflict with other employees, a change in employment or responsibilities, work overload and role ambiguity. A famous experiment which indicated that being tied to a responsibility added to physical stress is described in the research box below.

Research into work-related stress: 'executive monkeys'

Brady (1958) conducted an experiment that demonstrated that a burden of responsibility combined with a physical stressor can cause greater stress and stress-related illness than the physical stressor alone. Monkeys were restrained in a chair where they received an electric shock every 20 seconds. In the experiment 'executive monkeys' had a lever to pull. If it was pulled by a monkey within the 20 second period, it would avert the shock for that single period. The control group, which had no levers to pull but received the shocks, displayed no gastrointestinal abnormalities, while many of the 'executive monkeys' died of duodenal ulcers. Monkeys in the control and experimental groups received the same physical stressor, but only the 'executive monkeys' had the psychological stressor in terms of having to maintain their avoidance behaviour (lever-pressing). This is relevant to occupational stress, in that occupations carry with them different burdens of responsibility — and are also associated with different levels of stress-related illnesses.

- Many occupational stressors relate to the employees' perceived control of their situation — the role of control in the perception of stress is covered in Section 3 of this chapter.

Life events and stress

In terms of life events and elevated stress, some stress-related illnesses have been found to be more prevalent in participants during examinations and after bereavement. Holmes and Rahe (1967) investigated medical histories of people and interviewed them about their experiences; from this they compiled a famous list of common life stressors. The list was arranged in a hierarchical order from most stressful to least stressful and loosely assigned a score out of 100. An adapted version of the scale is displayed in Table 3.1.

Death of spouse	100	Divorce	73
Marital separation	65	Prison sentence	63
Death of parent or close family	63	Personal injury or illness	53
Marriage	50	Being sacked from work	47
Marital reconciliation	45	Retirement	45
Change in health of family	44	Pregnancy	40
Sexual difficulties	39	Gain of new family member	39
Business readjustment	39	Change in financial state	38
Death of close friend	37	Change to different work	36
Foreclosure of mortgage	30	Change in work responsibilities	29
Son or daughter leaving home	29	Trouble with in-laws	29
Outstanding personal achievement	28	Spouse begins or stops work	26

Beginning or ending school/college	26	Changes in living conditions	25
Change in personal habits	24	Trouble with boss at work	23
Moving house	20	Change of school/college	20
Change of recreation	19	Change in social activities	18
Change in sleeping habits	16	Change in eating habits	15
Holiday	13	Christmas	12
Minor breaches of the law	11		

Table 3.1 The stressful life events scale (adapted from Holmes and Rahe, 1967)

According to Holmes and Rahe, the scale can be used predictively. Adding up the scores from the scale for a person's stressful life events in one year should correlate with their physical health in the subsequent year. When Holmes and Rahe conducted correlational analyses to test this hypothesis, they did indeed find statistically significant correlations.

Evaluation of the stressful life events scale

While Holmes and Rahe did confirm that life events scores on their scale correlated with the physical health of participants, several criticisms have been levelled at it.

* The way in which life events were scored in devising the scale was, though reasonable in terms of being relative to other life events, quite arbitrary. A score of 50 for marriage, for example, doesn't really tell us much about the true extent or nature of the stress involved, only that it is *generally* more stressful than being sacked from work (scoring 47) and *generally* less stressful than personal injury or illness (scoring 53).

* A correlation does not indicate causality — someones's general susceptibility to stress or their general level of health may also be important factors. Indeed, Dohrenwend and Dohrenwend (1974) pointed out that 29 of the items on the scale could be linked with a developing illness in some way other than causal.

* Adding up a person's scores from the scale and finding a high score *may* suggest a health problem is imminent, but the nature of that problem is not apparent — different stress-related illnesses appear to be more or less associated with different forms of stressor.

* While Holmes and Rahe did find a statistically significant correlation between scores on the scale and subsequent measures of health, the correlation was quite small. Therefore, the number and type of life events that a person experiences has some association with subsequent health, but there is a lot of variance and individual differences in response to life event stressors that are not accounted for by the scale. The following section details some of these individual differences and the manner in which they modify the effects of stressors.

***

Describe one study of life changes and stress and give two criticisms of the study.   (6+3+3 marks)

***

2.2 INDIVIDUAL DIFFERENCES IN MODIFYING THE EFFECTS OF STRESSORS

Personality

Research by Friedman and Rosenman (1974) described on page 28 shows that Type A personalities are more prone to developing stress-related illness than other people. Assuming no confounding factors, this indicates that personality type can modify the effect of stressors. Recall also that Jenkins et al. (1978) examined specific components and behaviours of the Type A personality and found that certain characteristics correlated more or less with specific forms of cardiovascular disorder. In other words, people vary in the manner in which they respond to stressors and cope with stress.

Chesney and Rosenman (1980) found that **control** was an important factor that interacted with personality type to determine responses to stressors. Type A managers experienced greater anxiety when they were not in control, while other managers experienced greater anxiety when they were in control. The issue of perception of control in moderating stress outcomes is an important one and we shall return to the subject in Section 3.

Individuals differ in the way in which they are predisposed to respond to stressors. Gannon et al. (1987) exposed two groups of participants to stressors in the form of arithmetic problems. One group, chronic migraine sufferers, experienced headaches in response to the stressors far more than the second group who were occasional headache sufferers. This demonstrates that individuals have **predispositions** in terms of the nature and extent of their response to stressors, and the predisposition interacts with **environmental triggers** to determine outcomes.

Culture and gender and stress

Since cultures differ in their approach to occupation (for example, consider the mid-afternoon siesta that is a Spanish tradition, the current debate about cutting working hours in Britain to bring them into line with Europe, and differences in environmental conditions), we would expect some differences in stress across them. Philosophies differ also — consider and contrast the Yanamomo tribes, a war-like society that values aggression and raises its children to display negative emotions, and Buddhist cultures, where negativity is frowned upon. In the former, stress-related illness and anxiety disorders are less frequent than in the latter (who have their outlet for internal stress inhibited — see 'emotional discharge' in Section 3) (Oatley and Jenkins, 1998). Cultural differences have also been identified in terms of the relationship between Type A personality and stress-related illness. While the relationship may be reliable in America, Bass and Wade (1982) found that, amongst patients suffering from heart pain, Type A personalities tended to have normal coronary arteries.

There appear to be differences in stress according to gender as well as culture. In general, women appear to be less affected by stress than men, which some suggest is due to hormonal differences. It has been suggested that high oestrogen levels alleviate stress in women. A study by Hastrup et al. (1980) investigated stress responses at various stages of women's menstrual cycles, and concluded that in stages where oestrogen levels were highest, stress responses were lowest. However, this finding is correlational, so cannot confirm a causal mechanism. Other researchers suggest that men have more stress because they engage in more unhealthy behaviours than women.

'One of the most important things to understand about stress is that there are massive differences between individuals. Gender plays a big part.' Consider the extent to which psychology has shown how there are gender differences in our susceptibility to stress. (18 marks)

---

3 *Critical issue — stress management*

3.1 APPROACHES TO STRESS MANAGEMENT

Introduction

What can be done to manage the negative effects of stress, and how effective are stress management techniques? According to Lazarus and Folkman (1984), stress management can take one of two approaches, or a combination of the two:

- *Direct action* (problem-focused) can tackle the source of the stress (the stressor). This is effective when the stressor can realistically be removed or avoided.

- *Indirect action* (emotion-focused) can tackle the stress and the negative emotions generated by stressors. This is the only option if the stressor cannot be realistically removed or avoided.
- The *eclectic approach* combines the two (i.e. the stressor and the stress are tackled).

Direct action/problem-focused approaches

Taking control of a stressor through identifying it as such and developing strategies to remove or avoid it directly tackles the problem. A sense of control over stressors and stress is also important in terms of shaping the emotional response to a stressor (see below). Time management, life changes (for example, changing occupation or habits — itself potentially stressful), renegotiating responsibilities, seeking help to tackle the problem stressor (social support, which can also help with tackling the stress response), or in some other way addressing the direct source of the problem are all examples of direct action.

Indirect action

Clinically diagnosed stress can be tackled through prescribed drugs, though such treatment is often used, with restraint, as a treatment for serious cases where other methods are not appropriate or effective. Drugs are generally effective in the short-term, though they treat symptoms without addressing the underlying problem. There are also negative side-effects to many anxiolytic (anti-anxiety) drugs.

Relaxation training, such as using the **progressive relaxation technique (PRT)**, meditation, or self-hypnosis, act to reduce autonomic nervous system activity, and thereby alleviate symptoms of stress. A benefit of such techniques is that the individual has some degree of control themselves, without resorting to help from others or from medication. However, some of the techniques are difficult to learn, and require substantial time to acquire and use.

Biofeedback can be used to increase the efficiency of relaxation techniques, since control over involuntary muscles (normally beyond conscious control) can be learned. Biofeedback involves feeding back to the individual information about his or her physiological state (such as heart rate, skin conductance and blood pressure). Such variables can be controlled to some degree. Miller and DiCara (1967) paralysed rats with curare, to ensure that their physiological functioning could not be altered by any voluntary movement. The researchers provided rewards in the form of electrical stimulation of the pleasure-centre in the brain whenever the rats increased their heart rates. With this continued reinforcement (operant conditioning), the rats exhibited a significant increase in their heart rates. In terms of using this technique to reduce stress, it is not always practical, as it takes time and effort to learn. There is also some doubt as to whether involuntary muscles are really controlled through the process, as opposed to controlling unused voluntary muscles. However, the technique bestows control of the situation to the individual and is non-invasive.

Attributional therapy encourages individuals to reconsider the way in which they explain to themselves what is happening to them, and its significance. Maier and Seligman (1976) identified negative attributional styles, and therapies exist to address these. An important aspect of such therapy is in terms of identifying and addressing aspects of control (see below). An advantage is that once patients are trained in more positive appraisals, they can carry this positivity into any subsequent life events without reliance on the therapist. A disadvantage is that the therapist assumes that the stress is self-generated through appraisal, whilst it could be argued that some extreme life events have no positive aspects.

Locus of control (Rotter, 1966; Glass et al., 1969) has been found to be related to stress. Locus of control refers to whether people believe their experiences are internally or externally directed (for example, doing well in an exam could be attributed to personal ability — internally, or luck — externally). People with an external locus of control are more vulnerable to stress than those with an internal locus of control (this phenomenon is linked to **learned helplessness**, where a belief that nothing can be done about a stressor leads the individual to do nothing useful about it). Training people to adopt an internal locus of control can help in many cases. However, in some unavoidable and extremely stress-inducing situations, where the control is attributed, it may not provide such reassurance.

Q **Describe the role of control in the perception of stress.** (6 marks)

Kobasa (1979) examined business executives, some of whom became stressed and others did not, and attempted to identify what attributes were related to the latter's '**hardiness**'. She found that the hardy executives who coped with stress saw stressors as challenges to be met head on, and didn't try to avoid them or ignore them. Training can be provided to help people become more hardy in this way, and Kobasa's findings suggest that **assertiveness training** may be useful for alleviating stress. However, it requires dedication to acquire, which, ironically enough, makes hardiness training more useful to those already of a hardy nature!

Q **Explain two ways of managing the negative effects of stress.** (3+3 marks)

Describe the procedures and findings of one study into managing stress and give two criticisms of this study. (6+3+3 marks)

Meichenbaum (1985) devised what is called **stress inoculation training**. This helps people to develop and use cognitive/behavioural coping skills *in advance* of stressors manifesting themselves, in order to be prepared when they do. This is done through a structured programme with seven distinct goals. Nurses, police officers and teachers (commonly identified as particularly vulnerable to stress) have benefited from such training with reduced stress (Bishop, 1994). This is an eclectic approach, since it focuses both on dealing with stressors and on the stress response. The training is useful for dealing with moderate stress, but relies upon the individual's ability to learn effectively.

Q **'Stress will be one of the chief things we have to cope with in the 21st century and psychology will give us a key lead in how to help people cope.' What insights has psychology given us into the strengths and weaknesses of different methods of stress management?** (12 marks)

Emotional and/or physical discharge may help in terms of providing an outlet for the build-up of adrenaline associated with stress. Examples include expressing feelings uninhibitedly (emotional discharge — 'catharsis') or taking part in strenuous exercise (physical discharge). Clearly, expressing feelings uninhibitedly can get one into serious trouble in social situations (swearing at a judge is not advised!), and it is not always possible to take part in strenuous exercise (during an exam, for example).

1 *Abnormality*

1.1 DEFINING PSYCHOLOGICAL ABNORMALITY

Abnormality is one of the most difficult terms in all of psychology to define. This is mainly because psychologists have different ideas about what causes abnormality and how it manifests (or shows) itself. Some psychologists believe it is mainly due to 'failures' in a person's basic biology (for example, brain chemistry); others believe that it is due to 'faulty' learning; others believe it is caused by 'faulty' cognitions (such as perceptions and belief systems); still others believe it is the result of problems of the mind and the personality.

All of these different views of abnormality have enjoyed dominance at different times in history, and at any particular time their influence will vary across cultures. Fernando (1991), amongst others, argued that the model which at any particular time is dominant in the Western world will be the one which exerts most influence.

Some definitions

- 'Abnormal behaviour is behaviour that departs from the norm or is harmful or distressing to the individual or those around them. Abnormal behaviours are usually those that in some way violate society's ideas about what is an appropriate level of functioning' (Cardwell, 1996).
- Stratton and Hayes (1993, p. 1) offer a concise, yet sufficiently broad definition of abnormality by referring to multiple aspects of how the term abnormality is used. As such, it can be defined as: '(1) behaviour which is different from the norm (i.e. unusual); (2) behaviour which does not conform to social demands; (3) statistically uncommon behaviour, based on the assumptions of the normal distribution; (4) behaviour which is maladaptive or painful for the individual; or (5) the failure to achieve self-actualisation, the humanistic view'. Notice the bias (excepting point 5) towards behavioural abnormality. There are other limitations and problems with this definition; the authors themselves point out that 'such definitions lead to the classification of highly regarded individuals like artists and social reformers as abnormal'. You will no doubt note some overlap between this set of defining characteristics and those provided by Gross (1996), detailed below.
- Rosenhan and Seligman (1995) contended that normality is simply the absence of abnormality. This is an interesting inversion of the usual focus and points out that, in making decisions about what is abnormal (decisions which vary cross-culturally and historically), we are also making decisions about what we consider to be normal.
- Gross (2001) argues that there are nine ways of defining abnormality and you need to know about the following four:
  (1) *Deviation from the statistical average*. For example, there are fewer schizophrenics than non-schizophrenics in the general population.
  (2) *Deviation from the norm*. The term norm in this context is used not in the sense of a statistical norm (as in 1, above) but as carrying a value judgement of 'oughtness'. For example, people ought to behave in such a way that they are not a danger to others.
  (3) *The adequacy or mental health criterion*. Jahoda (1958) argued that abnormality can be defined as lacking certain features found in people with 'healthy' adjustment to life (for example, having a realistic self image).
  (4) *Abnormality as mental illness*. This is the view that a person's behaviour may be

classified as fitting the symptoms listed for a clinical mental illness. We will revisit this criterion in Topic 11 beginning on page 150.

Q | **Explain one approach to defining psychological abnormality.** | (6 marks)

The AQA(A) specification renames these four definitions as:

- statistical infrequency.
- deviation from social norms.
- a failure to function adequately.
- deviation from ideal mental health.

1.2 THE STATISTICAL INFREQUENCY DEFINITION

Definition

People with a particular mental disorder, such as depression or schizophrenia, are less numerous in a national population (e.g. England or India) than those without the mental illness. This definition goes no further than this: it makes no judgement, for example, about quality of life or the nature of the mental illness.

Evaluation

For

A positive feature is that no value judgements are made. So, for example, homosexuality — which was defined as a mental illness in some early versions of the Diagnostic and Statistical Manual of mental Disorders (DSM) (see Topic 11) — would not be judged to be 'wrong' or 'unacceptable', merely less statistically frequent in most populations than heterosexuality.

Against

- A key weakness is that many behaviours or characteristics would be regarded as abnormal. An example would be being a genius! The DSM recognises mental retardation (which would be associated with a very low IQ score) as a dimension of mental illness, but there is obviously an equivalent at the other end of the IQ scale.
- The definition ignores cultural or gender variation. For example, Orbach (2000) argued that an unhealthy obsession with body image and weight may be characteristic of a majority of young women in countries such as Britain at the moment, but in certain other cultures in Asia and Africa the incidence is extremely low. The statistical infrequency definition does nothing to explain this.
- There is no notion about how far one has to be away from the statistical norm to be defined as abnormal.

1.3 THE DEVIATION FROM SOCIAL NORMS DEFINITION

Definition

This definition focuses on the impact of certain behavioural patterns on other people. Examples would be antisocial (psychopathic) personality disorder and aggressive or erratic behaviour due to persistent substance abuse.

Evaluation

For

One of the major advantages of this approach is that it gives a social dimension to the notion of abnormality, which gives us an alternative to an emphasis on the isolated, 'sick-in-the-head' individual. Szasz (1963) argued, very controversially, that one of the main 'functions' of psychiatry has been to exclude from society those who are deemed to behave in a way which is unacceptable to others.

Against

- Attitudes towards mental illness vary enormously between different cultures. In India, for example, incidences of mental illness such as depression are significantly lower than in the West, but this may be because a lot of support is given within the structure of the family, so sufferers may not have the need to 'go-public' and see their doctor. In Japan, mental illness is seen as shameful and ex-patients are not allowed to work as cooks or bakers, to enter public baths or to hold a driving licence (Prentice, 2000).

- As Szasz's position makes clear, the notion of who makes decisions about what is and what is not socially acceptable behaviour is a very politically sensitive one. The abuses of categorisation of mental illness under Russian communism (as anyone who proclaimed views against the state) are well known and documented. In many cultures today it is not acceptable for women to be independent and to speak their minds, whereas very few people in our culture would regard this as abnormal behaviour or indicative of mental illness (Rack, 1982).

- Social deviation may be a good thing, as in the case of Germans who stood up against the Nazis in Germany in the 1930s and 1940s, or those who risked their lives opposing the white racist governments in South Africa.

Q | **Give two criticisms of the deviation from social norms explanation for abnormality.** (3+3 marks)

1.4 THE FAILURE TO FUNCTION ADEQUATELY DEFINITION

Definition

Rosenhan and Seligman (1995) say that we can identify certain characteristics of abnormality. None on its own would be sufficient to categorise a person as being mentally ill, but when they co-exist a person may be so classified. The more characteristics a person demonstrates and the greater the severity, the more likelihood there is of being classified as abnormal (Zimbardo et al., 1995). Characteristics include:

- psychological suffering
- irrationality and incomprehensibility
- vividness and unconventionality
- violation of moral and ideal standards
- maladaptiveness
- unpredictability and loss of control
- observer discomfort

Evaluation

For

This definition focuses on personal suffering and distress, thus drawing attention to the subjective experiences associated with mental illness and abnormality.

Against

- Several mental illnesses do not include many of the 'symptoms' listed; for example, many schizophrenics do not feel that they have a problem themselves, although others would view them differently.

- Many of the criteria are very culturally specific. Rice and Haralambos (2000) give the following example: 'What would you make of the following behaviour? A man refused to speak to his mother-in-law and father-in-law. If he found himself alone in the house with his mother-in-law, he would cover himself with a blanket until she left. You may find this behaviour dysfunctional, unpredictable and irrational. However, in terms of traditional Cheyenne Indian behaviour, it is normal and expected.'

1.5 THE IDEAL MENTAL HEALTH DEFINITION

Definition

Drawing on the work of Erikson, Jahoda (1958) argued that the concepts of normality and abnormality were unhelpful, and said instead that we should talk about what constitutes good mental health, in the same way that we can identify characteristics of good physical health. She believed that good mental health has the following six characteristics:
(1) high self-esteem and a strong sense of personal identity
(2) psychological growth or development (towards what Maslow called self-actualisation)
(3) the ability to cope with stressful situations in one's life
(4) autonomy and the ability to resist social pressures
(5) an accurate perception of reality
(6) adaptation to the environment one lives in

Evaluation

For

The approach is a good one insofar as it emphasises positive achievements rather than failures and distress.

Against

- Many of the characteristics are difficult to measure (in the objective way that a doctor, for example, can measure physical health).
- As with almost all of the definitions, there is the difficulty of **cultural relativism**, i.e. characteristics will vary between cultures. Comer (1998) grasps the essence of this when he says, 'Efforts to define psychological abnormality typically raise as many questions as answers. The major difficulty is that the very concept of abnormality is relative: it depends on the norms and values of the society in question.'

Describe the limitations imposed by cultural relativism on attempts to define psychological abnormality.

(6 marks)

---

2 *Biological and psychological models of abnormality*

Models which have been developed to explain abnormality can be classified into two main groups, biological (medical) models and psychological models.

2.1 BIOLOGICAL MODELS OF ABNORMALITY

There are several biological/medical models of abnormality, but all share a common assumption that abnormalities (including mental illnesses) are caused by physical malfunction. Just as a person can be suffering from a heart disorder, and receive drug treatment or surgery to help alleviate the problems, so mental illness can be viewed as resulting from physical causes, such as those arising from brain chemistry 'problems' or genetic inheritance.

In the West, the medical model of mental illness has dominated the field of mental health for the past 200 years (Prentice, 2000). During the past 100 or so years this was largely associated with the development and widespread usage of **psychiatry**. The beginning of modern psychiatry is generally attributed to the work of Kraepelin (1883), who believed that mental illnesses were caused by physiological and physical factors. These mental illnesses, such as dementia praecox (the original term for schizophrenia), could be identified by common groups of symptoms, and were independent of each other. **Psychiatrists** believe not only that mental illnesses have physical causes, but also — because of this — that they can be cured (or at least held stable) by physical treatments. By contrast, **clinical psychologists** subscribe to psychological models of mental illness. But exactly *what* physical factors do biological/medical models put forward to explain mental illnesses? Eysenck and Flanagan (2000) contend that there are four groups:

- *Infection*. For example, Barr et al. (1990) found that there was an association between the incidence of schizophrenia in children and the mother having influenza during her pregnancy.
- *Genetic factors*. For example, twin studies have been carried out to explore the influence of genetic inheritance in certain mental illnesses. McGuffin et al. (1996) found that with monozygotic twins (who are genetically identical), if one of the twins had depression, there was a 46% likelihood the other would too, whereas the figure fell to 20% in dizygotic twins (who have half of their genes in common).
- *Biochemistry*. An example of this is the Dopamine Hypothesis, which is based on findings from several studies (e.g. Iversen, 1979) that people with schizophrenia have excessive amounts of the neurotransmitter dopamine in their brains.
- *Neuroanatomy*. For example, Chua and McKenna (1995) found that people with schizophrenia had smaller brains with larger ventricles than non-schizophrenics.

2.2 IMPLICATIONS FOR TREATMENT OF BIOLOGICAL MODELS

Given that these models are based on the belief that mental illnesses are *caused* by physical/physiological factors, it follows that the *cure* will lie in rectifying these physical problems.

Rice and Haralambos (2000) describe four groups of treatment associated with the biological/medical model: drug treatment; gene therapy; electroconvulsive therapy; and brain surgery.

Drug treatment
The four main groups of drugs used to treat mental illnesses are:

- antimanic drugs (such as Lithium). These are used, for example, to control mania in bipolar depression
- antidepressant (stimulant) drugs (such as Prozac)
- antianxiety (also called anxiolytic) drugs (such as Valium)
- antipsychotic drugs (such as Chlorpromazine, which is used to treat schizophrenia)

Gene therapy
A project which aims to map the complete genetic make-up of humans, the Human Genome Project, was begun in 1990. If successful, gene manipulation may be a way of preventing the occurrence of mental illnesses, assuming that genes play a significant part in the cause of the abnormality in question.

Electroconvulsive therapy (ECT)
Although originally used in the 1940s for the treatment for schizophrenia, it is more commonly and effectively used today for depression. In ECT, a 70–150 volt electric shock is applied for up to one second to either one or both sides of the brain. This produces a general convulsion, which lasts for approximately one minute. Typically, treatments are given two or three times per week for three or four weeks (Gross, 1996).

Brain surgery
The technique is only used as a last resort, usually in cases of severe depression or obsessive-compulsive disorder, where other techniques have been tried and failed.

Nevertheless it has been estimated that up to 50,000 cases have been recorded in the USA alone. The technique of surgically cutting out or destroying tissue which links the frontal lobes with the subcortical areas of the brain (pre-frontal lobotomies) was pioneered in human schizophrenics by Moniz in 1935. The surgical technique has been significantly refined in recent years — these days electric probes are used to destroy specific tissue, instead of the scalpel.

General evaluation of the biological/medical model

For

- As an explanatory model, it can be regarded as scientific as it focuses upon physical and physiological factors (for both cause and treatment) in the same way as medicine does for physical disorders or problems. Genes and brain chemistry and function can be reliably measured and manipulated. This contrasts with, for example, the psychodynamic model (see below) which is metaphysical.
- Patients may find it reassuring that their 'condition' can be attributed to a physical deficiency (such as overproduction of dopamine for schizophrenics) rather than something 'wrong with them' (as a person).
- As noted above, treatments are often effective.

Against

- Physical/physiological irregularities associated with mental illnesses may be caused by the illness rather than be the cause of the illness.
- The model is reductionist. That is to say, it reduces things down to basic units of physical and physiological functioning. In so doing it misses the larger picture, such as what Szasz (1962) called 'problems of living'.
- It may encourage patients to adopt a passive view of their illness, whereby they depend on a doctor to 'do something to them' rather than playing an active part in their own cure (as in many forms of counselling).
- Most of the treatments focus only on patients' symptoms rather than any underlying cause(s). The psychodynamic model, for example, has the opposite focus.
- More than most other treatments, biological/medical ones are ethically and morally contentious. Obvious examples include the consequences for the patient of side-effects and dependency as well as those noted above relating specifically to gene therapy and lobotomies.

Describe the assumptions made by the biological/medical model of abnormality and give two criticisms of these. (6+3+3 marks)

To what extent can the causes of abnormality be understood in terms of the biological/medical model? (18 marks)

2.3 PSYCHOLOGICAL MODELS OF ABNORMALITY

There are several psychological models of abnormality, which can essentially be reduced to three broad perspectives — **psychodynamic**, **behavioural** and **cognitive**. The perspectives offer different explanations for how abnormality arises in the first place; in line with this, the treatments also differ.

The emphasis on cause and treatment of mental illnesses in these models is, unlike in the biological models, centred on the **psychology** of the individual.

Psychological explanations of causation and treatments offered differ across the three perspectives: unresolved conflicts are the focus of the psychodynamic model; inappropriate learned behaviours are the focus of the behaviourist model; and unhelpful or unwanted thoughts and perceptions are the focus of the cognitive model. Each is detailed more thoroughly below.

2.4 THE PSYCHODYNAMIC MODEL OF ABNORMALITY

Freud proposed that the human mind or psyche is governed by three aspects of our personality: the **id**, **superego** and **ego**. The id is the source of our animal instincts, strong urges and drives that are essentially insatiable, and is an innate inherited aspect. The superego is supposed to be the social conscience, and develops as individuals learn the rules and norms that govern society in their culture. Clearly these two aspects of personality are going to run into numerous conflicts — the id urging selfish and amoral behaviour to satisfy primal needs, whilst the superego strictly admonishes such behaviour in line with the morality of society. In order to resolve these unconscious conflicts, the third aspect of personality, the ego, develops to allow for balance, to allow the id and superego to be expressed in appropriate ways at appropriate times.

2.5 IMPLICATIONS FOR TREATMENT OF THE PSYCHODYNAMIC MODEL

Since the psychodynamic model of mental illness outlined above assumes that illness is the result of unresolved unconscious conflict, the treatments are aimed at first identifying the nature of the conflict, and then resolving it. Since the conflict is **unconscious**, the patient cannot be consciously aware of it, so various methods are used to elicit information that allows the psychoanalyst to identify and resolve the patient's issues.

Dream analysis
Description

Freud believed that dreams were the 'royal road' to the unconscious mind, and that the images and events of dreams, if analysed by the trained psychoanalyst, could, through their symbolism and deeper meaning, reveal facts about the patient's inner conflict. Thoughts otherwise repressed (for example, if too traumatic to consider consciously) in the unconscious mind 'bubble up' in dreams and can thus be scrutinised.

Free association
Description

Dreams are not the only forum in which the unconscious mind can surface, according to psychodynamic theorists. By encouraging a patient to 'free associate', to speak freely without reservation, contemplation or inhibition about a particular subject, the therapist has access to what is called the patient's 'stream of consciousness'. The resulting information can then be analysed in much the same way as the content of dreams.

General evaluation of psychodynamic models
For

- The theories underlying the models and their applications are extensive and have remained popular for over a century. There are also many examples of successful outcomes using such therapies. Even if this can be attributed to recovery based on the placebo effect, a positive outcome is still a positive outcome.
- Empirical evidence confirms that many patients with mental illnesses did indeed have histories of trauma in childhood (then, of course, many non-patients were not asked if they had traumatic childhoods).
- The patient would usually feel no blame for the disorder — not only are the conflicts informing their illness commonplace and part of human nature, there is also a strong allocation of blame towards parents and caregivers.

- The psychodynamic models were the first explanations of mental illnesses that were psychological in nature and challenged some of the assumptions of the biological model.

Against
- The patient has little 'ownership' or responsibility attached to the problem — exonerating patients of their behaviour can be helpful, but can also be challenged on moral and practical grounds. This also means there is a reliance upon experts who may be few and far between, and thus likely to charge considerably for their services.
- The theory and the evidence supporting successful treatment is anecdotal and un-scientific.
- The theory is reductionist and deterministic (instincts are biologically driven and innate, though clearly there is a social and cultural influence in the model in terms of the superego).
- Patients without sufficient verbal skills cannot be treated with these methods, and some mental illnesses constrain insight to the extent of making such treatments redundant.
- The theory upon which the models are based can be criticised for attaching far too much weight to sexual factors (Freud's theories evolved in a culture that supported his theories on sexual obsession, but since then they have been challenged as being untenable in other cultures).

Give two criticisms of the implications for treatment of abnormality from the psycho-dynamic model.
(3+3 marks)

2.6 THE BEHAVIOURAL MODEL OF ABNORMALITY

The behaviourist perspective emerged as a reaction against the introspective mind-based theories that preceded it. Behaviourists wanted to move away from unscientific psychology, of which the psychodynamic model covered previously is an example. The emphasis for behaviourist psychology is not on the workings of the mind, personality, or the history of an individual, but purely on **observable** and **measurable** behaviour.

Behaviours, whether they are 'normal' or 'abnormal', are all acquired in the same way, through **conditioning**. Associations form when presentations of stimuli are repeatedly paired, so an innate (unconditioned) response to one stimulus may be transferred to a paired stimulus (classical conditioning). Additionally, the consequences (positive and negative reinforcement, and punishment) of our behaviour inform the likelihood of that behaviour being repeated (operant conditioning). Bandura (1986) extended such ideas by proposing that behaviours can be vicariously reinforced when we observe behaviours and their consequences in others (social learning theory).

Therefore, abnormal behaviour is seen as being acquired and learned through condi-tioning. An example of this is the case of Little Albert, who through manipulating paired associations was taught to fear harmless stimuli. Behaviourists believe that such behaviours can be **unlearned** by applying the same principles (i.e. using classical and operant conditioning manipulations to cause learning of more useful or adaptive behaviours) — this is known as **counter-conditioning**.

2.7 IMPLICATIONS FOR TREATMENT OF THE BEHAVIOURAL MODEL

Since behaviour is the currency of the model, and *not* thoughts or personality, even the descriptions of mental illnesses (under other models) are referred to as inappropriate or maladaptive behaviours rather than mental illnesses or thought disturbances. Therapies are aimed at *counter-conditioning*, *modifying* or *extinguishing* these unwanted behaviours. Primary behavioural therapies are discussed below.

Aversion therapy

This is a treatment for addictions and unwanted dependencies, such as serious drug addictions, as well as alcoholism and nicotine dependency. The maladaptive behaviour (taking the drug, drinking alcohol, smoking cigarettes etc.) is repeatedly paired with an unpleasant stimulus (such as an **emetic** substance, which induces nausea and vomiting). This creates a negative association with the craved substance and leads to avoidance of it. This can be regarded as classical conditioning in that an innate response to the emetic is transferred through association onto the target stimulus (alcohol etc). It can also be regarded as having operant conditioning properties, since the vomiting becomes, through association, regarded as a consequence of the target stimulus.

Systematic desensitisation (SD)

Used by Wolpe (1958) and other behavioural therapists, this therapy is used to remove phobias. In the behavioural model of a phobia, fear and anxiety have become a behavioural response to the phobic object. Therefore, an application of classical conditioning is used to replace the unwanted fear and anxiety associated with the phobic object with an incompatible response — typically relaxation. The patient is taught deep muscle relaxation techniques and instructed to use them when exposed (in various degrees of valence, from weak to strong) to the object of their phobia. So, at first, a spider phobic may read the word spider, then look at a photograph of a spider, then be in the same room as a spider, etc. At each stage, patients are instructed to use the relaxation techniques they have learned, and will go on to the next stage once they can maintain a relaxed state in the current stage. Eventually, through repeated pairings of exposure to the stimuli with relaxation and no fear, the fear is eliminated.

Implosion and flooding

Both these therapies are aimed at treatment of phobias and are practically quite similar. Based upon the principles of classical conditioning, in which associations formed through repeated pairings are *extinguished* if the stimulus is presented without its associate, both therapies involve maximal exposure to the feared stimulus for a prolonged time until the fear subsides. With implosion, the exposure is imagined (patients imagine their most feared scenario vividly), whilst with flooding, the exposure is real. From the social learning angle, some therapists use principles of modelling to treat patients, themselves being immersed in the feared scenario while being observed by the patient. The patient then learns to imitate the therapist's more appropriate behaviours.

Token economies

In institutional settings, operant conditioning is often used to shape behaviour. This is in the form of rewards given to those behaving appropriately. The rewards are generally tokens that can be exchanged for positive privileges (such as cigarettes, books, etc.). Following Thorndike's Law of Effect ('behaviours positively rewarded are more likely to be repeated'), the idea is that the behaviours rewarded with tokens will be repeated.

Q **Describe the implications for treatment of the behavioural model of abnormality.** (6 marks)

General evaluation of the behavioural model

For

- The underlying theory is extensive and widely supported. The therapies have also achieved some high success rates.

- Patients arguably feel less judgementally labelled by being described as having learned maladaptive behaviours as opposed to being 'mentally ill'.
- The model is sensitive to individual differences and social and cultural context, since the individual behavioural history of patients has shaped their maladaptive behaviour.

Against
- Many of the therapies can be challenged as being distressing and unethical.
- Since only behaviour is addressed, it has been argued that only the symptoms are treated, not the underlying problem. Thoughts and feelings are not considered.
- The model focuses on the influences of environment and learning, yet ignores the genetic element of many disorders (e.g. schizophrenia).
- The model and treatment approaches are reductionist and limited in scope.
- Much of the supporting evidence and theory rests better in terms of non-human animals than humans.

2.8 THE COGNITIVE MODEL OF ABNORMALITY

The cognitive model of abnormality was founded by Ellis (1962) and Beck (1963) and challenged the behavioural approach. Cognitive psychologists argue that between the stimulus and the response (the only components considered in behaviourism) there are mental processes — cognitions, appraisals, thoughts — and it is these processes that inform the way a person feels about the stimuli.

Abnormalities (emotional disturbances, such as anxiety and depression) are argued to result from maladaptive, distorted, irrational, illogical or just unhelpful thoughts, beliefs, and attitudes. An example of an illogical error is thinking '*everything* has gone wrong in my life', when one thing has gone wrong — this is termed **over-generalisation**. **Polarised thinking** is another example, when people think in extremes of black and white (people don't allow something to be considered 'slightly disappointing', only 'totally dreadful').

2.9 IMPLICATIONS FOR TREATMENT OF THE COGNITIVE MODEL

It is acknowledged that everyone engages at some point in irrational and unhelpful thought processes. Problems that require treatment arise when the extent of these negative thoughts becomes intolerable or maladaptive for the individual or others. The aim of cognitive therapies is to address these faulty or unhelpful thought processes and replace them with more positive adaptive cognitive processes, a procedure known as **cognitive restructuring**.

Cognitive restructuring
Developed by Beck (1976), cognitive restructuring involves identifying the unhelpful (and usually irrational) thoughts that a depressed person may have, and replacing them with more realistic and useful thought processes. For example, *over-generalisations* and *polarised thoughts* are questioned and modified, which increases the confidence and self-esteem of the patient, challenging the person's negative self-image. Similar to this is Meichenbaum's **stress inoculation training** which challenges and adjusts the negative internal dialogues that people often hold.

Rational-emotional therapy (RET)
Similar to Beck's therapy (cognitive restructuring), Ellis (1962) developed a theory around the idea that patients possess irrational or unreasonable beliefs about their life events that have a negative effect. He described the 'ABC' of undesirable emotion (A = activating event → B = beliefs about the event → C = consequences). 'B' is the aspect which RET challenges. The therapist aggressively questions the rationale of the unreasonable belief

(for example, 'Who says you're a complete failure if you don't get an A in all your exams?'), forcing the patient to consider how unreasonable such thoughts are. As in the example, the therapy tends to be used on patients with anxiety, which may be caused by self-imposed perfectionism.

General evaluation of the cognitive model

For

- Many mental disorders are, as assumed by this model, associated with cognitive biases and dysfunctional thoughts (Gustafson, 1992).
- The therapies give some ownership of the problem to patients — they are essentially given highly transferable coping skills. Also, patients are not negatively labelled, just helped with their thinking.
- The model accounts for more than the stimulus–response (S–R) approach, since appraisal in between is considered.

Against

- Social conditions are largely ignored — a person's thinking takes all the 'blame'.
- As with the behavioural model, critics fear that the underlying problem is left after tackling what they suggest are merely symptoms.
- The model has been criticised for assuming that thought processes are the cause rather than a symptom of the problem. However, very recent research has suggested that cognitive biases may be not only central to certain disorders such as anxiety, but *causal* (e.g. Mathews, 2000; Ward, 2001).
- The genetic and biological contributions to disorders are largely ignored by the model and totally ignored by the treatments described.

3 Critical issue — eating disorders

In the previous section, you read about how the different models of abnormality have different explanations of, and treatments for, disorders in general. The rest of this chapter will deal with a specific pair of eating disorders, **anorexia nervosa** and **bulimia nervosa**, explaining how the models explain and treat them. Both these eating disorders are far more common in the Western world than in any other society, and the overwhelming majority of sufferers are female (for anorexia, adolescent females; for bulimia, 20–30 year old females).

These eating disorders have increased in frequency over the past three decades (Garner and Fairburn, 1988; Cooper, 1994), arguably exacerbated by media representations of slim women as the ideal, although Tolstrup (1990) describes cases diagnosed before the 1600s.

3.1 THE CLINICAL CHARACTERISTICS OF EATING DISORDERS

The clinical characteristics of the two main eating disorders are taken from the DSM-IV (*Diagnostic and Statistical Manual*, 4th edition).

Anorexia nervosa

- Patient has a body weight less than 85% of expected weight.
- Patient has intense anxiety about becoming fat (despite being underweight).
- Patient exhibits body-weight distortion, in terms of rating a low body-weight as overly desirable and/or not having realistic beliefs about the dangers of being so underweight.

- Patient suffers with amenorrhoea, the absence of menstruation. Three or more consecutively skipped periods is an indication of anorexia (confirmed by the above criteria).

Bulimia nervosa

- There is a lack of control over eating behaviour, and there are episodes of binge eating where far more food than normal is eaten within a two hour period.
- Bingeing is followed by behaviour to compensate for it (purging). This is typically self-induced vomiting, but may also include skipping meals, using laxatives and exercising excessively.
- This binge–purge activity may also occur in those who would not be diagnosed as bulemic — diagnosis requires that the binge–purge activity occur at a frequency at or above twice a week over a three month period.
- There is body-image distortion, as with anorexia.
- The condition is distinct from anorexia, with the binge–purge activity occurring extraneously to episodes of anorexia.

Q **Describe the clinical characteristics of either anorexia nervosa or bulimia nervosa.** (6 marks)

3.2 BIOLOGICAL (MEDICAL) EXPLANATIONS OF ANOREXIA NERVOSA AND BULIMIA NERVOSA, INCLUDING EVALUATIONS

Genetic predisposition

There is compelling evidence of a genetic component in both the main types of eating disorder. Holland et al. (1984) found 55% concordance in identical (monozygotic) twins compared to only 7% in non-identical (dizygotic) twins. The fact that identical twins do not *always* both exhibit the conditions suggests that genetics is not the only factor (or we would have 100% concordance). See the research box at the end of the topic for more detail on this research.

Hypothalamus

One of the functions of the hypothalamus is to regulate the internal physiology of a human, maintaining **homeostasis**. Homeostatic drives include those concerned with feeding, so it is suspected that the hypothalamus may be implicated in these eating disorders (e.g. Keesey and Corbett, 1983). There is no direct evidence of this, but the idea is supported by cases where a damaged hypothalamus has been observed alongside loss of appetite and disturbances to menstruation.

Hormonal imbalance

Amenorrhoea (absence of menstruation) sometimes occurs before weight loss occurs. This could be indicative of a general disorder of the endocrine system, which may be partly causal in some eating disorders — this ties in with the hypothalamus being implicated, since endocrine dysfunctions are often associated with hypothalamic dysfunction. Fava et al. (1989) found anorexics had different levels of noradrenaline, which partially corroborates this notion. There is not any *direct* evidence of this explanation, however, and the occasional association does not imply causality.

Neurotransmission

Some researchers have suggested that dopamine may be involved in eating disorders (dopamine is frequently implicated in numerous mental illnesses including schizophrenia, Tourette's syndrome and obsessive-compulsive disorders). Low levels of serotonin have been associated with binge eating (Jimerson et al., 1997), and bulimia is most effectively treated by serotonin-active antidepressant drugs (Walsh et al., 1997).

3.3 PSYCHOLOGICAL EXPLANATIONS OF ANOREXIA NERVOSA AND BULIMIA NERVOSA, INCLUDING EVALUATIONS

Psychodynamic explanations

Freudian theory suggests that eating is a substitute for sexual expression (though this is highly contentious). As such, and given that most cases of anorexia occur in adolescence, eating disorders have been described (e.g. Bruch, 1979) as an attempt to repress sexual impulses. Overbearing or abusive parents may lead the adolescent to resist the move to adulthood, and not eating is argued to be a manifestation of this resistance (eating = sexual = adult...therefore to avoid adulthood, avoid eating). Bruch (1987) also suggested that overbearing parenting (with parents wanting the child to remain heavily dependent on them) may lead to the adolescent rebelling and expressing **autonomy** in a transparent and manageable way, by refusing to eat. As with much of psychodynamic theory, while some of the arguments sound plausible, others are based on wildly conjectured assumptions (e.g. that eating is a substitute for sexual expression), and there is little scientific evidence to support them.

Behavioural explanations

Social learning theory (e.g. Bandura, 1986) tends to support the popular layperson's explanation of eating disorders, that they are the result of modelling (in both the psychological definition of the term, and partially the occupational one!). The media portrays successful and attractive people (particularly women) as slim. Adolescents are highly suggestible and seek role models, so the media may influence them to starve to achieve their goal. This is supported by Lee et al. (1992) who found that there are very few cases of anorexia in China, where family values are considered well above personal appearance and personal success. (See the research box at the end of the chapter for more detail about Lee et al.'s study.) Additionally, behaviourists argue (in line with operant conditioning) that the attention received from losing weight (whether admiration from peers or concern from parents) may well reinforce the slimming behaviour. This explanation has the advantage that it can explain why there has been such an increase in eating disorders over the past few decades, since this timing coincides with the rapid growth and accessibility of multiple forms of media. Also, behavioural treatments tend to be very successful, supporting the theory underlying them. However, this explanation ignores the influence of biology and genetics, which evidence suggests play a part, and if media exposure was all that was required for triggering eating disorders, the problem would be far more rampant in the West than it is.

Cognitive explanations

The diagnostic criteria for anorexia and bulimia lend themselves well to a cognitive explanation — both include reference to **distorted body image**. In order to qualify as one of these eating disorders, a patient must exhibit such dysfunctional thinking, so cognitive explanations focus on the irrational thinking that is associated with eating disorders. Garfinkel and Garner (1982) found that patients diagnosed with eating disorders overestimated their body size compared to controls, supporting the notion that eating disorders are associated with dysfunctional appraisals. However, association does not imply causality, and the dysfunctional thinking in eating disorder patients may be a symptom rather than a cause of the problem.

Q Describe one psychological model which attempts to explain eating disorders.   (6 marks)

Research into eating disorders

Holland et al. (1988) investigated whether anorexia had a genetic factor. Thirty-four pairs of twins were sampled, where one of the twins had anorexia. If anorexia was 100% triggered by genes, we would expect 100% of the twins to share the anorexia, but they did not. However, there was concordance between the twins, with many cases of both twins developing anorexia. In MZ twins (monozygotic, 100% genetic sharing), 56% of the siblings of anorexics were themselves anorexics; in DZ twins (dizygotic, 50% genetic sharing), this concordance rate was 7%. It was therefore concluded that there was some genetic predisposition, and that manifestation presumably depended upon environmental triggers. It must be remembered that many twin studies share a similar flaw — that the twins not only share genes, but mostly tend to share environment too. However, there were some twins raised apart, and in these cases, the concordance was still higher than one would expect.

Cultural differences are evident in eating disorders. Lee et al. (1992) conducted a study investigating the incidence of anorexia bulimia in Hong Kong, and found surprisingly few cases. They proposed various explanations for this disparity:

(1) The Chinese tend to eat more low-fat foods than people in the West.
(2) The Chinese culture has a very different definition of success. In the West, success is associated with personal wealth and achievement, including personal appearance and career progression. However, in China, the emphasis on success is on family growth and stability.
(3) Dieting is uncommon, and fatness is not stigmatised with negativity.
(4) There appears to be less exposure to role models for females in Chinese culture. Surveys revealed that knowledge of self-induced vomiting as a weight control method was much less common than in the West.

The explanations mostly refer to socio-cultural factors based upon what constitutes success, and how it is portrayed by the media and in public values. However, there is also reason to believe that some of the disparity can be explained in genetic terms. The Chinese tend to be slimmer than Westerners, and tend to weigh less at birth. Therefore, there are fewer people of larger size to engender consideration of weight control, whether through recommended channels (sensible dieting) or dysfunctional means (self-induced vomiting). Furthermore, the preference for low-fat foods relative to tastes in Westerners may be genetically predisposed. Such genetic predispositions for food preferences have been found with regard to alcohol, which is far less popular in China than in the West.

Q **Describe the procedures and findings of one research study into eating disorders.** (6 marks

---

1 Conformity and minority influence

We may define conformity as 'a change in belief or behaviour in response to real or imagined group pressure when there is no direct request to comply with the group nor any reason given to justify the behaviour change' (Zimbardo and Leippe, 1991). The point about conformity occurring when there is no direct request to comply with the group clearly differentiates conformity from obedience. Many students get confused over the difference between these two concepts.

Q **Give a definition of conformity.** (3 marks)

According to Jahoda (1959) there are three key features to conforming behaviour:

- the amount of emotional or intellectual 'investment' a person has in the issue involved: put simply, how important it is to him or her
- a person's behaviour: whether he or she goes along with the group or not
- beliefs and attitudes: whether a person actually agrees with the position of the group or not

Clearly the first and third are 'inner' (mental) factors, whereas the second one is 'external' (behavioural).

On the basis of the interrelationship between these three factors, Jahoda was able to develop the model given in Table 5.1, which classifies eight different types of conformity and independence.

	Initial investment high on issue		Initial investment low on issue	
	Public and private agree	**Public and private differ**	**Public and private agree**	**Public and private differ**
Adopts group position	Independent consent	Compliance	Conformity	Expedient conformity
Does not adopt group position	Independent	Undermined	Compulsive resistance	Expedient resistance

Table 5.1 Types of conformity and independence

1.1 WHY DO PEOPLE CONFORM?

Conformity studies show that there is considerable variation between *different individuals* in the extent to which they display conformity. There is also variation between different behaviours of the same individual on *different occasions and in different situations*. Some of the key factors which have been shown to determine whether or not an individual is likely to conform or be independent are as follows:

- *Individual differences.* Personality characteristics can be very influential. People with low self-esteem, need for approval, feelings of insecurity, high anxiety or feelings of self-blame are all associated with high conformity. Sex differences have been found in many studies, with women consistently being found to conform slightly more than men. However, this may be due to the nature of the task. Sistrunk and McDavid (1971) tested conformity with tasks using images of stereotypically male tools (e.g. a wrench) and stereotypically female tools (e.g. types of needlework) and found that each sex conformed more than the other on the 'unfamiliar' images.

● *Cultural factors*. Smith and Bond (1996) showed that people who score high on a collectivist scale are more conformist than those who score low. For example, Berry (1967) found that the Temne people of Sierra Leone conformed significantly more than the Eskimos of Canada. He explained this by reference to the nature of economic subsistence in these two cultures: in the former the people rely on a single crop which is harvested intensively once a year and requires complete co-operation between the people; by contrast the Eskimos hunt and gather on a largely individualistic basis.

● *Normative and informational influences*. People often have feelings of group-belonging-ness, such as a need to be accepted or valued by the group; this is known as normative influence. On other occasions individuals may simply be unsure or lack confidence in a task and may then look to the group for guidance or direction. This is an example of informational influence. Normative and informational influences constitute the main emphasis of the Dual Process Dependency Model of Conformity (Hogg and Turner, 1987).

● *Situational determinants*. In experiments such as the one carried out by Asch (1952) (see below), it was found that the *number of people* in the group in which the individual was placed was important. Some research suggests that as the size of the group increases (for example, from 3 to 10 people) so conformity increases. Hogg and Vaughan (1998), however, contend that conformity reaches its full strength in three to five people consistently opposed to the individual; any increases in the group size beyond this has little effect. It has been shown that if opposition is not unanimous (i.e. the individual has another person in the group who agrees with him or her), conformity rates fall dramatically. Therefore **group unanimity** is another important situational determinant.

Although Sherif's (1935) studies, comparing individual and group responses to a visual illusion, were pioneering and were some of the first experimental studies of conformity, there were two major shortcomings:

● The situation was highly artificial and lacked ecological validity (see page 64).
● Because there was no correct answer, it is not surprising that the individuals looked to other members of the group for help in making their judgements.

The classic conformity study (Asch, 1952)

Asch believed that Sherif's results may simply have been caused by the ambiguity of the illusion stimuli and decided to see what would happen if the stimuli were clear-cut. He tested 123 American male college students, who worked in groups between seven and nine in size. In each trial the members of the group were shown two cards: one with a single 'reference' line, and a second with three comparison lines, one of which was the same length as the reference line.

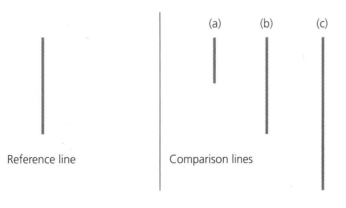

Figure 5.2

Only one member of each group was a genuine participant; the others were confederates of the experimenter and on certain trials unanimously gave a wrong answer (such as (a) in the example above). How did the genuine participants respond? Seventy-five per cent of the participants conformed to the (incorrect) group decision at least once; 5% conformed on every trial. The average conformity rate was 37%.

Q | **Describe two factors which have been found to affect conformity.**   (3+3 marks)

Evaluation

- As with Sherif's studies, the task was trivial, and so in terms of the Jahoda model personal investment would have been low.
- The participants were paid to take part and so may have felt obliged to go along with what was happening.
- In terms of ethics, the participants were deceived as they were not told what the true purpose of the study was.

Q | **Give two criticisms of one study of conformity.**   (3+3 marks)

Describe the aims and findings of any one study of conformity.   (6 marks)

1.2 MINORITY INFLUENCE

Minority influence occurs when a minority of members in a group 'rejects the established norm of the majority of group members and induces the majority to move to the position of the minority' (Turner, 1991).

Q | **What do psychologists mean by the term 'minority influence'?**   (3 marks)

Identify factors which have been found to increase minority influence.   (6 marks)

The pioneering work in the social psychological investigation of minority influence was carried out by Moscovici. In a series of studies, he established that certain factors tend to characterise successful minority influence. Important examples are:

- The minority must hold a consistent view amongst themselves.
- They must stand firm in the face of opposition against their view(s).
- They must hold a clear view from the outset, rather than changing in mid-event.
- They should not be seen to have a vested interest in the issue (like a small number of people trying to persuade others to buy something which would bring them financial gain).
- They will be more successful if they are perceived to have made personal or material sacrifices as a result of holding their view.
- The minority should not appear to be rigid or dogmatic.
- The minority will be more successful if their view is consistent with the spirit of the times.

Why does minority influence work?

Minorities often appear to have deeply held **convictions** (as illustrated through many of the factors listed immediately above) and often occupy a **difficult position**. An example would be Nelson Mandela, who was imprisoned for much of his life for steadfastly opposing the racist regime in South Africa. Because of factors such as these, minorities are often thought of as highly principled, rather than people who take the easy way in life and just 'go along' with the crowd. Minorities often cause the majority to think about issues they may otherwise not think about (Greenpeace activists are a good example).

On the influence of a minority (Clark, 1994)

Clark carried out a study based on the film *Twelve Angry Men*, which illustrates minority influence. The film is set entirely in a jury room as the 12 jurors debate the guilt or innocence of a youth accused of murdering his father. Initially the youth's guilt seems fairly clear, but one of the jurors continually expresses doubt and uncertainty about the evidence and piece-by-piece it is all painstakingly scrutinised and shown to be problematic. At the end of the film the lone juror, subjected to intense pressure by the other jurors to come over to their view, has convinced them that there is too much doubt surrounding the reliability of the two eyewitnesses and the uniqueness of the murder weapon for the youth to be convicted.

Clark was interested in how minority influence can work in jury settings. He had student jurors read a summary of the film (which they were unfamiliar with) and asked them to decide whether the youth was innocent or guilty.

Some of the students were not told of the lone juror's arguments but were told that one of the jurors was unconvinced of the defendant's guilt. Some others were told of his arguments but were not told that other jurors subsequently changed their minds.

The results showed that although initially convinced of guilt, this was affected by the information that one of the jurors was unconvinced and was affected by knowing his arguments. Furthermore, the knowledge that other jurors changed their minds also influenced the verdicts given by the students.

Describe the aims and procedures of any one study of minority influence. (6 marks)

Evaluation

- The study was carried out on students only; the results may not be generally applicable. For example, students may have higher than average IQ scores compared to the general population.
- The study was a simulation of a jury at work and may not accurately reflect how it works in reality.

Obedience to authority

Obedience is a form of social influence, as is conformity, but here the person changes behaviour because of the direct instruction of another person. Obedience almost always involves external (behavioural) change, whereas conformity is often a result of internal (attitudinal) change, such as in many of the cases of minority influence.

Give two differences between conformity and obedience. (3+3 marks)

2.1 RESEARCH STUDIES

The most famous researcher into obedience was Milgram. He distinguished between conformity and obedience with the following example relating to someone who has just joined the military. 'He scrupulously carries out the orders of his superiors. At the same time he adopts the habits, routines and language of his peers. The former represents obedience and the latter conformity' (Milgram, 1974). Unlike conformity, obedience is generally to a single other person rather than a group.

It should be noted that the specification concentrates on obedience to *authority*. In the study described below the orders are being given by figures of authority (a scientific researcher at a prestigious university and a doctor). This authority will be *culturally specific*. For example, whereas the scientific researcher may carry high prestige in the West, he or she may carry relatively little in a highly religious culture in the East, where spiritual leaders would be more highly esteemed.

Probably the most famous experiment ever (Milgram, 1963)

Milgram's study into obedience to authority is the all-time classic experiment in the history of social psychology. He obtained 40 male volunteers via a newspaper advertisement to take part in a learning experiment at Yale University. They were studied individually and were paired with a stooge (a 47 year-old accountant trained for the part). A draw was rigged so that the volunteer was always the 'teacher' and the stooge the 'learner'. The experimenter instructed the volunteer to punish the learner each time he made a mistake by administering an electric shock. The shock was to increase in intensity by 15 volts each time a mistake was made, up to a maximum of 450 volts. In fact, no shocks were administered; the screams of pain which were heard from the learner had been pre-recorded. They were followed by silence after 345 volts had been administered, with the teacher having been told earlier that the learner suffered from a heart complaint.

Prior to carrying out the experiment, Milgram had asked staff and students to predict how many of the participants would continue to the maximum 450 volts. The staff predicted 0.1%; the students 1.2%. The actual response was 65%!

Evaluation

Milgram's study of obedience (and his many subsequent ones) has been questioned in terms of both their experimental and ecological validity (see below). However, the biggest criticism has been in terms of the ethics of the work. Participants were deceived about the true purpose of the study and many suffered considerable distress at the time (although they were counselled and the vast majority later said that they were glad they had taken part in the study). Critics such as Baumrind and Bettelheim said that the studies were inhumane.

Obedience in the real world (Hofling et al., 1966)

Hofling et al. studied obedience to authority in a real-life setting. The study was carried out on 22 night nurses working in psychiatric hospitals in the USA. Each received a telephone call from a person posing as a doctor. He instructed the nurse to administer 20 mg of a particular drug to a specified patient before he arrived on the ward to see the patient. Despite the fact that the maximum prescribed dosage of the medicine was 10 g and that the medicine was an unauthorised drug for the ward in question, 21 of the 22 nurses were prepared to administer it and were only prevented from doing so on the intervention of one of the Hofling team. Furthermore, the instruction was illegal on two other counts: nurses were not supposed to accept instructions given over the telephone and they accepted instructions from a doctor they had never heard of.

In many respects, the Hofling et al. study is even more informative and disturbing than Milgram's studies, in that it was carried out in a real-life setting. In a later part of the research, Hofling and his colleagues interviewed a number of experienced and student nurses and asked how they would respond in the above scenario. Thirty-one of the 33 said they would not follow the doctor's instructions. This gives a startling illustration of the disparity between what people say they will do and what they actually do, a point which Milgram contended was a strong justification for his own work.

2.2 THE ISSUES OF EXPERIMENTAL AND ECOLOGICAL VALIDITY

Milgram's research, in particular, has been examined in terms of the issues of its validity. The term validity is considered in more detail on page 63 (Topic 6).

Experimental validity

This concerns whether the experimental situation is believable. All experiments are unreal to the extent that they are set up by the researcher and the participants are generally aware of this. However, it can often be the case that they can mirror real-life situations to such an extent that participants can 'suspend reality' and act as they would in a real-life situation. Clark's research on jury behaviour (page 51) is a good example of this.

The critical question concerning Milgram's research is whether the volunteers *believed* that they were actually administering shocks to the teacher. If they did not, the research is practically worthless as they were just acting. Orne and Holland (1968) argued that Milgram's studies lacked experimental realism, as the participants must have realised that something untoward was happening. Why, for example, did the experimenter not do the job of the teacher and administer the shocks himself?

Further strong support for the experimental validity of Milgram's studies comes from the fact that Rosenhan carried out a replication in 1969; nearly 70% of the participants said they had believed that what they were doing in the study was for real.

Ecological validity

This is also known as external validity. The question here is whether work such as Milgram's has any *real-world* significance, or is just a product of an experimental situation.

Smith and Bond (1998) give a summary of near-replications of Milgram's scenarios in the USA, UK, Italy, Germany, Australia, Spain, Austria, Holland and Jordan. Obedience rates varied from over 90% to just 16%, but they do not really answer the question as they were all experiments of one form or another.

More significant is the study carried out by Bickman (1974), as this was a field study carried out in a real-world setting (New York). Three male researchers gave orders (such as 'Pick up this bag for me') to randomly selected pedestrians. One researcher was wearing a sports coat and tie, the second a milkman's uniform, and the third a uniform which was similar to a policeman's.

Bickman found that the pedestrians were more likely to obey the orders given by the person looking like a policeman. This supports Milgram's emphasis on the importance of authority in obedience.

It is interesting to note that the Hofling et al. study appears, as a field study, to be of higher ecological validity than Milgram's studies (which were laboratory experiments). Several studies have replicated Milgrams's findings, whereas those replicating the Hofling et al. scenario (e.g. Rank and Jacobsen, 1977) have tended not to produce the same results.

What are the differences between experimental validity and ecological validity?	(6 marks)
Consider the ecological or experimental validity of any one study of social influence.	(6 marks)

2.3 WHY DO PEOPLE OBEY?

Psychological research has shown that there are many factors which may lead to obedience. Some of these relate to a person's nature, others to the situations they find themselves in.

- *Personality*. As with conformity, it has been shown that certain personality types are more likely to obey commands from authority. In particular, the authoritarian personality has been shown to be extremely deferential to authority.
- *Credible authority figure or setting*. In a later version of the Milgram scenario, he carried out the experiment in a run-down office instead of a prestigious university. Although obedience rates were still high, they were lower than in the original experiment. In the Hofling et al. study, the doctor clearly held a position of higher status than the nurses.
- *Locus of responsibility*. Many of the volunteers in Milgram's experiments constantly sought assurance that the experimenter was responsible for any injury caused to the learner before they would carry on. In the Hofling et al. study, the 'doctor' promised to sign an authorisation form when he arrived to inspect the patient.
- *An agentic state*. When asked to explain what he found in his studies, Milgram put a lot of emphasis on what he called the agentic state. By this he meant that in certain circumstances or conditions we come to see ourselves as an agent for another person, someone who does their duties for them. Soldiers carrying out orders may see themselves as the agent of their army so that they can follow orders, ignoring their own individual consciences.
- *Being bound by a 'contract'*. Milgram's volunteers may have felt that they had entered into a 'contractual' relationship with the experimenter where they agreed to follow his instructions. To renege on this would be to cast doubt on his competence. This would have been strengthened by the fact that on each occasion the volunteer was only being asked to do something slightly worse (a 15 volt increase) than he had done before. In the Hofling et al. study the nurses may have felt that it was unacceptable to challenge the authority of the doctor because of the contractual relationship that exists between nurses and doctors.
- *Early socialisation*. Milgram emphasised that throughout our childhood — from being told to eat up our food to discipline at school — the habit of unquestioning obedience is inculcated. Furthermore, social order is dependent upon some degree of obedience.

Much research has concentrated on why we 'toe the line', and yet there is another side to the coin.

Identify factors which have been put forward to explain why people obey authority figures.

(6 marks)

2.4 WHAT FACTORS ARE ASSOCIATED WITH INDEPENDENCE AND RESISTANCE?

- *Morality*. Psychologists such as Kohlberg have suggested that there are hierarchical levels of moral reasoning and that people with the highest levels, such as Mahatma Ghandi, will have the inner strength and principles to resist what they perceive to be unjustifiable social influence and coercion.
- *Individual characteristics*. Krech et al. (1962) found that independence was associated with a number of individual characteristics such as higher intelligence, low anxiety and a realistic perception of one's self.
- *Group solidarity*. A study was carried out by Gamson et al. (1982) which involved people working in groups, making videos and signing statements which could be used in court proceedings. Many became increasingly suspicious about the true purpose of the study and one gave knowledge of Milgram's studies as a reason for refusing to obey the

instructions of the experimenter. This suggests that people may draw strength from being in a collective position. In a variation of the Milgram scenario he gave the volunteer a supporter (a co-teacher) who refused to comply with the instructions. Obedience fell massively.

- *Agentic shift*. If people are reminded of their responsibilities in situations, obedience to aberrant orders decreases (e.g. Hamilton, 1978).
- *Zeitgeist (spirit of the times)*. It has been argued that the Asch and Milgram findings were children of their times. For example, Asch was working after the Second World War when the McCarthy purges against communism in the USA were at their height, and conformity to American values was seen by many as the only safe way to survive.

Describe two factors which are associated with independent behaviour. (6 marks)

Critical issue — ethical issues in psychological research

3.1 ETHICAL RESPONSIBILITY

The studies of obedience to authority carried out by Milgram in the 1960s aroused a great deal of debate amongst psychologists about ethical responsibilities. Flanagan (2000) defines ethics as 'concerns relating to what is acceptable human behaviour in pursuit of certain personal or scientific goals'. In this context we are particularly interested in how participants are treated in psychological research.

Ethical responsibilities can be viewed in *absolute* or *relative* terms. The former means that some research (such as Milgram's) should never be undertaken because of the distress it caused many of the participants when they were taking part in the study. The latter — a position occupied by most psychologists — is that we need to balance the costs against the benefits of the research, and if the benefits outweigh the costs, then the research may be justified. Milgram argued that his research was legitimate because, although participants may have been temporarily distressed, they were given extensive de-briefing and offered counselling, but — most importantly — the study gives us insights into human nature that we could not otherwise gain. Remember that staff and students predicted obedience rates of 0.1% and 1.2%, respectively, whereas the actual figure was 65%.

Before the 1960s ethical monitoring was left to the professional judgement of individual psychologists, but subsequently psychological associations such as the British Psychological Society (BPS) and the American Psychological Association (APA) have drawn up sets of ethical guidelines which psychological researchers should adhere to. However, the guidelines are just that, they are not rules or laws. Their function is to protect participants and the 'good name' of psychology.

What is meant by the term 'ethics'? (3 marks)

3.2 BPS GUIDELINES

The most recent set of BPS guidelines (1993) relating to research with human participants contains the following recommendations.

- *Introduction*. Researchers and investigators should have mutual respect for each other. Some potential research may endanger this. Ethical guidelines clarify what is acceptable and unacceptable research.

- *General*. Psychological research should be viewed from the perspective of the participants; the views of such people could be sought as the psychologists may be unaware of their values and concerns. Psychological research should not compromise the well-being and dignity of participants.
- *Consent*. Psychologists should endeavour to inform participants of all aspects of the study, which may influence their decision as to whether they wish to take part. No attempt should be made to coerce them into participating or to remain in the study.
- *Deception*. Misleading participants about the true nature of the study or withholding important information from them is unacceptable, if it is likely to cause distress once they have been debriefed.
- *Debriefing*. Once a participant's role in a study has been completed, he or she should be fully informed about all relevant aspects of the study and allowed to ask questions of the researcher to complete his or her own knowledge and understanding of what the study was about and their role in it.
- *Withdrawal from the study*. The researcher must make it clear to all participants that they are free to withdraw at any stage. This is still the case if the participants have received payment for taking part. Furthermore, participants have the right to withdraw their consent retrospectively and may request that their results are retracted and, if necessary, destroyed.
- *Confidentiality*. Unless there are contrary legal reasons, participants have the right to anonymity; if results of a study are published, their own results or contribution to the study should not be identifiable.
- *Protection of participants*. Participants should be subject to no greater harm or stress than that which they could reasonably be expected to encounter in their everyday lives. Participants must be protected from stress and psychological and physical harm by all possible means.
- *Giving advice*. If, during the course of carrying out a study, a researcher discovers something about a participant which he or she is unaware of and which might affect their future well-being, the researcher is obliged to inform the participant. If the researcher does not have the necessary professional competence to deal with the situation, he or she must seek someone with such competence.
- *Colleagues*. If a psychologist becomes aware that one of his or her colleagues is carrying out research which might breach any of the above guidelines, he or she should encourage that person to reappraise the appropriateness of the research.

'Guidelines such as those given by the BPS are an unnecessary constraint on the work of psychologists. They are professional people and we can be confident of their own judgement in these matters.' In the light of your knowledge about social psychological research into conformity or obedience, discuss the appropriateness of this viewpoint.   (12 marks)

3.3 THE CASE FOR NOT ADHERING TO THE GUIDELINES

Focusing specifically on three of the guidelines — consent, deception and protection of participants against harm — we can consider how research (including social psychological investigations into social influence) has sometimes not adhered to the principles above and how this has been justified.

Informed consent

The following are some situations in which informed consent cannot be obtained (Eysenck and Flanagan, 2000).

- Children, or people who have cognitive, perceptual or psychological difficulties, may not fully comprehend what they are being told.

- In situations such as those in the Asch and Milgram studies described above, full knowledge of the purpose of the experiments (without which fully informed consent is impossible) would result in the study 'not working'. For example, Milgram's volunteers would presumably have had no reservations in going up to 450 volts if they knew the learner was a stooge and was not actually being shocked at all. This point also applies to deception.
- In field experiments and many observational studies, many participants do not even know they are part of a study as it is taking part in a natural, real-life environment.
- Some retrospective studies use data which is already 'in' and is in the public domain.
- In certain studies informed consent cannot be given because the participants would not be able to anticipate their own behaviour and feelings before taking part in the study. Milgram's obedience would again be a good example.

Deception
- Menges (1973) considered over 1000 experimental studies carried out in the USA and contended that in only 3% of them were the participants given full and accurate information about the study they were about to take part in.
- In many situations some degree of deception, necessary for the experiment 'to work', is relatively harmless and causes no distress to participants.
- Thorough debriefing after a study can sometimes rectify misunderstandings arising out of earlier deception. This was one of Milgram's key justifications for deception in his own obedience research.
- The knowledge gained is so insightful or scientifically important that the use of deception can be justified. This is another of the best-known justifications of Milgram's work.

Protection of participants from harm
- Central to Baumrind's (1964) stinging criticisms of Milgram's work was the distress many of the participants displayed. They were stuttering, sweating and digging their fingernails into their own flesh. One participant experienced a seizure.
- Milgram responded that he had not anticipated that such a high proportion of participants would have continued until the end. However, this does not answer the question as to why he did not stop the experiment once he did realise this and could see the distress suffered by participants.
- Values change with the times. Many psychological studies carried out in the past would be rejected on ethical grounds today. This applies not only to studies carried out on humans, but also on animals.

Q **Consider the relevance of ethical issues in the context of social influence research.** (12 marks)

Quantitative and qualitative research methods

Quantitative methodologies are concerned with measuring (quantifying) variables in a numeric fashion. This methodology has the advantage that data generated can be analysed scientifically and in a transparent way. For example, from quantitative measures of IQ in men and women, we can calculate a mean score for men and women and directly compare them to see if there is a difference. A disadvantage of such quantitative methods is that by reducing variables down to simple numeric measures, some of the rich context of life can be lost. In short, this approach has high **reliability** but has problems in terms of **validity** (see section 2.3 for definitions of reliability and validity).

Qualitative methodologies are concerned with analysing behaviours, arguments or dialogues within their contexts. Data are not reduced to numbers or measurements, but are analysed as a whole. Data are analysed for common themes and meanings. A popular way of obtaining qualitative data is by using interviews. Some interviews are highly structured and use **closed** questions, such as 'Do you think all war is unjustified? YES/NO'. Questions formed in this way limit the range of answers, so effectively the data can be coded with numbers and treated as quantitative. However, such restrictions of answers is more common in questionnaires, since the point of interviews is that they allow rich, elaborated data to be gathered. Therefore, many interviews will use **open** questions, such as: 'In what situations do you think war is justifiable?' This allows the respondent to give a detailed and considered response, including attitudes and opinions. An advantage is that the rich context of the data is retained. However, a disadvantage is that findings are less easily generalised, since the methods do not result in data that can be analysed statistically in terms of probability. In short, this approach has high validity, but has problems with regard to reliability.

1.2 KEY METHODS

Experiments — types of experiment and their advantages and disadvantages

Experiments involve the deliberate and controlled manipulation of one or more **independent variables (IVs)** (refer to section 2 for definition) in order to study their effects upon one or more **dependent variables (DVs)**. Only the independent variables are varied — all other **extraneous** (unwanted and unaccounted for) variables are (as much as possible) controlled, in order to establish a **causal link** with the dependent variables. So, for example, participants may be tested on recall (the dependent variable) after being given either coffee, alcohol or water. The drink provided is the independent variable (the experimenter has manipulated this in order to measure its effects on the dependent variable, recall). All other variables will be held constant (such as room temperature, lighting, instructions provided, etc.). This means that any difference in recall performance will be down to one of two things only — either the independent variable (drink given) or possibly (though less likely, especially with larger samples) natural participant variation between the three groups. Furthermore, in a very strict experiment, it is possible to minimise the chances of one group having participants that naturally differ from those in other groups by pre-testing and matching ability across groups, or having a very large sample with random allocation to groups.

Laboratory experiments are tightly controlled, allow effects of extraneous variables to be strictly controlled, and can be **replicated** by other researchers to verify findings. However, they are artificial (we don't have all our real-life experiences in scientific laboratories!) and are therefore *not* **ecologically valid** — we cannot necessarily generalise our findings from the laboratory to the 'real world'. Being in an experimental situation might cause participants to behave or respond differently from how they would under normal circumstances. For example, participants might want to be regarded positively (impression management), might want to behave in the ways in which they think the experimenter wants them to (experimenter bias), or might have pre-conceptions as to how they should try to react in psychological experiments (demand characteristics).

Field experiments are similar to laboratory experiments (IVs are manipulated to observe their effects upon DVs) except that they are conducted in the field — real-life settings — and participants are unaware that they are involved in an experiment. This has the advantage of making the experiments less artificial — experiments in natural settings have greater ecological validity. Other problems of the laboratory experiment (e.g. demand characteristics and experimenter bias) are eliminated (assuming participants remain unaware that they are being studied). However, field experiments tend to be more problematic ethically, since **informed consent** cannot be obtained (participants aren't aware of their participation). They are also less easy to control, they suffer more from the effects of extraneous variables, and are costly and less easy to replicate.

Natural experiments are sometimes described as **quasi-experimental**, since they do not involve deliberate manipulation of the IV by the experimenter — the IV varies *naturally*. For example, experimenters do not directly manipulate sex and age in order to see their effects upon a dependent variable. People can still be compared on a dependent measure though, so a causal link remains the focus of this type of experimentation. However, extraneous variables that come along with natural group memberships can more easily confound the results.

Investigations using correlational analysis

Such investigations are concerned with studying **relationships** between two or more factors. Two factors might be **positively related** (for example, height and weight — people who are taller *tend* to weigh more), **negatively related** (for example, depression and self-esteem — more depressed people *tend* to have lower self-esteem), or not related at all (for example, IQ and the number of freckles). Correlational investigations involve collecting and analysing data to determine the nature and strength of such relationships.

These investigations are convenient where manipulation of variables would be difficult or unethical; they can tell us the strength and direction of relationships, can identify patterns amongst variables to inform subsequent experimentation, and can allow prediction of the value of one variable from the value of its covariate.

However, cause and effect cannot be established; two variables might be related only because they are both influenced by a third variable, and only **linear** relationships can be measured through simple correlations. An example of two variables being related, but only because they are both influenced by a third variable, could be as follows. A researcher measures height and liking for football, and finds a positive correlation. This suggests an association (taller people tend to like football more). Remember it doesn't suggest causation (we can't say either that being tall makes people like football, or that liking football makes people taller!). Furthermore, the association is best explained not in terms of a relationship between the two measures, but as influenced by a third variable that impacts upon both. In this case it is gender — males tend to be taller than females, and tend to like football more than females. Interpreting correlations is therefore sometimes difficult, because you have to accept that the association between any two variables may not be meaningful, as they might both be influenced by a variable you haven't measured.

Naturalistic observations

Behaviour is observed in its natural environment, without interference or manipulation from an experimenter.

This suggests that such studies have high ecological validity and are more free from experimental artefacts, such as experimenter effects and demand characteristics. This is particularly true of '**participant observation**', where the observer over a long time attains membership of the sub-group being observed, leading to natural and uninhibited behaviour without the need to be covert. The method also allows study of behaviours that would be unethical to engineer.

However, this is only the case if the participants are unaware that they are being observed (which brings its own ethical problems, since participants cannot both be unaware of observation and give informed consent). If participants are aware that they are being watched, their behaviour can become less natural and less spontaneous. Cause and effect cannot be established, observers may be biased (effectively seeing what they want or expect to see), extraneous variables cannot be controlled, and replication is difficult. Additionally, depending upon the number of participants and behaviours that are being observed, more than one observer is usually required — this is problematic since behaviours might be reported differently from different observers (a problem with **interpreter reliability**).

Observational designs (other than naturalistic observations) are as follows:
- *Participant observation* refers to observations where the observer is a member of the group being observed. For example, a researcher observing the subculture and behaviour of marijuana smokers integrated himself into the group and was accepted amongst them. Observations where the observer isn't a participant are called non-participant observations.
- *Experimental observation* refers to observations in a controlled environment. For example, Ainsworth's strange situation experiment and Harlow's observation of primate behaviour with two artificial mothers can be described as experimental (they are in controlled environments, with manipulations of independent variables, as in true experiments).
- *Disclosed or undisclosed observation* (also known as overt or covert) simply refers to whether participants are aware or not that they are being observed. Undisclosed or covert observation can be done through hidden cameras or one-way mirrors. However, these undisclosed designs are clearly more problematic in terms of ethics (no informed consent, and invasion of privacy).
- *Content analysis* is undertaken when books, diaries and other sources are analysed; this is clearly a more indirect method of observing behaviour.

Questionnaire surveys

A cost-effective and simple way to gather data is to use a questionnaire survey. Questionnaire surveys are generally used to *sample* some information (such as the general public's political preferences). In using such techniques it is important to observe ethical guidelines (such as those published by the BPS) and laws (such as those under the Data Protection Act) on confidentiality.

A survey is relatively cheap, simple and quick to administer. Information/data can be gathered about **intangible** characteristics (concepts and constructs that we can't directly observe, such as attitudes to crime or opinions about social equality). Results of surveys can inform future study, and can provide a simple measure for comparison between groups.

Surveys are often plagued by reliability and validity issues. A questionnaire relies upon the researcher's own definition and understanding of the construct being measured (which may be biased, inaccurate, too loose or too narrow). Closed questions (where respondents select from answers provided) are common in surveys and can lead to responses that don't fully represent the respondent's genuine opinion or position.

Questionnaire designs are as follows:
- *Closed or open questions*. Closed questions are posed in a way to allow only a limited range of answers, and often invite the respondent to tick or circle their chosen response. For example, 'Do you think your street is subject to more crime than the surrounding area? YES/NO (please circle answer)'. Open questions are asked in order to invite more detail and a wider range of responses from the respondent. For example, 'Describe how you feel about the level of crime in your community'.
- *Likert or Likert-type scales*. Similar to closed questions, these invite respondents to answer on a scale provided. For example, 'How serious do you consider the crime problem to be in your street? 1 (not at all serious) — 2 (not very serious) — 3 (serious) — 4 (very serious) — 5 (extremely serious)'.

Interviews

Interviews range from highly structured question and answer sessions (essentially, a survey or test administered orally) to very loose, informal conversations. Surveys or tests completed by interview have an advantage over self-completion surveys or tests in that misunderstandings of questions can be clarified, but they carry a risk that experimenter effects may arise. On the other hand, looser forms of interview can gather more detailed information, but are open to researcher bias and are problematic with regard to reliability and validity.

Advantages of this method include the high level of detail that can be acquired, the flexibility of the questions that can be asked, the high ecological validity, and its use as a tool for generating ideas for subsequent experimental research.

Disadvantages include the problems of reliability and validity, difficulty in replicating, limited ability to generalise from findings, the potential bias of interpretation and 'leading' from the interviewer, and the potential for demand characteristics.

Interview design — interviews can be structured, unstructured or semi-structured:
- *Structured*. All questions are decided and prepared beforehand. There is as little deviation from the order and phrasing of these questions as possible. This allows interviews of different people to be more comparable, but such lack of flexibility restricts the interviewer from following up interesting avenues suggested by the interviewee's answers.
- *Unstructured*. The interviewer has a few questions prepared, but bases later questions on what answers he or she receives. This allows the interview to follow any interesting directions suggested by particular answers, but means that multiple interviews are less comparable, and that the answers may be led more by the specific questions in that interview.
- *Semi-structured*. Harder to define, this design rests somewhere between structured and unstructured. This allows for elements of control and standardisation across interviews, whilst allowing interesting answers to be followed up with spontaneous questions. Some regard semi-structured interviews as the same as unstructured ones.

Research design and implementation

2.1 AIMS AND HYPOTHESES

The aim

The question or questions that a piece of research is designed to answer provides the aim. Research is, for the most part, carried out to address a particular question that empirical observation has raised. Research is informed and shaped by previous findings, theories and our observations of the world.

Hypotheses

A hypothesis is a very specific and precise prediction made about the results of the research and must be testable. Such a prediction is informed by theory and previous research.

The **experimental** or **alternative** hypothesis (H1 being the first and, where there are multiple predictions, H2, H3, H4 and so on) is the name given to the prediction that the researcher makes or wants to test.

Hypotheses can be **one-tailed** or **two-tailed**. Two-tailed hypotheses predict a difference, relationship, or effect, but *not* the *direction* (e.g. 'There will be a significant difference between men and women on IQ score' — two-tailed). One-tailed hypotheses are the same, but predict the direction of the difference or relationship (e.g. 'Women will score significantly higher on the IQ test than will men' — one-tailed, and very controversial too!).

For every experimental/alternative hypothesis, there is a **null hypothesis**, which states that there *won't* be any significant difference or relationship amongst the variables. Add *not* in the right place in your experimental hypothesis for an instant null (e.g. for the examples used above, 'There will *not* be a significant difference between men and women on IQ score' and 'Women will *not* score significantly higher on the IQ test than will men'). Having an alternative and a null hypothesis allows us, through testing, to support one *or* the other — we can achieve clear outcomes (though never conclusive *proof*, only probabilities).

2.2 RESEARCH DESIGNS

People differ in various ways, so when they are involved in experiments, we can assume that they will not provide consistent results. In order to account for natural variation amongst people on measures we take, we use research designs to try to remove their confounding influence. There are broadly three types of research design, detailed below. Essentially, these designs relate to how the participants are allocated to groups or conditions, and also whether an individual fulfils one condition or both/all of the conditions.

- *Independent samples* (also known as '**between groups**' and '**unrelated**' samples or design). This design consists of having two (or more) independent groups of participants. Participants are randomly (or naturally in the case of independent variables such as gender) assigned to groups to allow comparisons between them. For example, of 100 participants, we might have 50 in our experimental condition and 50 in our control group. This theoretically tackles natural variation between participants (individual differences), since we can often assume that variation amongst people will be spread across both groups (unless we have **sampling bias**). There are also fewer demand characteristics, since a participant does not get measured in all conditions and thereby get an idea of what the experiment is about. There are no **order effects**.

However, since participants only fulfil one condition, more participants are required for the other conditions, whereas in repeated measures fewer people are needed as they are measured more than once.

- *Repeated measures* (a type of **related** design). All participants are measured in both conditions. This has the effect that individual differences (subject variables) can show up in all conditions and therefore be accounted for. This design is more economical; since we can use the same participants in both conditions, we need fewer of them. However, participants are more likely to be able to work out the purpose of the experiment (since they see both conditions) and results might therefore suffer from demand characteristics. Also, order effects may arise, unless we deliberately counterbalance the order of presentation of conditions amongst participants.
- *Matched pairs* (a type of **related** design). Participants across the conditions are allocated to account for any possible confounding influence from subject variables. So, if we think sex and age might confound our measures, we could ensure that all participants exposed to condition A are matched in terms of sex and age in condition B. The two separate groups we have are **controlled** in terms of how individual differences arise in each. There are also no order effects and less chance of demand characteristics, since participants are only involved in one condition.

2.3 VARIABLES AND CONTROLS

Definitions of variables

- *Independent variable (IV)* is the term used to describe the variable that is manipulated by the experimenter to study its effect upon the DV. Some IVs occur naturally (such as with age and gender).
- *Dependent variable (DV)* is the term used to describe the variable that is measured to see if it differs according to the IV. We predict that the DV 'depends' upon the IV.

Good hypotheses are stated in such a way that specific mention of the IV and DV are made, in an operational manner. This means that the descriptions of the variables reflect the way they are measured in our experiment. For example, it is not precise enough to predict that 'Participants using imagery rehearsal methods will have better memories than controls'. 'Better memories' could be operationalised thus: 'Participants using imagery rehearsal methods will recall more words than controls'.

Problems in research

Problems centre on issues of **reliability** and **validity** and good research must control for **extraneous variables** (factors other than the IV that can influence the DV). The sampling method is also important, and all these facets combined impact upon the extent to which we can **generalise** findings from our sample to the population (the 'real world').

- *Reliability*. A reliable measure will produce the same score when measuring the same participant or phenomenon. **Internal reliability** is a term applied to questionnaires that purport to measure the same construct — if all the items on a questionnaire are measuring the same thing, scores on such questions should correlate well. **External reliability** refers to whether a measure produces a similar score on a second use. So, if a person completes a trait anxiety test on Monday, he should score similarly in the test on Friday — again correlating the scores is the preferred method to ascertain external reliability.
- *Validity*. A valid measure is one that actually does measure what it purports to. An anxiety questionnaire that doesn't ask questions that appear to be about anxious feelings may not be valid (at least, it isn't **face valid**). Experts can advise on the content of the questionnaire (**content validity**). Experiments are also described as having

varying degrees of validity. **Experimental validity** refers to experiments where strict control over any extraneous variables ensures that differences in the DV can be confidently attributed to deliberate manipulation of the IV. **Ecological validity** refers to how much the experiment and its findings can be generalised and applied to the 'real world'. The closer the conditions and procedures of the experiment are to the outside world, the more ecologically valid the study is (naturalistic observations generally have better ecological validity than laboratory experiments).

Minimising problems, maximising reliability and validity, and control

- **Pilot studies** (conducting the research on a small representative sample before full testing) allow researchers to iron out procedural problems and get a feel for any revisions to the method that are required; they can provide some measures on reliability and validity.
- **Standardisation** is important when conducting research — instructions given to different participants in a particular condition should be identical, to ensure that the only things that vary in the experiment are the deliberately manipulated ones (IVs).
- **Selecting best design** — some experiments are best done as repeated measures, matched pairs or independent designs. The design should fit the subjects, practical considerations and ethical guidelines. Remember that different design types are more or less vulnerable to subject effects (individual differences).
- **Counterbalancing** is used in **repeated measures** designs to counter order effects. If all participants are to do procedure A followed by procedure B, then whatever happens in procedure A might affect the results in procedure B. Therefore, half the sample do procedure A followed by procedure B, and half do the procedures in the reverse order. This allows order effects to be balanced.
- **Single blind** — refers to when participants are unaware of the purpose of the experiment, so that demand characteristics don't interfere with results.
- **Double blind** — refers to experiments where the experimenter, as well as the participants, isn't aware of all the conditions and aims of the study, so that the impact of demand characteristics and experimenter bias are minimised.
- **Randomisation** — truly random samples are the best way to ensure an unbiased sample. A truly **randomised sample** would be one where participants are selected from the relevant population at random and also allocated randomly to conditions. A **systematic** sample would be sampling every tenth person on a class register — there is an element of chance involved in this, but it isn't truly random, since not all members of the population have an equal chance of being chosen. **Opportunity sampling** is selecting participants based on availability — market researchers questioning people in the street is an example of this. It is not truly random, since not all members of the target population are likely to walk down a particular street. A **stratified sample** is one where variables that are likely to affect measures taken are accounted for. So, for example, if age was predicted to influence results and the researcher wanted a sample representative of all ages in a population, he or she may sample a desired number of participants from each age range. The desired number of participants per age range would be randomly chosen from people in that age range, unlike in **quota sampling**. In quota sampling, people are not chosen from a list of people with the desired characteristics — the first people with those characteristics that are found are included in the sample (so it's less random, and can be seen as a cross between stratified and opportunity sampling). A **volunteer** sample is simply made up of anyone that volunteers. This isn't completely random, however, since people who volunteer (in response to newspaper advertisements, for example) tend to be different in many ways from non-volunteers, in terms of motivation and their abilities (I might

volunteer for a memory experiment because I think I have a good memory — if I'm correct in my perception of my memory, and so are the other volunteers, the sample will have better memories than a random sample would).

- **Extraneous variables** should be controlled as much as possible — if measuring participants over different days, things like room temperature might affect results, so we would ensure it was consistent (unless of course temperature was our IV in which case we'd *want* to manipulate it to be different).

Researchers should ensure that, unless under exceptional and justifiable circumstances, this research does not breach the BPS ethics guidelines (see page 55).

3 Data analysis

3.1 ANALYSIS OF QUALITATIVE DATA

Qualitative data may be derived from naturalistic observations, questionnaire surveys, unstructured interviews, case studies or from analysing text or conversation for themes (rather than frequencies, for example).

Such data are analysed generally in terms of common themes or identification of important strands of meaning. This might be highly structured and based on an established qualitative methodology, or might be highly personal.

Such qualitative analyses are mostly subjective interpretations — generally of low reliability, but high validity.

3.2 ANALYSIS OF QUANTITATIVE DATA

In quantitative analysis, we are often interested in comparing scores on a DV in one group or condition with scores in another group or condition. Individuals usually differ *within* a group or condition, so we don't have a single score for each group for our comparison — this is why we generate **measures of central tendency**, values that hopefully represent 'typical scores' for our groups or conditions. We are also interested in the spread of the scores in our data — for this we have **measures of dispersion**. Both measures of central tendency and measures of dispersion are integral elements in statistical formulae used to calculate the probability that differences in our data may have arisen by chance alone.

Data types
- *Nominal data* represent a category (e.g. colour preference: 1 = red, 2 = blue, and so on).
- *Ordinal data* represent order or rank (e.g. position in a race: 1st, 2nd, 3rd, etc.).
- *Interval data* represent a score on a continuous scale (e.g. scoring in an IQ test), without an absolute zero.
- *Ratio data* are the same as interval data, but with an absolute zero time in seconds (zero = no time).

It is important to identify what type of data we have in order to decide what type of analyses and descriptive statistics will be appropriate and valid.

Measures of central tendency
- The **mean** is the result of adding up scores and dividing by the number of scores added. This is only a suitable measure where the data are of **interval** or **ratio** type. If your data were **nominal** or **ordinal**, a mean would not make sense. You could *not* take the mean of colour preference where 1 represents 'red' and 2 represents 'blue'. (What

would a mean colour preference score of 1.5 really *mean*?) The mean is very sensitive to **distortion** by extreme values. (Calculate the mean of 3, 3, 4, 5, 5 and 5,980 — does the mean value provide a 'typical' score?)

- The **mode** is the most common score in a data set. It is less prone to distortion by extreme values, but ignores much of the data (The mode of 3, 3, 3, 8, 10, 34, 12, 23 and 15 would be 3 — but how effectively would that describe the scores?)
- The **median** is the middle score, when scores are ranked in order. (In the example in the mode description, the median would be 12 — intuitively a better description of those *particular* scores than the mode is.) Like the mode, the median is less prone to distortion by extremes than the mean, but is a more crude measure of central tendency. It is useful for ordinal data, however.

Measures of dispersion

- The *range* shows the difference between the lowest and highest value in a data set. Like the mean, this is easily distorted by extreme values. The scores 4, 5, 4, 5, 4, 5 and 1,000 have a large range, but only one score varies to a large degree. Variance and standard deviation are more descriptive, as they both indicate how the scores are spread out around the mean.
- The **variance** is deduced as follows: (1) subtract each score from the mean to obtain differences; (2) square these differences; (3) calculate the average of these squared differences. The variance gives a rough measure of dispersion — the larger the value, the more spread out from the mean are the scores.
- The **standard deviation** *(SD)* is the square root of the variance (best done on a calculator, this one!). This is the most useful measure of dispersion, because it tells us by how much the majority of scores deviate from the mean. If our mean was 10 and the SD was 2, nearly all the scores would be between 8 and 12, with only a few outside this range.

Variance and SD are only appropriate calculations for normal distributions and interval/ratio level data.

Interpreting correlation coefficients

- Correlation coefficients resulting from running correlational analyses range from −1 to + 1. The scale below shows what the coefficients mean about the relationship tested (coefficients can be any number between the ones shown on this scale).

Perfect negative	Negative	None at all	Positive	Perfect positive
−1	−0.5	0	+0.5	+1

- The closer a correlation coefficient is to zero, the weaker the relationship.
- The nearer it is to −1 or + 1, the stronger the relationship.
- Positive relationships mean that as one variable increases in value, so does the other.
- Negative relationships mean that as one variable increases, the other variable decreases.
- Correlations can be represented graphically by a **scattergraph** — scattergraphs show clearly the nature of relationships. Dots represent actual scores of the two variables, so we can see what the general trend is. A **line of best fit** helps us see the nature and strength of the relationship. Figure 6.1 shows a scattergraph. It shows a strong positive correlation — as the variable on the x-axis increases, the y-variable also tends to increase.

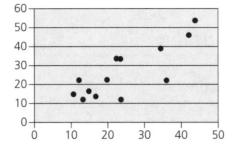

Figure 6.1
A scattergraph
showing a positive
relationship

Graphical representations

- *Displaying DV means*. IV is on the *x* (horizontal) axis, DV on the *y* (vertical) axis. If the IV is categorical (i.e. nominal, like gender), a **bar graph** (Figure 2a) is appropriate. The bars represent each level of the IV, and should not touch adjacent bars (which would imply a continuity that isn't present in nominal data). If the IV is of interval or ratio level, a **line graph** (Figure 2b) is the appropriate option.
- *Displaying frequencies*. If the variable to display is categorical, a **frequency bar graph** (Figure 2c) is appropriate. As with mean bar graphs for categorical IVs, bars shouldn't touch adjacent bars. If the IV is interval level, a special type of bar graph, called a **frequency histogram** (Figure 2d) is appropriate. It is like a normal bar graph but the bars actually touch — since the IV on the *x*-axis is interval level, it is appropriate to suggest continuation visually in this way. If you have a lot of intervals on the *x*-axis, to make the display clearer a **frequency polygon** (Figure 2e) would be used (the eye can scan such a line more easily than lots of very thin bars).

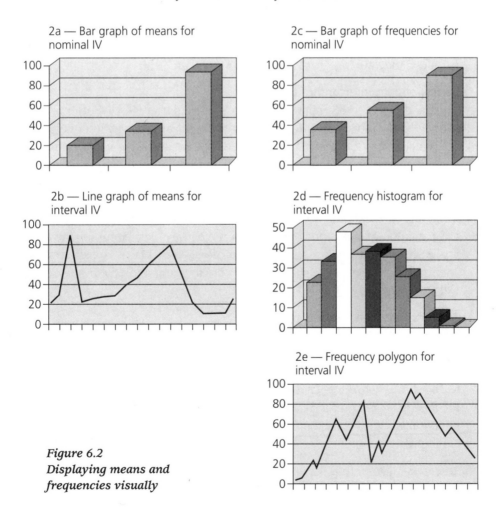

Figure 6.2
Displaying means and
frequencies visually

1 Attribution of causality

1.1 ATTRIBUTION THEORIES

Social cognition is concerned with how we can understand our social world by considering the ways in which we interpret, analyse and remember information, especially information about people.

Kelley's attribution theory

Kelley (1967) suggested that we attribute the behaviour of others to either **situational** (external) or **dispositional** (internal) factors. For example, we might attribute an aggressive act as a response to provocation (situational) or as an expression of hate (internal). Three things help us decide causality:

- *Consensus*. Behaviour shared by many people is deemed to have external causes (if a group of other people is also fighting, then one person's aggression is attributed to the situation).
- *Consistency*. If a person consistently behaves in a particular way, then later acts of that behaviour are attributed to internal factors (if a person is aggressive often and in a variety of settings, we assume that he is normally a violent person).
- *Distinctiveness*. If a person's behaviour differs significantly in a certain context, then such distinctive behaviour is attributed to the situation (if a long-known friend shows aggression for the first time, then we assume that he is being unduly provoked).

For Kelley, when we attribute causality, we apply our knowledge of the way things co-vary (or correlate) — our perceived relationship between the behaviour of others and the situations they are in.

Correspondent interference theory

Jones and Davis (1965) built on the work of Heider (1944), who emphasised that attributions tend to focus on **intentionality**: whether an act was intentional and deliberate or unintentional. Jones and Davis argued that we are more likely to make dispositional attributions rather than situational attributions. When we decide that an act was deliberate, we look to see if there are corresponding traits that would support the action. Moreover, we are more likely to assign internal attributions if we are affected directly in some way by the action. However, the theory was modified after research indicated that social factors influence attributions in a major way. For example, one study found that final year social science students were more likely to blame the system for poverty and unemployment than were students from engineering and economics courses (Guimond and Palmer, 1990).

Weiner's three-dimensional model

Weiner (1988) developed a model of attribution that focused on emotional reactions to actions, and in particular attributions of success and failure. For each outcome, we determine causality based on the following three aspects:

- *Locus* — whether the cause of the emotional reaction is external or internal (E or I)
- *Stability* — whether the cause is stable or unstable and changes over time (S or U)
- *Controllability* — whether the cause of the emotion is controllable or uncontrollable (C or U)

Research suggests that these are useful dimensions of attributions of causality and that they can influence **expectations of future behaviour**. For example, Mikulincer (1988) gave participants a number of problems that had no solutions. It was found that those who had been given explanations that implied stable attributions subsequently performed significantly better on easy problems than did participants given unstable ones.

> **Key study: Attributions of abused children by their parents**
>
> Stratton and Swaffer (1988) provide research evidence that highlights the social and personal impact of the consequences of the attribution process. Parents of abused, non-abused and disabled children observed their children at play in a controlled environment. The children were each given the same problem to solve which required a considerable amount of sustained effort. In interviews after the observation, mothers of abused children tended to say that they saw themselves as less in control of their child's behaviour, and attributed more internal causes for their child's behaviour than did parents from the other two groups. The implication of this finding is that the way parents attribute the causes of their child's behaviour may be responsible for child abuse. Parents who see their child's behaviour as uncontrollable are more likely to become frustrated and aggressive towards the child than those who feel that they have control.

Outline and evaluate two theories of attribution. (24 marks)

Describe one theory of attribution. Evaluate the extent to which research supports this theory. (12+12 marks)

1.2 BIASES IN THE ATTRIBUTION PROCESS

Fundamental attribution error

People are not only more likely to give extra weight to **dispositional** factors over **situational** factors, they often erroneously overestimate them, even in controlled laboratory experiments. Ross (1977) termed this the fundamental attribution error. In a study by Jones and Harris (1967), American students heard arguments that either supported or opposed Fidel Castro (whose political stance once seriously threatened the USA). Other students, irrespective of their attitude towards Castro, read these arguments. Even though the students were told this, they still believed that those who read pro-Castro essays were in favour of him and those that read anti-Castro essays were against him. The situational factors were ignored.

Actor–observer effect

In contrast to the above, when explaining *our own* behaviour, we are more likely to use situational attributions. In a study by Orvis et al. (1976), college-age male and female couples were asked separately to describe disagreements in their relationship and to offer explanations for them. When accounting for their own behaviour, the participants tended to highlight situational factors (e.g. money problems or sleep problems). However, when accounting for their partner's behaviour, they preferred dispositional accounts (e.g. selfishness or low commitment).

Self-serving bias

Sometimes we make attributions that are favourable to ourselves and protect our self-esteem. For example, we tend to attribute our successes to internal causes and our failures to external causes. Although the self-serving bias is motivated to protect self-esteem, people with depressogenic tendencies are more likely to attribute their failures to stable factors in themselves, such as a lack of ability (Metalsky et al., 1987). One self-serving bias is known as the 'belief in a just world' — the belief that people get what they deserve (Lerner, 1977). For example, victims are blamed for their own misfortune (such as unemployed people, rape victims, people infected with HIV). It has been argued that through this self-serving bias, by blaming victims we label them as bad and since we are good, these bad things will not happen to us. Furnham (1992) found that susceptibility to the belief in a just world bias was positively correlated with wealth and social status.

Q Discuss two errors and/or biases which occur in the attribution process
(e.g. self-serving bias, fundamental attribution bias). (24 marks)

---

2 Social perception

2.1 PERCEPTION OF THE SOCIAL WORLD

This refers to how we perceive people (ourselves and others) and social situations. It therefore contrasts with what is called object perception, which is dealt with in Topic 8.

Cook (1971) locates this within the nature/nurture debate by identifying two overarching theories of how we perceive others, the Intuition Model and the Inference Model.

The Intuition Model
The Intuition Model is based on three assumptions:
- Social perception is innate. We are born with the ability to make sense of the social world; it is not something we learn how to do.
- Social perception is global. We perceive people as wholes rather than by their particular features such as their class, intelligence or sex appeal. This is similar to the gestalt model of object perception.
- Social perception is 'direct', i.e. it is unmediated by cognitive processes. This is similar to Gibson's direct theory of object perception.

Evaluation
Cook concludes 'These three claims all have some degree of truth, although two of them — that perception is direct and that it is innate — apply only to judgements of emotional states. The third — that perception is global — is true of many judgements, but is not a necessary feature of perception'. The model is clearly of only limited value.

The Inference Model
The Inference Model is based on the assumption that people share commonalities (such as beliefs and preferences and even their nature) with other members of the social groups to which they belong. An example would be: 'Men like football. Colin is a man. Therefore he will like football'.

Or one could say: 'People who engage in little eye contact are shy, nervous or insecure' (these are called Associations). 'Jo is engaging in little eye contact' (these are called Identifications), 'therefore she is shy, nervous or insecure' (these are the Inferences).

Evaluation
Cook (1971) says 'The inference model has given rise to much research already and could inspire much more. It is also reasonably clear and logically sound'. However, it does lend support to possible prejudice by seeing people of certain groups as having common characteristics.

Impression formation — Asch's configural model
Research in this area concerns the question: 'How do the perceptions, thoughts and motives of one person become known to other persons?' (Asch, 1952, p.143).

Asch (1946) argued that an impression consists of a set of traits, where some traits **(central traits)** have more of an influence than others. For example, when forming impressions of others, some people give more weight to traits such as intelligence, while other people are swayed by a sense of humour, and so on.

> **Key study: Primacy and recency in impression formation**
>
> Asch (1946) presented two types of trait lists of hypothetical people to participants. A six-trait list consisted of either three positive traits followed by three negative traits (intelligent, industrious, impulsive, critical, stubborn, envious), or the negative traits followed by three positive traits (critical, stubborn, envious, intelligent, industrious, impulsive). After seeing the lists, participants had to rate the person with these characteristics. It was found that ratings were predicted by whether the first three traits were positive or negative: if the first three traits were positive, the person was rated as more liked than if the first three traits were negative, *regardless of the nature of the last three traits*. This indicates a clear primacy effect in the formation of an impression of a person. Furthermore, the study revealed that when asked to recall the traits just listed (in a surprise recall task), participants showed a recency effect in their recall of the traits (they recalled the last three significantly better than the first three). This suggests that the primacy effect occurs 'on-line', in the sense that it occurs immediately and while the traits are being presented. It does not appear to be based on the information in immediate memory. The implication is that once formed, an impression can be impervious to new information, even when that information is easily retrievable from memory.

Two psychological processes illustrate the nature of social perception particularly well, social representations and stereotyping. Both clearly demonstrate the influence of social and cultural factors upon how we perceive the social world around us.

2.2 SOCIAL REPRESENTATIONS

We can define social representations as 'shared beliefs…within social groups, which serve to organise and direct social action…They create a base of shared knowledge which allows us to communicate directly with one another' (Hayes, 2001).

The notion of social representations was introduced by the French psychologist Serge Moscovici in the early 1960s. It built upon the work of the sociologist Emile Durkheim, who wrote at the turn of the last century (1898) about collective representations. Both conceptions centre on the notion of shared ideas or beliefs, i.e. the notion that any individual's beliefs are not wholly exclusive to him or her but are based on those of a given culture and time. Your parents may espouse the values of the sixties culture of love or the eighties culture of dog-eat-dog entrepreneurialism. Both were dominant cultural beliefs at the time. Many of you reading this who are British Asian will be only too familiar with the clash between the cultural beliefs of traditional Asian and 'contemporary' Asian beliefs and the impact it has upon your lives.

Social representations can be shared by very large groups (e.g. all Muslims) or by much smaller groups.

> **Key study: Social representations**
>
> Moscovici (1961), in one of the very first studies into social representations, explored the way in which Parisian students had incorporated Freudian ideas of psychoanalysis (such as symbolism in dreaming and Freudian slips) into their everyday thinking. He identified three stages through which social representation developed:
> - the scientific stage: when the beliefs were adopted by professional scientists
> - a second stage: when the beliefs were more disseminated and accepted into a wider community

- the ideological stage: when the beliefs were held at a broad level as an explanation for how things were as they were, for example how the unconscious mind influences a person's behaviour and the explanation of motivated forgetting (see Topic 1).

It is interesting to note that in the final stage the social representations are often not articulated or discussed, they are just 'taken for granted'. Another example of a 'taken for granted' social representation is the once widespread belief that women should not have the same human rights as men. This was rarely stated, and certainly not challenged, until relatively recently in our culture, and is still prevalent in many countries.

Social representations are made up of two elements: a **central core** (technically called a figurative nucleus) and outer, **peripheral** elements. The central core is the essential part of the belief and rarely changes. An example for a Christian would be that there is a God. Peripheral elements might concern debates about whether priests should marry or whether women can become priests.

Evaluation

- Moscovici has been frequently criticised for having shifting definitions of aspects of social representations, which are seen by some as unclear and inconsistent.
- Moscovici has been criticised for appropriating a theory from another discipline (Durkheim's collective representations).
- It is unclear where social representations actually 'live' — inside the heads of the holders (cognitive) or in the folklore, media and stories of a culture (e.g. autobiographical accounts of male striving and success), which 'sit around' the individual (a social location).
- Social representation research has given us very good insights into the way people make sense of their world (e.g. Jodolet's 1991 work on perceptions of mental illness in a small French community).
- Social representations is a good example of European social psychology which, compared to the majority of North American social psychology, tended to focus more at a genuinely social level (as opposed to an individual in a social setting).

2.3 SOCIAL AND CULTURAL STEREOTYPING

The term stereotyping has been with us for a long time. It was first used by Lippman in the 1920s who defined it as 'pictures in our heads', arguing that it gives only a 'very partial and inadequate way of representing the world'.

Perhaps the definition which best summarises stereotyping is that given by Tagiuri (1969): 'The general inclination to place a person in categories according to some easily and quickly identifiable characteristic such as age, sex, ethnic membership, nationality or occupation, and then to attribute to him qualities believed to be typical to members of that category'.

Stereotyping can be seen as a form of **cognitive shorthand** (or perhaps less positively, laziness) whereby we try to make quick and easy judgements about people on the basis of their membership of certain groups. Although it is easy to see how this can lead to prejudice (seeing all women as romantic and weak), stereotypes do often contain an element of truth.

Brislin (1981) (cited in Gross 2001) says: 'Stereotypes should not be viewed as a sign of abnormality. Rather, they reflect people's need to organise, remember and retrieve information that might be useful to them as they attempt to achieve their goals and to meet life's demands'.

Key study: Stereotyping

The first study into stereotyping was carried out on a hundred university students at Princeton in New Jersey, USA (Katz and Braly, 1933). The students were asked to choose from a list of adjectives (such as intelligent, sly, ambitious, musical), which suited the following ethnic groups: Americans, Chinese, English, Irish, Italians, Japanese, Germans, Turks, Negroes and Jews.

The first traits ascribed to Americans were industrious; intelligent; materialistic; ambitious; progressive. For Japanese the top five were: intelligent; industrious; progressive; shrewd; sly. Perhaps the most shocking one was the list for Negroes: superstitious; lazy; happy-go-lucky; ignorant; musical.

Later replications were carried out in 1951 and 1967.

One of the most disturbing features of the original study was that many of the students who were quite happy to ascribe traits had had no personal contact at all with some of the ethnic groups they were judging.

Evaluation
The study was ground-breaking and showed the power of stereotyping for the first time. However, the prevalence of the stereotypes may have been exaggerated by the 'forced compliance' of the methodology (students having to make the judgements at all and being given a specific list to choose from).

Discuss research into stereotyping. (24 marks)

Most studies on stereotyping have been carried out in the USA (as has the majority of studies in social psychology). One of the reasons why North Americans may be particularly concerned about stereotyping is that it is the most individualistic culture in the world and as such encourages the perception of each individual as an individual, as opposed to a member of a group as is the case in collectivist cultures.

Discuss one approach to explaining social and cultural influences on the perception of the social world. (24 marks)

Prejudice and discrimination

Prejudice may be defined as 'the positive or negative evaluation of a social group and its members' (Smith and Mackie, 2000). It is about *prejudging* people on the basis of their perceived social group. Discrimination refers to 'positive or negative behaviour directed toward a social group and its members' (Smith and Mackie, 2000). Prejudice is an attitude that is often translated into discriminatory behaviour.

3.1 THE ORIGINS OF PREJUDICE

Evaluation

This approach has led to a number of questionnaires that measure (a) prejudice towards minority groups (Ethnocentrism or E-scale) and (b) the attitudes of the authoritarian personality (Fascism or F-Scale). Adorno et al. found that the two scales are significantly and positively correlated with each other, and that high scorers on the F-scale had been treated harshly during childhood. However, the theory ignores the role of group norms and the wider social context (Billig, 1976). Also, Adorno et al. carried out interviews with high scorers to validate their theory — yet knowing the interviewee's score beforehand may lead to biased questioning and biased interpretation of responses. Altmeyer (1998) has produced a modified F-scale, the Right-Wing Authoritarian scale, which focuses on authoritarian submission, authoritarian aggression, and conventionalism. The scale positively correlates with prejudice towards the gay community and criminals.

Social identity theory

Tajfel (1969) proposed that we develop a social identity based on *membership of certain social groups*. The theory is based on three main cognitive components:

- *Categorisation*. Basic to human cognition is the need to categorise and place things into meaningful groups (such as reading handwritten text, recognising familiar faces, recognising different cultures, and so on). In a social context, categorisation can lead to stereotyping.
- *Assimilation*. As children we adopt the social evaluations of our parents, and then as we develop we gradually assimilate broader social norms.
- *Search for coherence*. Another basic cognitive process is to infer meaning from the events that happen to us and to others, and to understand the world around us.

According to Tajfel, these three mechanisms combined can lead to stereotyping and prejudice, quite early on in life. Individuals identify with a group in a meaningful and personal way, since groups are often defined by their power, status and influence. People will often attempt to justify their group identity and in so doing may consider other groups to be weaker — or just different — and will denigrate them. Differences between groups can become accentuated and exaggerated, and in times of social difficulty, such as economic depression, such accentuation can lead to intergroup conflict, with the rivalry becoming very intense.

Evaluation

Several studies suggest that social identity and group membership can have powerful effects on attitudes towards the self, the group and outgroups. For example, Hirt et al. (1992) found that social identity can strongly influence self-esteem, and Pettigrew (1959) found that local group norms can sometimes predict prejudice better than individual personality attributes (see Key study). However, Rabbie et al. (1989) found that self-interest can sometimes override social identity and lead to outgroup favouritism, for example when the outgroup provides for the individual.

Realistic conflict theory

According to Sherif (1966), prejudice is also an aspect of group identity, but only arises out of *conflicting interests* between groups. Support for the theory comes from a study by Sherif et al. (1961), who found that when competition was introduced into groups who already had a sense of group identity, hostility emerged. However, other studies show that hostility between groups does not emerge when the groups have formed friendships or are known to each other (Tyerman and Spencer, 1983).

Key study: Cultural norms and prejudice

Pettigrew (1959) distributed the F-scale, an anti-Semitism scale, and an anti-Negro prejudice scale to people in four northern and four southern US towns. The research was investigating whether people from the north and people from the south of the USA differ in terms of their authoritarian personalities, and whether such differences could account for the fact that people in the south are regarded as more prejudiced. He found that people from the south were more prejudiced against Negroes than were people from the north, but they did not differ in the amount of prejudice towards Jews. This finding might be taken as evidence that prejudice could be determined by local norms. For example, while the authoritarian personality in the southern towns might be prejudiced specifically towards Negroes, the same authoritarian personality in northern towns is prejudiced, but is less specific. One important observation from this study was that conformist personalities in the northern towns were least prejudiced, but that conformist personalities in the southern towns were most prejudiced. This suggests that local norms can have more of an influence than individual personality in the formation of prejudiced attitudes.

Outline and evaluate two explanations of the origins of prejudice. (24 marks)

3.2 THE REDUCTION OF PREJUDICE AND DISCRIMINATION

Theories of prejudice are most useful when they suggest ways in which it can be reduced. Indeed, one test of a theory is whether such suggestions actually reduce prejudice.

Having common goals

If Sherif (1966) is correct that prejudice arises when groups are in conflict, then it may be possible to reduce prejudice through the sharing of common interests. Sherif et al. (1961) showed that having two groups work towards a common goal resulted in friendlier attitudes towards members of the opposite group. However, the drawback is that if, in their joint effort, they are unsuccessful in their common pursuit, their prejudice could actually increase.

> **Key study: Aronson and Osherow (1980) — The jigsaw classroom**
>
> The name of this study is taken from the fact that a jigsaw is made up of individual pieces that are equally important in completing it. Aronson and Osherow (1980) attempted to reproduce this philosophy in a Texan school that had recently been segregated. Children had to work in small groups on tasks to acquire knowledge that they would later be tested on. Each member of the group learned one aspect of the information, which they then had to teach to the other members of the group. The findings from this cooperative learning strategy were encouraging. The children showed a reduction in prejudice and increases in self-esteem. However, the effects were not as large as hoped; this was due to the fact that the project was conducted over a short period. Furthermore, if their tasks were not achieved well, recriminations and an increase in prejudice occurred. Subsequent replications of this method at other schools found that when progress at a task was poor, the minority group members tended to get blamed for it, and this often served to reinforce existing prejudices.

Contact

Allport (1954) argued that prejudice could be reduced by increasing the amount of contact between groups. This suggests that stereotypes are often based on *faulty assumptions* and that by being in social contact with members of a group, the assumptions become questioned. In addition, social contact reinforces the view that the similarities easily outnumber any differences. Although studies show that social contact can reduce prejudice (e.g. Deutsch and Collins, 1951), Allport accepted that by itself it is not enough, and that cooperative activities, coupled with institutional support, should also be provided.

Decategorisation

Since categorisation is considered an important cognitive process that can lead to stereotyping in Tajfel's (1969) social identity theory, it follows that social contact could be more effective in reducing prejudice if the nature of social categories could be made *less distinctive* (Brewer and Miller, 1984). Slavin (1983) reports that teaching methods that encourage cooperation (such as in the jigsaw classroom study) reduce prejudice by blurring social categories. However, the research suggests that while decategorisation breaks down prejudice towards individuals, it is not often generalised to the individual's group.

Empathy

Individuals may be prejudiced partly because they have never been the subject of prejudice. In this approach it is argued that the experience of what it is like to be a victim of prejudice can reduce such attitudes. The evidence generally supports this view. For example, Elliot (1977) conducted a classroom experiment in which children were divided into two groups, based on eye colour. The children were then told that those with blue eyes were superior in several ways to those with brown eyes. Subsequently, blue-eyed children taunted the brown-eyed children and did better in class. The children were then debriefed and told that it was an exercise in understanding prejudice and discrimination. In a follow-up study, Elliot (1990) reported that these children thought that the exercise had made them more tolerant of others and actively opposed to prejudice.

Q **Discuss research into studies which have attempted to reduce prejudice or discrimination.**   (24 marks)

---

4 Relationships

4.1 ATTRACTION

Physical attractiveness

A popular belief is that some people are simply more attractive than others. However, research suggests that, as well as differences within and between cultures in what is considered as physically attractive, our attractions to others are largely influenced by our attitudes towards them as individuals. For example, information about a person can bias a subsequent rating of how attractive they are seen to be (Owens and Ford, 1978).

Evolutionary theory

Men attach more importance to physical attractiveness than women do (Feingold, 1990). This may be because, in order to maximise the likelihood of passing on their genes, men select women who appear to be better able to have healthy children. Beautiful women are considered to be free of disease and genetic defects. Buss (1994) argues that psychological mechanisms have evolved to make men seek mates who are physically attractive. On the other hand, women have evolved to seek mates who are willing to commit their resources to them and their children. Thus women seek men who are dominant, have status and are wealthy, rather than men who are physically attractive.

Interaction

We tend to be attracted to people with whom we have positive interactions. *Proximity* (living or working close to someone) can increase the chances of positive interactions. For example, in a study by Festinger et al. (1950), friendships tended to be formed by people living close to each other. Furthermore, people who lived in locations that increased the chances of interactions generally, were considered to be more liked. One reason why interaction increases perceived attractiveness is that of *familiarity* — rather than breeding contempt, as the proverb suggests — breeding liking. In one study, a group of women sat in on lectures, with some attending more lectures than others. Women who attended more lectures were rated as more attractive than women who attended fewer lectures (Moreland and Beach, 1992).

Similarity

According to Smith and Mackie (2000), similarity leads to attraction for three main reasons:

- 'Birds of a feather flock together'. We tend to interact with people who are similar to us. Pairs of college couples and friends tend to be similar on many variables, such as age, religion, race and social class (Hill et al., 1978).
- We tend to assume that similar others will like us. In addition, being liked by someone is one of the strongest reasons for liking that person (Condon and Crano, 1988).
- Similar others share the same beliefs and attitudes. People like similar others even before they have met them (Byrne, 1971).

The matching hypothesis

According to Walster et al. (1966), people tend to be attracted to others who they consider about *equal* in terms of attractiveness. Murstein (1971) found that married partners were often rated as being very similar in terms of attractiveness.

Reinforcement and need satisfaction theory

For a relationship to work there must be some **reward** or **benefit** in it. One way in which attraction can occur is through direct positive reinforcement: people who reward us, especially verbally, are seen as more likeable and attractive (Lott and Lott, 1968). It is argued that people who become associated with pleasant experiences are more liked than people who become associated with unpleasant experiences. This can occur even when someone is not the cause of pleasantness, as the study by Griffith and Veitch (1971) demonstrates. In that study, people who met in a hot, crowded room were not attracted to each other, even though their personalities were similar. In relationships, people may directly exchange benefits, such as cooking a meal in order to obtain help with the car. In other relationships, rewards may occur through a mutual activity that both enjoy, such as playing tennis. Clark and Mills (1979) refer to such relationships as exchange relationships. They distinguish between exchange and communal relationships. In the latter, partners are directly concerned with each other's welfare, and provide benefits for the sake of caring, rather than to receive a reciprocal benefit.

Discuss one approach to explaining interpersonal attraction.	(24 marks)
'We like certain people because we find them rewarding and they satisfy our needs.' **Critically consider the extent to which this view of relationships has been supported.**	(24 marks)
Outline and evaluate the theories relating to the formation of relationships.	(24 marks)

4.2 MAINTENANCE OF RELATIONSHIPS

Self-disclosure

Important in developing and maintaining a relationship is to reveal **personal** and **sensitive information** about oneself to the partner. According to Sprecher (1987), we tend to monitor this closely and try to match the amount of information revealed. There appear to be different levels of self-disclosure, depending upon the point in the relationship (Knapp, 1984). Early on, it concerns fairly neutral topics and occasionally a topic is 'floated' to see if the other person is willing to discuss it. As the relationship develops, there is less adherence to the norms of self-disclosure. For example, early on in the relationship a partner will respond to self-disclosure with more self-disclosure, while in developed relationships a partner responds to self-disclosure with offers of support and understanding (Archer, 1979).

Maintenance strategies

According to Dindia and Baxter (1987), who interviewed 50 married couples, there are at least 49 strategies that couples use to maintain their relationships. These include: talking about the day, paying compliments and reminiscing. The range and frequency of such strategies become less as the relationship progresses, and this is either because the relationship does not require such frequent effort at maintaining it or because people who have been married for a long time take each other for granted.

Levinger's (1980) Stage Theory of Maintenance

This model is based on the idea that a developing relationship becomes progressively more intimate. The five stages are:

A *Acquaintance*. The first stage involves all of the factors associated with attraction.

B *Build-up*. Self-disclosure encourages interdependence and couples begin to evaluate each other in terms of the benefits of developing a long-term relationship.

C *Continuation*. As the relationship develops further, the couple's lives and lifestyles become enmeshed through engagement, marriage, living together, sharing each other's friends and family.

D *Deterioration*. For some relationships, imbalances in costs and benefits can lead to its breakdown.

E *Ending*. If relationship difficulties are not resolved, then it will end.

Evaluation

Levinger assumes that relationships always follow this staged sequence, but the evidence is that there are large differences between couples in relationship development (Brehm, 1992). However, the model does not offer explanations as to why relationships improve over time and then deteriorate, or why they go through these stages.

Social Exchange Theory

Thibaut and Kelley (1959) developed the **first stage model** of the development of relationships; it focuses on the strategies used by individuals at various stages to determine the costs and rewards:

- *Sampling*. Before a long-term relationship is developed, individuals, especially teenagers and young adults, explore the benefits and costs of different types of relationships, either by direct experience or by observing or hearing about the experiences of others.

- *Bargaining*. At the beginning of a relationship, couples give and receive various types of reward and in various amounts. The purpose at this stage is to determine whether the relationship is 'profitable' and so worth pursuing.

- *Commitment*. Having determined the benefits of the relationship, the amount of sampling and bargaining is reduced and commitment is given to developing the relationship.

- *Institutionalisation*. The developed relationship becomes established in terms of mutual and social expectations. In other words, the couple 'settle down' together.

Evaluation

Thibaut and Kelley assume that a relationship is a form of 'social contract' in which a person **bargains** for the **best deal.** In this view, social rewards are seen to be exchanged for caring actions; if the costs are greater than the rewards, then a person will consider terminating the relationship. Homans (1974) extended the economical metaphor of the model to include the principle of satiation: that we place greater value on receiving reward and approval in areas where we feel most insecure. However, Duck and Sants (1983) have criticised the theory as being based too much on individual personality and individual needs, and ignoring the social aspects in which the relationship develops. Thus, what is important for the maintenance of a relationship is how the couple talk to each other and how they interpret events in the relationship (see Key study: Murray and Holmes).

The basic rules of relationships

Argyle and Henderson (1984) studied friendships in four different countries and found that, although some aspects of these relationships are different, there appear to be six **main implicit rules** that strong friendships adhere to:

- Rule 1: Defend and support your friend in his or her absence.
- Rule 2: Share your successes with your friend.
- Rule 3: Show emotional support for your friend.
- Rule 4: Confide in and trust your friend.
- Rule 5: Offer your friend help when he or she is in need.
- Rule 6: When you are together, try to make your friend happy.

Their research findings included the observation that although obeying these six rules was insufficient alone to maintain a relationship, breaking one of them was almost guaranteed to end it.

Key study: Murray and Holmes (1993) — Maintaining relationships through storytelling

It has been argued that relationships are more likely to be successful if the partner's faults are regarded as favourably as possible. In other words, instead of criticising the other person for his or her faults, one tries to see the positive or even humorous side. Murray and Holmes (1993) found that dating and married couples were happier in their relationships when they idealise their partners, which involves seeing virtues in their partners that their partners do not see in themselves. Seeing the best in a partner does not involve denying a partner's faults. Rather, it involves elevating the importance of the partner's virtues and minimising the importance of the faults within their relationships. For example, satisfied, secure couples tend to turn their partners' faults into virtues and construct 'Yes, but' refutations that minimise faults. Impressively, the stability of relationships was found to be dependent on individuals forming such impressions of their partners.

4.3 DISSOLUTION OF RELATIONSHIPS

There are a number of theories of how relationships break down.

Lee's Stage Model

Most stage theories are based on the assumption that the breakdown of a relationship occurs slowly over time, rather than suddenly. Through studying a large number of break-ups in premarital relationships, Lee (1984) identified five stages:

(1) *Dissatisfaction*. Problems within the relationship are identified by one or both partners.
(2) *Exposure*. The problems identified in stage 1 are exposed and brought out into the open.
(3) *Negotiation*. These problems are then discussed and possible resolutions negotiated.
(4) *Resolution attempts*. Both partners attempt to resolve the problems using the strategies identified in the previous stage.
(5) *Termination*. If attempts at resolution are unsuccessful, the relationship is likely to end.

Lee found that the stronger the relationship, the more time would be spent working through the stages, especially the exposure and negotiation stages. It is likely that this is because a good relationship is worth fighting for.

Duck's Phase Model

A similar staged model is provided by Duck (1982) who assumed that passing from one stage to the next occurs when a **threshold** is met:

(1) *Intrapsychic phase*. 'I can't stand it any more.' Thoughts about the negative aspects of the relationship or the other partner occur, but are not expressed.

(2) *Dyadic phase*. 'I'd be justified in withdrawing.' Thoughts about the negative aspects are now expressed and discussions begun about how to resolve the problems.

(3) *Social phase*. 'I mean it.' When the problems cannot be resolved, the couple discuss how to end the relationship.

(4) *Grave-dressing phase*. 'It's now inevitable.' After the relationship has ended, each partner provides an account of how and why it ended to the outside world.

Evaluation of stage theories

Unlike Duck's model, which is essentially a model about how relationships break down, Lee's model accounts for how relationships can be retrieved after difficult problems. The models are useful for identifying the current stage of a relationship difficulty and in suggesting ways in which it can be repaired. Duck (1994) suggests that couples in the intrapsychic stage should focus on why they were attracted to each other in the first place. Neither account, though, explains how couples get to each stage; they are mainly descriptive.

External and internal risk factors

Duck (1992) identified two factors that make a relationship more prone to dissolution:

- *internal factors* — distasteful personal characteristics, such as bad habits and untidy behaviour; changes in attitudes and interests; pre-existing differences that come to the fore, such as different religious, cultural, educational, socio-economic and racial backgrounds; marrying at an early age; and poor social and relationship skills that are often the result of poor role models, such as people from divorced or dysfunctional family backgrounds
- *external factors* — jealousy, either real or imagined; deception and infidelity; boredom, in the sense that one's partner ceases to provide stimulation; and relocation

---

Q Outline two explanations of either the maintenance or dissolution of relationships and assess the extent to which research supports these. (24 marks)

4.4 PSYCHOLOGICAL EXPLANATIONS OF LOVE

Psychoanalytic theory

For Freud (1901), adult love has its origins in the Oedipus and Electra complexes. The child's socially unacceptable sexual longing for the opposite sex parent is pushed into the unconscious and reveals itself through defence mechanisms, for example in the transference of affection from the parent to the spouse. As with most early Freudian theories, this account is based on attempts to explain neuroses in a small section of a particular population (middle-class Europeans at the beginning of the 20th century) and it is virtually impossible to test empirically.

Love as distinct from liking: Rubin's theory

Most contemporary theories of love attempt to distinguish between **different forms** of love. Rubin (1970) argued that love and liking are distinct states and developed two scales to measure each of them: the Rubin Love scale and the Rubin Liking scale. In the love scale, love is considered as being based on a desire to care for someone, having dependent needs on them and feeling absorbed in them. In the liking scale, liking is considered as being based on respect and similarity of attitudes.

Evaluation

If these are discrete scales, there should be a low correlation between the two. However, significant positive correlations have been found with the scales, such that feelings of liking and loving for a lover were similar, as they were for one's mother, for one's friend and for one's father (Sternberg and Grajek, 1984). An interesting finding by Rubin is that men conceptualise love as related to sex, while women conceive of love as more to do with intimacy and attachment.

Limerence: love as infatuation

Tennov (1979) identified a particular type of love that often appears in popular culture, such as literature, film and music, but which could be considered as largely **dysfunctional**. He used the term 'limerence' to refer to unrequited love that is based on infatuation. Such love is said to be passionate and all consuming. It is obsessive and often based on fantasy and imagined togetherness. It can only exist if it remains unfulfilled — should a relationship start, attraction would soon cease.

Evaluation

The theory can explain why banned teenage relationships can flourish, since obstacles presented by parents can lead to infatuation.

The colour of love: Lee's different types of love

Lee (1976) identified several kinds of love, depending upon the *type* of relationship.
- *Eros*. This is an idealised love, where one has a clear mental image of an ideal partner and is searching for someone who fits it.
- *Ludus*. This is a form of love based on fun and enjoyment, but not commitment.
- *Storge*. This form of love is based on friendship that develops into an intimate and affectionate relationship.
- *Mania*. This is a very intense love, characterised by possessiveness and jealousy.
- *Agape*. This is an altruistic form of love, in the sense that love and caring is given without any expectation of receiving love in return.
- *Pragma*. This is a practical form of love, in which the emotional feelings for the partner are not held to be more important than other aspects, such as his or her occupation or background.

According to Lee (1976), an individual can have more than one type of love, depending upon the nature of the relationship; and the type of love in one relationship can change into another form over time. Breakdown of a relationship can occur when two partners have different types of love in the same relationship.

Evaluation

Attitudes to love are not fixed, but dependent upon whether someone is currently in love. Hendrick and Hendrick (1988) found that people who said that they were currently in love with someone had a more altruistic attitude towards love than those who said they were not currently in love, in the sense that they were more concerned with erotic and agapic love.

Sternberg's Triangular Theory of Love

According to Sternberg (1987), a relationship will emphasise two or more of the following:
- *Intimacy*. This refers to the feelings of closeness in a relationship and caring for the welfare of one's partner. It is also characterised by good communication within the relationship.
- *Passion*. This refers to the physical and sexual attraction couples feel for each other. It also includes other needs, such as self-esteem and self-fulfilment.
- *Commitment*. This refers to the short-term expression of love and to the long-term efforts at maintaining the relationship.

Sternberg argued that these components have an order of importance, depending upon the stage of a relationship. In the short term passion is most important, while in long-term relationships intimacy and commitment are the most important. In addition, different types of love are defined, based on the presence or absence of each component (see Table 7.1).

Type of love	Intimacy?	Passion?	Commitment?
Liking or friendship	Yes	No	No
Romantic love	Yes	Yes	No
Compassionate love	Yes	No	Yes
Empty love	No	No	Yes
Fatuous love	No	Yes	Yes
Infatuated love	No	Yes	No
Consummate love	Yes	Yes	Yes

Table 7.1 Sternberg's Triangular Theory of Love

As can be seen from the table, the strongest form of love is consummate love, since it involves all three components. Sternberg argued that one reason why relationships fail is that people commit in the short term for short-term reasons, rather than looking at the long-term needs of the relationship.

Describe one psychological explanation for love. To what extent has this explanation been shown to be accurate?   (12+12 marks)

4.5 CULTURAL AND SUBCULTURAL DIFFERENCES IN RELATIONSHIPS

Most of the research has focused on heterosexual relationships in the UK and the USA. However, relationships need to be understood in context; hence there may be significant differences in the relationships of different cultures and subcultures.

Differences between Western and non-Western cultures are summarised below.

Individualist versus collectivist

Goodwin (1999) argued that the main cultural difference between Western and non-Western cultures is that the former are individualist (individuals make their own decisions and are responsible for themselves), while the latter are collectivist (individuals consider themselves as a member of several social groups, including the family, and are obliged to follow the decisions of the group). For example, people from individualist cultures tend to marry for personal reasons, while individuals from collectivist cultures tend to marry for social status (Hsu, 1981) — although there is a degree of marrying for social status in the former and a degree of personal choice in the latter.

Voluntary versus involuntary relationships

Love is considered significantly more important in marriages in Western than in non-Western culutres (Lebine et al., 1995). Furthermore, Chinese people tend to think that the Western view that marriages should be based on romantic love is overly optimistic (Shaver et al., 1991). However, the evidence suggests that arranged marriages have about the same marital happiness as those based on romantic love (Yelsma and Athappily, 1988).

Permanent versus impermanent relationships

In some cultures divorce is extremely rare. For example, the divorce rate in China is less than 4%, compared to 40–50% in the USA. It has been argued that high divorce rates are based on the philosophy that one should strive to seek one's ideal partner (Simmel, 1971). Also, social groups in collectivist cultures may provide a more supportive background for a relationship (Brodbar-Nemzer, 1986).

Age differences

Despite cultural differences, Buss (1989) identified one similarity that appears across the 37 cultures studied, which is that most men prefer younger partners while most women prefer older partners. Buss argues for a socio-biological explanation: men and women find those features that maximise the likelihood of producing offspring the most attractive. Younger women are more likely to be able to have healthy children and older men are more likely to be in a good position to provide for the offspring. However, Howard et al. (1987) offer an alternative explanation based on social status rather than sociobiology. Traditionally, for most cultures, men have greater social status than women; therefore women are more likely to wish to marry for social status (and older men tend to have more status than do younger men). Since women have lower status, the way that they compete for men is by offering youth and beauty.

Monogamous and polygamous relationships

In some cultures it is normal for men to have more than one wife. This form of polygamy is referred to as polygyny. Although most societies value monogamy more than polygamy, human sexual behaviour tends to be polygamous across cultures (Eysenck, 2000).

Critically consider the extent to which relationships have been shown to be different in Western and non-Western cultures. (24 marks)

4.6 GAY AND LESBIAN RELATIONSHIPS

Similarities between homosexual and heterosexual relationships

A popular misconception among heterosexuals is that gay and lesbian relationships are invariably short term. However, the evidence is that, similar to heterosexuals, 50% of gay men and 65% of lesbians are in a long-term relationship at any given moment (Peplau, 1991). Gay and lesbian couples and heterosexual couples report being in love with their partner to about the same degree overall; however, gay and lesbian couples report liking their partner more than do heterosexual couples.

Differences between homosexual and heterosexual relationships

Homosexual couples are more likely than heterosexual couples to have a sexual partner outside their main relationship. In one study, for couples together for at least ten years, the numbers reporting having sex with someone outside their relationship were 22% of wives, 30% of husbands, 43% of lesbians, and 94% of gay men (Blumstein and Schwartz, 1983). Another difference is that gay and lesbian relationships are founded more on equity of status than are heterosexual relationships. Where there is unequal status between a couple, gay men and lesbian women are more likely to break up than are heterosexuals (Blumstein and Schwartz, 1983). A major difference between heterosexual and homosexual relationships is that the latter have to deal with outside hostility, and this hostility from society is a major reason why homosexual couples are less likely than heterosexual couples to cohabit (Kitzinger and Coyle, 1995). According to George and Behrendt (1987), many gay men harbour the same 'homophobic' fears as heterosexual men: many gay men believe that sex with other men is unnatural, sinful and immoral. In addition, due to societal prejudice, many gay and lesbian individuals lead double lives, such that they may hide their sexual orientation from their family and work colleagues (Dahlheimer and Feigal, 1991). As such, gay couples receive less social support from their family than do heterosexual couples (Kurdek and Schmitt, 1987), and gain more social support from friends than family (Kurdek, 1988). Clearly, such attitudes cause significant problems for gay relationships, which is one reason why gay and lesbian couples are more likely to break up than are heterosexual relationships (McFarland, 1997).

Q

'Gay relationships have more in common with heterosexual relationships than differences.'
Discuss the extent to which psychological research has supported this statement. (24 marks)

Further research

Sadly, the main reasons why studies of gays and lesbians were initiated were first, to understand how best to turn them into heterosexuals, and second, to understand the spread of HIV infection. However, just as research into heterosexual relationships can help us understand and deal with break-ups in marriages, there is also the need to understand homosexual relationships better than we currently do to deal with break-ups in those too.

4.7 INTERNET RELATIONSHIPS

There are several modes of communication on the internet: e-mail, usenets and chat.

E-mail

Electronic mail is a form of message writing that is delivered via the **internet**. People with internet accounts have an e-mail 'address' (such as 'JohnSmith@Coolmail.com') and are able to send mail to other people with internet accounts if they know their address. E-mail is read at the recipients' leisure, i.e. they can choose to read their mail at any time — they do not have to read it the moment it is received. E-mail is most similar to writing and receiving letters by post ('snail-mail'), but differs in that e-mail exchanges can take place over minutes rather than days or weeks, and the conventions of writing messages are such that one writes in a less formal way than is done in snail-mail (although internet communication does have its own informal rules, known as netiquette). However, as with letter writing, non-verbal signals usually picked up in face-to-face communication are not present, and neither are voice intonations available as they are with telephone conversations. Because of these missing elements, misunderstandings are common. It has also been suggested that people communicate with more assertiveness and aggression in e-mail than they do with either face-to-face or telephone conversations when dealing with other people.

Usenets

There are over 14,000 newsgroups on the internet and these are organised around themes or particular topics. Messages are posted onto a usenet site; users read existing messages and submit their own. There are several problems with this form of communication, as identified by Bloom (1998), such as lack of confidentiality (messages containing personal information can potentially be accessed by the entire internet community), and the validity of the information offered (for example, an unqualified individual may offer advice that is inappropriate or even dangerous if followed). Usenet communication can lead to interpersonal relationships that are continued in several forms. Parks and Floyd (1996) report that of 176 individuals questioned, about two-thirds pursued a relationship beyond the usenet medium. Most of this was through e-mail, one third was through the telephone, and one third actually met in person. Internet relationships are based more on rapport, similarity and mutual self-disclosure than on physical attractiveness (Cooper and Sportolari, 1997).

Chat rooms

A chat room is a **virtual room** on the internet where a number of people can 'chat' by sending and receiving typed messages almost instantly. Usually, the room is limited to about 30 to 50 people at any one time, and every message can be seen by all members of the room. On some systems, members can send private 'instant messages', which can only be read by the recipient. Individual rooms can also be created by users, to limit the number of people to a select few. According to Branwyn (1993), the most common use of chat is for people looking for relationships or erotic encounters (cybersex).

Cyberaffairs

Griffiths (1999) identifies three types of cyberaffairs:

- *Sexual arousal*. Some people meet on the internet (but not in person) for sexual arousal, and this is achieved by exchanging sexual dialogue. Such encounters may be brief or regular.
- *Emotional contact that leads to off-line encounters*. Some relationships are formed that are based on personal and emotional interest, and these can become precursors to off-line (face-to-face) contact.
- *On-line relationships*. Some relationships that are formed on the internet go no further, and this is usually because of geographical distance.

Griffiths (2000) argues that an internet relationship can become **addictive**, since it offers anonymity and escape. It is also a convenient medium for people who are shy or people whose lifestyle inhibits them from meeting other people in the usual way.

Problems with internet relationships

The first obvious problem is that some people may (and do) claim to be someone they are not. In the extreme, this may lead to exploitation by paedophiles, or may result in the unwanted receipt of sexually explicit messages. Although the latter can occur with the telephone and conventional mail, internet users are less easy to trace.

Discuss psychological research into 'electronic' friendships. (24 marks)

Pro- and antisocial behaviour

5.1 NATURE AND CAUSES OF AGGRESSION

Definition of aggression

Aggression can be defined as 'any form of behaviour directed towards the goal of harming or injuring another living being who is motivated to avoid such treatment' (Baron and Richardson, 1993). Psychologists have identified several forms of aggression:

- person-orientated aggression, which is designed to harm someone
- instrumental aggression, in which aggression is used to obtain something
- proactive aggression, which is aggression that is deliberately initiated
- retroactive aggression, which is an aggressive reaction to something

Aggression can be both physical and verbal, and is usually defined by an *intention* to hurt someone.

Social learning theory

In this perspective (e.g. Bandura, 1973), aggression is seen as a *learned* behaviour that results from direct or indirect reinforcement or imitation.

- *Observational learning*. If a person is seen to be rewarded for behaving aggressively, others may learn that aggression can be useful (vicarious reinforcement). Observers may then imitate the actions at some later time. Thus the behaviour is acquired by observing the actions of others and the outcomes that follow.
- *Parental influence*. Patterson et al. (1989) compared the parental styles of families with at least one aggressive child and those of families without problem children. The key difference was the use of reward and punishment. The coercive home environment

consisted of: little demonstration of affection; overt use of aggression by parents; little use of positive reinforcement (e.g. approval); regular use of physical punishment, shouting and teasing. These results suggest that parental use of positive and negative reinforcement can determine the levels of aggressive behaviour in their children.

● *Video games.* After playing aggressive video games, 9 and 10 year-old girls, but not boys of the same age, tend to show increases in aggression (Cooper and Mackay, 1986). Much younger children of both sexes tend to show increases in aggression after playing such games (Silvern and Williamson, 1987; Irwin and Gross, 1995). These results imply that the behaviour may be imitated, especially in younger children.

Evaluation

There is evidence to show that aggressive behaviour may be learned. The theory can account for individual variation, as well as aggressive behaviour demonstrated in certain situations only (through context-dependent learning, in which reinforcement is only given in certain contexts). However, the approach is limited, since research shows that some aspects of aggression are innate, as demonstrated by twin studies (e.g. McGue et al., 1992).

Key study: Bandura, Ross and Ross (1961) — Bobo doll

Young children watched an adult behave aggressively towards a Bobo doll (a limbless object that wobbles about when hit but does not fall over). Other children watched an adult who did not behave aggressively to the Bobo doll. The children were then moved to another room which included several toys and a Bobo doll. Those children who observed the adult aggression were significantly more likely to show aggression to the doll. The claim is that this is evidence for observational learning of aggressive behaviour. However, later research has shown that children are more likely to imitate aggression towards a doll than they are towards another person (Durkin, 1995), and this may be because punching a Bobo doll represents play fighting.

Frustration–aggression hypothesis

One idea is that aggression follows from frustration (Dollard et al., 1939).

● Doob and Sears (1939) showed that when people imagine frustrating situations, they subsequently report feeling angry. However, the problem with this as supportive evidence is that anger does not *always* lead to aggression. Pastore (1952) distinguished between justified and unjustified frustration, and showed, through a series of experiments, that only the latter leads to aggression.

● Aggressive cues, rather than frustration, may also lead to aggression. For example, in mock electric shock experiments with students (Berkowitz and LePage, 1967), the mere presence of guns can elicit more aggressive acts than in their absence.

Evaluation

Berkowitz (1989) modified the original frustration–aggression hypothesis and developed a cognitive-neoassociationist approach. An aversive event is first interpreted and then promotes a flight or fight response. If the event is interpreted as an intentional threat, then aggression (or flight) may be elicited. However, if the event is interpreted as unintentional or non-threatening, then non-aggressive feelings are elicited.

Deindividuation

This concept can be defined as 'the loss of a sense of personal identity that can occur when we are, for example, in a crowd or wearing a mask' (Eysenck and Flanagan, 2001). Such a loss of identity can lead to aggressive behaviour because individuals feel less constrained by normal social conventions. In Zimbardo's (1973) prison simulation study, students were divided into prisoners and guards and enacted these roles over several days. Guards became increasingly deindividuated and hence more aggressive as they continued in the role.

Evaluation

The problem with the approach is that deindividuation does not always lead to aggression. For example, in Zimbardo's study, the students with the role of prisoner, although also deindividuated, became increasingly passive rather than aggressive.

Relative deprivation theory

This approach is defined as 'the theory that feelings of discontent arise from the belief that other individuals or other groups are better off' (Smith and Mackie, 2000).

People find it difficult to assess objectively how well they are faring in terms of their status and the resources that are available to them in everyday life. Therefore, people make social comparisons and these determine how satisfied they are. For example, someone may be entirely happy with a new Ford Ka, until the next-door neighbour turns up in a shiny new Mercedes Benz. Often social comparisons are made between groups and these may result in a sense of relative deprivation. For example, the 1960s was a time of both economic boom and intense social disorder in the USA; this may be because African Americans saw their economic situation lagging behind that of Whites (Sears and McConahay, 1973).

Relative deprivation may lead to conflict and violence. The theory has been used to account for conflicts between unemployed youths and the authorities in Australia (Walker and Mann, 1987), gay and lesbian and straight groups in Toronto (Birt and Dion, 1987), French and English speakers in Canada (Guimond and Dube-Simard, 1983), and Muslims and Hindus in India (Tripathi and Srivasta, 1981).

Q Outline two social psychological theories of aggression and assess the extent to which research supports these.

(24 marks)

5.2 ENVIRONMENTAL STRESSORS AND AGGRESSIVE BEHAVIOUR

Temperature

Room temperature has been shown to influence how willing participants in an experiment were to give a mock electric shock to another person (Baron and Bell, 1976): the higher the temperature, the less likely they were to give the shock. The reasoning is that high temperatures induce stress, making them less likely to add to that stress by agreeing to give the shock. However, in naturalistic settings, Anderson (1989) found that the incidence of assault, rape and murder tended to increase as the temperature increased.

Key study: Glass et al. (1969) — noise as a stressor

Noise may lead to increased stress, arousal and frustration. Glass et al. (1969) gave students a number of tasks under various conditions: loud or soft noise that occurred either predictably (at regular intervals) or unpredictably (at irregular intervals). Some of the tasks could not be solved and were used to elicit frustration. Galvanic skin responses (GSRs) were recorded as measures of arousal or stress. GSRs were lower in the predictable condition, where students also made fewer errors and persisted longer at the insoluble tasks than in the unpredictable condition. Those in the no-noise condition made fewer errors. The results show that noise can add further stress to an already stressful situation.

Evaluation

The presence of unpredictable and uncontrollable noise is one of a number of environmental factors that have their effects by increasing an individual's level of arousal. For example, the mere presence of weapons can increase aggression even more strongly in people who are already angered (Berkowitz, 1993). Furthermore, high states of arousal can lead to misinterpreting a bump or jostle as an act of aggression (Dodge and Somberg, 1987). Increases in arousal may also lead to the selection of short-term problem solving strategies (e.g. aggression) rather than more carefully thought-out (non-aggressive) solutions (Gray, 1999).

Overcrowding

Several studies have linked overcrowding with aggression. For example, nursery children showed increased levels of aggressive behaviour as the number of children in a nursery rose (Loo, 1979). Rats show similar behaviour: when the number of rats living in an enclosure was increased, so too was the amount of aggressive behaviour (Calhoun, 1962). Although in some situations crowds can enhance pleasure (as at a sporting event), in many other cases they may promote aggression, since the presence of a crowd appears to enhance one's current mood (Freedman, 1973).

Discuss research into the effects of environmental stressors on aggressive behaviour.   (24 marks)

5.3 ALTRUISM

Altruism can be defined as 'voluntary helping behaviour that is costly to the person who is altruistic' and **empathy** as 'the ability to share the emotions of another person, and to understand that person's point of view' (Eysenck and Flanagan, 2001).

Empathy–altruism

Eisenberg et al. (1983) argued that empathy is a key aspect of moral development. Batson (1987) argued that altruistic behaviour results from an ability to empathise. When someone is in distress, we may have an empathetic concern (sympathy for the person and a motivation to help) and a personal distress (concern about our own discomfort and a motivation to reduce it). According to the theory, if empathetic concern is stronger than personal distress, this will lead to helping behaviour.

Evaluation

An early criticism was that people might show helping behaviour, not through empathetic concern but through a desire for social approval. However, there is a substantial body of evidence from developmental psychology to show that, as children's ability to empathise increases, so too does their thinking and behaviour become more altruistic. Smith et al. (1989) developed an alternative theory, which suggested that helping behaviour results from the feelings experienced by seeing the joy of others who have been helped. However, the theory is difficult to test.

Negative-state relief

Cialdini et al. (1987) argue that helping behaviour occurs because people who *empathise* with someone in distress feel sad and wish to reduce their own sadness. In their negative-state relief model they further argue that people in a negative mood are more likely to help than people in a positive or neutral mood, but only if the costs are not too high. However, there is evidence that sadness does not always lead to helping behaviour (Thompson, Cowan and Rosenhan, 1980). This theory then argues that empathy only leads to altruistic behaviour for selfish reasons! However, Lerner and Lichtman (1968) have shown in the laboratory that people engage in altruistic behaviour, even when there is no obvious personal gain.

Sociobiology

A sociobiological explanation of any behaviour is one in which it is argued that the behaviour has *evolved*, since it promotes survival of the species. An important dilemma for sociobiological theory is accounting for altruistic behaviour, since by definition it is a behaviour that is likely to promote the survival of others rather than oneself. However, such an explanation might be that an altruistic act is likely to be returned at some later time (reciprocal altruism). Whether this can explain acts of human altruism has been questioned. It is likely that, since people think about their behaviour, it will be influenced by empathy, social norms and individual choices, rather than an inbuilt tendency to expect reciprocation for helping someone in distress.

5.4 BYSTANDER INTERVENTION

Diffusion of responsibility

Darley and Latané (1968) attempted to account for the behaviour of 38 witnesses to a murder, all of whom failed to intervene or even telephone the police. The much publicised murder, which took place in a middle-class area of New York, was of Kitty Genovese, a 28 year-old woman who was heard to call out for help over a half-hour period. The conclusion that Darley and Latané came to was that, if there are many observers to a crime, each person feels less responsibility for providing assistance.

> **Key study: Darley and Latané (1968) — the diffusion of responsibility**
>
> Participants were led to believe that they were having discussions with other people about their personal problems, communicating via headphones and a microphone. The discussions, which were tape recordings, were to be held with various numbers of people: one, two, three or six others. They were told that one of the other persons was prone to seizures. During the conversation, one man was recorded as saying that he was about to have a seizure and asked for help; 100% of participants who thought that they were the only other person sought help, but only 62% of participants who thought that there were four others who had heard it sought help. Furthermore, participants were unaware that the size of the group had the effect of determining whether help would be sought, and although some of the participants in the larger group sizes did not seek help, they were more aroused and anxious than those who did seek help. The study demonstrates that people are less likely to assist when several people witness an event requiring urgent help than when they are the only witness. Thus, responsibility for seeking help is diffused among the group.

Situational factors

A bystander may be unwilling to help if an event appears to be ambiguous. For example, a person falling to the ground may be having a heart attack or may be drunk. Helping behaviour may then occur, when the bystander perceives that it is an emergency (Brickman et al., 1982). A bystander may be unwilling to help when it is perceived that two people (an attacker and a victim) are related and may put it down to a lover's quarrel, as the study by Shotland and Straw (1976) suggests.

Individual differences

- *Knowledge*. According to Huston et al. (1981), people are more likely to help if they feel that they have the necessary skills and expertise.
- *Gender*. Men are more likely than women to offer help when there is either an element of danger or when there is an audience (Eagly and Crowley, 1986). Further, men are more likely to help women than they are to help men, particularly attractive women. In contrast, women are just as likely to help men as they are to help women.
- *Personality*. Although personality factors do not generally tend to predict the likelihood of offering help, one study suggests that helpers are other-oriented rather than self-oriented (Dovidio, Piliavan and Clark, 1991).

Models of behaviour

A number of models of bystander behaviour have been suggested and these focus on the stages involved in deciding whether or not to help.

The decision model

Latané and Darley (1970) suggested a decision model that consists of a series of questions. Helping behaviour only follows when one answers 'yes' to each of the following:

- Is something wrong?
- Is assistance needed?
- Should I accept responsibility?
- What kind of help is needed?
- Should help be carried out?

This model accounts for the research evidence that there are not one but several reasons why bystanders do not intervene. Since there are several questions that require a positive response before a final decision to help is made, the model accounts for why bystanders often fail to offer assistance. More research is required, though, in determining the thought processes that occur at each stage. Furthermore, the model does not include an emotional component but instead over-emphasises the rational aspects of decision making.

Arousal/cost–reward model

Piliavin et al. (1981) include emotional aspects of the decision process through their arousal/cost–reward model, which consists of five steps.

(1) Someone's need for help grabs a bystander's attention.
(2) He or she experiences autonomic arousal.
(3) An attempt is made to label or interpret this sense of arousal.
(4) He or she calculates the rewards and costs associated with helping or not helping.
(5) A decision is made and acted upon.

The costs and rewards of helping or not helping are displayed in Table 7.2.

	Cost	Reward
Decide to help	• May be harmed physically • May be delayed	• Personal satisfaction if one has the expertise required • Praise from the victim
Decide not to help	• Guilt • Ignoring one's responsibility to help • Criticism	• Able to carry on as normal without any delay

Table 7.2 Costs and rewards of helping or not helping

This model is more complete than the decision model and is supported by the evidence that bystanders do tend to weigh up the costs and rewards of deciding whether or not to help. One problem is that bystanders tend to act impulsively and their responses are likely to be considerably slowed by the process of weighing up the costs and rewards. It is possible, though, that bystanders do not consider all of the costs and rewards, but only some of them. The model also assumes that arousal is necessary before help is given and this is not always the case (e.g. an experienced police officer may offer help without becoming aroused).

Q

Outline and evaluate two explanations of altruism and/or bystander behaviour.   (24 marks)

5.5 CULTURAL DIFFERENCES IN PROSOCIAL BEHAVIOUR

Individualism and collectivism

Western countries place greater emphasis on personal success and competition than do non-Western societies (see Table 7.3).

Feature	Individualism	Collectivism
How the people see themselves	Unique and separate from the society	Connected to society through social roles and relationships
Personality	Unchanging and constant, across different situations	Adaptable and able to change according to the situation
Aspect of self considered to be important	One's abilities, thoughts, feelings, personality traits	One's social status, social roles and relationships
Desirable behaviour	Self-expression, self-interest, being an individual	Fitting in with others, acting according to social conventions, promoting group goals

Table 7.3 Individualism versus collectivism

West versus East

One might expect that altruistic acts are less common in the West. Indeed, Darley (1991) argued that people in Western societies are more concerned with self-interest; and most of the research which shows that bystanders often fail to help has been carried out in the USA. Whiting and Whiting (1975) showed that 100% of Kenyan children between 3 and 10 years were high in altruism, but only 8% of a similar US sample were altruistic. Eisenber and Mussen (1989) reviewed a number of bystander studies and found large differences between cultures, such that children of Mexico and Southwest America appear to be more cooperative and considerate of others than are US children.

Influence of culture

If a culture places greater emphasis on competition and personal success, it is likely that cooperative behaviour will be reduced. Further, children in collectivist societies are usually given greater family responsibilities, such as looking after younger children. These responsibilities may encourage the development of cooperative behaviours early on. Also, since cooperation is more expected in collectivist cultures than it is in individualistic cultures, behaviour may be more about conforming to these expectations than representing acts of altruism (Fijneman et al., 1996).

Within-culture differences

Interpersonal Reactivity Index: Davis (1983) developed a measure of empathetic concern and personal distress and found that those high on empathetic concern were significantly more likely to watch TV charity 'telethons' and more likely to make a donation than those low on empathetic concern.

Discuss research into cultural differences in prosocial behaviour. (24 marks)

5.6 MEDIA INFLUENCES ON PRO- AND ANTI-SOCIAL BEHAVIOUR

'The media' is a term that refers to various sources through which popular culture is presented, such as books, newspapers, television, the radio, music, films and videos. Most research has concentrated on the influences of television, since most people have access to it and view it on a regular basis.

Disinhibition

Most of the time people tend to inhibit their anti-social tendencies. However, exposure to media in which people behave in antisocial ways may counteract the effects of personal inhibition (a process known as disinhibition), by making the behaviour appear socially acceptable. This can also occur in a positive way; a scene, for example, that shows a bystander offering help may disinhibit tendencies to avoid offering help.

Desensitisation

According to Franzoi (1996) and others, a particular antisocial act, such as unwarranted physical aggression, may initially provoke **arousal** in the viewer. However, after watching several hundred such acts on television, arousal may no longer occur and we become *less responsive*. Indeed, Thomas et al. (1977) found that the physiological reactions of young children to a violent television programme were significantly reduced if they had just watched a video of young children behaving aggressively. Reduced arousal may lead to acceptance of such behaviour as normal.

> #### Key study: Josephson (1987) — cognitive priming
>
> Many different types of experiment show that thoughts and feelings can be made more likely to occur if people have been previously exposed to stimuli of a similar content. Aggressive images in the media may provide such cognitive cues for aggressive behaviour. In this study, Canadian boys watched a violent television programme in which snipers communicated with each other through walkie-talkies. Another group of boys watched a non-violent programme. All of the boys then played a hockey match, with some of the boys receiving the referee's instructions before the match via walkie-talkies and others through tape recordings. The walkie-talkies acted as cognitive primers for aggression, since the boys who had watched the violent programme and who had received instructions via walkie-talkie were more aggressive in the match than boys who had watched the violent programme but who received instructions through tape recordings.

Stereotypes

Television can increase (or decrease) prejudice through the use of stereotypes. Examples include the use of foreign accents by the 'bad guy', the adventure movie that shows the black person being the first to die (and hence portraying black people as weak), and so on. Positive stereotypes also exist, such as showing women as caring, and fat people as jolly. Counter-stereotypes, although rare, may decrease prejudice, such as seeing women judges and single fathers.

Displacement

Gerbner and Gross (1976) found that people who watch a lot of television rate the outside world as much more *dangerous* than it really is. This may be because programme makers are more likely to create extremely dangerous situations than everyday situations. Furthermore, news programmes tend to focus more on extreme acts of violence than on positive news. The effects of showing a range of antisocial behaviours whose frequency is much less in reality is known as the **deviance amplification effect**.

Positive effects of television

Several studies indicate that television can promote prosocial behaviour (Friedrich and Stein, 1973; Sprafkin et al., 1975). For example, children who were shown *The Waltons* (a programme about a US family whose members are seen to behave in very positive and cooperative ways to each other) were more likely to behave in a more prosocial way than other children who had not been shown the programme (Baran, 1979).

The absence of television

If television does have a negative influence on viewers, one might expect *less actual violence* in societies or areas where television reception is not possible. According to Hennigan et al. (1982), in the 1950s, when some areas received television earlier than others, the level of recorded violence was higher in receptive areas than non-receptive areas. Furthermore, in non-receptive areas, later reception was associated with an increase in recorded thefts.

Key study: Charlton (1998) — the introduction of television in St Helena

The people of the island of St Helena in the Atlantic received television for the first time in 1995. The introduction of TV to this island was predicted by some to lead to subsequent rises in aggression, as children would model themselves on TV characters (a significant proportion of whom are seen to behave aggressively). Charlton (1998) reports on a series of studies designed to test this claim. Children were observed in a number of settings, such as being secretly videoed playing at school. The researchers failed to find any imitation of the violence seen on television by these children. Charlton claims that these children were immune to the effects of violence on television because they had come from stable home and community backgrounds.

Evaluation

Although useful in showing that the prediction of increased aggression was unfounded, the study may only report on relatively short-term effects of television. The long-term effects of prolonged exposure to TV violence are unknown.

'Claims that the media make people, including children, behave in antisocial ways have little support from psychological research.' Discuss. (24 marks)

Discuss research into the effects of the media on prosocial behaviour. (24 marks)

Describe one research study on the effects of the media on either pro- or antisocial behaviour. Assess this study in terms of its strengths and weaknesses. (12+12 marks)

TOPIC 8 Physiological psychology 2

Brain and behaviour

1.1 METHODS OF INVESTIGATING THE BRAIN

Methods of investigating the brain and its influence on behaviour can be categorised as **invasive** or **non-invasive**.

Invasive methods involve direct manipulation or stimulation of the brain, or surgery. Non-invasive methods are techniques that can measure the activity of the brain without the need for direct manipulation or surgery.

Invasive methods

- **Electrical stimulation** of the brain involves insertion of electrodes into a particular location in the brain. The targeted neurones are stimulated with brief electrical activity and the consequent behaviours or experiences of the organism are recorded. For example, stimulation of the visual cortex causes perception of flashing lights, and stimulation of the auditory cortex causes perception of sound, etc. This method is useful to determine the *function* of a particular brain region — for example, Penfield and Rasmussen (1950) identified the major sensory projection, motor and somatosensory areas of the brain. Problems include the fact that it requires minor surgery to attach electrodes, and that it is difficult to be sure that only *selected* neural areas are activated due to the scales involved.

- **Chemical stimulation** — neurotoxins and neurostimulants are drugs that block/stimulate certain **neurotransmitters** (such as dopamine). Effects upon behaviour are recorded after administering such drugs. This is useful in devising drug treatments for specific mental illnesses. For example, drugs inhibiting dopamine activity help schizophrenics, while drugs stimulating dopamine activity make their symptoms worse. Problems of the method are that it relies on imprecise trial and error and that much research relies upon data from studies of animals. Some researchers (e.g. Fisher, 1964) argue that neurotransmitters have different functions in different species.

- **Ablation** is a technique where a region of the brain is removed and the effects observed. Ablation can be used to identify which region is involved in what behaviour or process. Clearly there is an ethical problem of inflicting ablation deliberately; furthermore, the method is not very precise, and there are problems extrapolating data from animals to humans.

- **Lesioning** involves cutting connectors or tissue in the brain to disrupt functioning. Lesion methods include aspiration (fine removal of outer layers of cells through suction), sectioning (delicate cutting using tailored surgical tools), and radio-frequency lesioning (destroying tissue with heat from radio-frequency current). Cryogenic blockade is an alternative technique achieving similar results, where neurones are *nearly* frozen in order to stop their firing. As with ablation, these methods can be used to identify which region is involved in what behaviour or process. All but the last method cause structural damage (however minor) and this is obviously an ethical problem in using such methods.

Non-invasive methods

- **Electrical recording** involves attaching electrodes to the skull in order to detect electrical activity (EEG or electroencephalography). Some uses of the method involve inserting electrodes directly into the brain (invasive EEG), but obviously this shares the problems of the invasive methods detailed above. While it tells us nothing about the structure or specific areas of the brain that are active, EEG provides a gross measure of electrical activity in the brain and so can be used to identify and explore different states (such as sleep or alertness).

- **Scanning** the brain is done by means of either a PET (positron emission tomography) or a CAT (computed axial tomography) scan. PET scans work as follows: active neurones use up glucose in firing — patients are injected with a radioactive imitation of glucose (2-deoxyglucose, 2-DG). The active neurones take up the 2-DG, but cannot use it, as only real glucose will do. Therefore there is a radioactive build-up of 2-DG in active areas that can be seen using the scanning equipment (the 2-DG subsequently breaks down over time). Such a method is harmless and allows researchers to see which areas of the brain are active at any given time. CAT scans involve taking many X-ray pictures that are compiled by specialised computer equipment — this provides a detailed representation of the structure of the brain, but tells us nothing about which areas are active.
- **Imaging — MRI (magnetic resonance imaging)** creates high-resolution images constructed from the measurement of waves that hydrogen atoms emit when they are activated by radio-frequency waves in a magnetic field; a detailed 3D picture of the brain can be formed. This is useful for identifying structure, but cannot tell us which parts of the brain are active.

Table 8.1 summarises the strengths and weaknesses of these techniques.

Technique	Strengths	Weaknesses
Electrical stimulation	Useful for determining function	Invasive (minor surgery) Problem of scale*
Chemical stimulation	Useful for developing treatments for mental illnesses, less invasive than cutting (ablation/lesioning)	Relies on a lot of guesswork (trial and error); relies on studies of animals (problems of generalising)
Ablation	Useful for determining function	Ethical problems with deliberate ablations, problems generalising from animals, problems of scale*
Lesioning (aspiration, sectioning, radio-frequency lesioning)	Useful for determining function (very accurate with radio-frequency lesioning)	Ethical problems — causes structural damage, problems of scale*
Cryogenic blockade	Useful for determining function Doesn't cause lasting structural damage	Problems of scale*
Electrical recording (EEG)	Provides a gross measure of activity, useful for identifying states	Tells us nothing about structure and function of individual brain regions
Scanning (PET, CAT)	PET scans provide information as to which areas are active CAT scans provide detailed structural information	PET scans may show which areas are active, but don't provide a very clear picture of structure CAT scanning gives a clear picture of structure, but tells us nothing about function. Very expensive equipment
Imaging (MRI)	Very clear, high-resolution pictures of the brain	No idea which areas are active Very expensive equipment

*Problems of scale refers to the fact that when stimulating or cutting a particular part of the brain, it is difficult to be sure that only the targeted area is affected (the target might be incredibly small, and where it stops and the adjacent region begins might be hard to distinguish).

Table 8.1 Comparison of methods of investigating the brain

Outline one invasive and one non-invasive method of investigating the brain and assess each of these in terms of their strengths and weaknesses. (24 marks)

1.2 LOCALISATION OF FUNCTION IN THE CEREBRAL CORTEX

Introduction and definitions

Various areas of the brain, particularly the cerebral cortex, have been shown, through research methods detailed in Section 1.1, to be implicated in certain functions — in other words, certain functions are **localised** within specific brain regions. Examples of such localisation of function are presented in Table 8.2.

Some functions of the brain do not appear to be localised in this way, but are instead described as having **distributed function** — in other words, no one particular region is responsible for the function. Early research into memory led Lashley (1929) to believe that memory was a function distributed in this way (because his research failed to find a specific location responsible for the function). He argued that a large region of the cortex (called the association cortex) served a general function, processing and linking information from other more specific regions. Since then, with advances in the methods available for investigating the brain, doubt has been cast on Lashley's conclusion of distributed function for memory.

Forebrain

Cerebrum	Thinking, planning, perception, memory
Thalamus	Sensory processing and relay
Hypothalamus	Maintaining homeostasis
Pituitary gland	Coordination of endocrine activity and brain
Limbic system	The four Fs of motivation; emotion

Midbrain

Tectum	Visual and auditory fibres
Tegmentum	Sensorimotor fibres

Hindbrain

Cerebellum	Coordinated movement, skill learning, including speed of language and cognition
Reticular formation	Attention, arousal, movement, sleep
Pons	Sleep, dreaming, attention
Medulla	Breathing, heart rate, digestion, autonomic functions

Spinal cord

White matter	Somatosensory nerve fibres
Grey matter	Pain responses, spinal reflexes

Table 8.2 Examples of localised function in the central nervous system (adapted from Hayes, 2000)

Important findings from research into localisation of function

- *Motor processes.* Movement is primarily controlled through a localised region referred to as the motor cortex. This is a band of tissue across the top of the brain. Each hemisphere is responsible for controlling the *opposite* side of the body (**contra-lateralisation**), and each part of the body is represented in the motor cortex by a specific sub-region. The size of the region for a body part is directly related to the complexity of the movements possible by that body part (so hands, which are capable of very complex and diverse movements, have a relatively large region in the motor cortex). As Table 8.2 shows, the **cerebellum** is also important for coordination of precise movements.

- *Sensory processes*. Different sensory processes have been found to be localised to specific regions of the brain. Visual processing occurs in the visual cortex (occipital lobe), auditory processing occurs in the auditory cortex (temporal lobe), and sensations of touch, temperature and pain are processed in the somatosensory cortex (which is next to the motor cortex and is organised in the same way, with body parts that are most sensitive having greater representation in the cortex).
- *Language processes*. Different structures have been discovered that deal with language processes, and these structures are located in regions that make functional sense (i.e. they are near to other structures that assist such processes). **Broca's area** is involved in the production of speech, and is located near the motor cortex (which itself is involved with the sort of movements required to translate speech 'plans' into actual speech). **Wernicke's area** is concerned with speech comprehension, and is located near to the auditory cortex (which itself would receive the speech).

1.3 LATERALISATION OF FUNCTION IN THE CEREBRAL CORTEX

Introduction and definitions

In the same way that many specific psychological functions are localised within a specific brain structure, various more general functions are lateralised. That is, groups of functions are associated with either the right or the left hemisphere (side of the brain). The right and left hemisphere are connected by the **corpus callosum**, a large set of axons that allows information from each side to be transferred to the other. This is important because while one side may be responsible for a particular function, other functions reliant on shared information may be located on the other side. Much of what we know about lateralisation of function has been discovered by observing the behaviour of people who have had their corpus callosum damaged or removed — this is generally known as **split-brain** research.

Important findings from research into lateralisation of function

Structures of the brain involved with language processes are mostly located on the left hemisphere, as are those associated with analytical skills. However, emotional content of heard speech and emotional inflection of produced speech appears to rely more upon the right hemisphere, as do understanding and visuo-spatial functions (Rasmussen and Miller, 1977).

The left hemisphere is connected to muscles and sensory receptors on the right side of the body, and the right hemisphere to the left side of the body. In the majority of people, the left hemisphere is dominant (right-handedness).

Visual pathways (from the eyes to the brain) and auditory pathways (from the ears to the brain) are not lateralised — in other words, the left eye/ear feeds information to *both* hemispheres, as does the right eye/ear. Motor functioning is also not lateralised.

Split-brain patients have revealed such lateralised functions through studies of their behaviour and performance. A famous example of such research is that conducted by Sperry (1961) — see the research box below.

> **Research into split-brain functioning**
> Split-brain patients who also had their optic connections cut (so each eye only transferred information to the opposite hemisphere) were shown written text to just their left eye.
> The words were therefore only 'seen' by the right hemisphere. The text could *not* be read (Sperry, 1961). Language processes are lateralised to the *left* hemisphere — in this case, only the *right* hemisphere had the information, so the patients couldn't read it.

A common criticism of much split-brain research is that the findings do not necessarily apply to 'normal' brains. Since it is unethical to sever the corpus callosum of a healthy person, the majority of the participants of such studies consist of severe epileptic patients (in whom the severing has been shown to relieve symptoms by restricting the spread of the seizure across hemispheres). It may be that the brains of such patients differ in their localisation and lateralisation from the brains of non-afflicted individuals.

Discuss research into the location of function in the cerebral cortex.	(24 marks)
'The brain has been shown to be divided in terms of asymmetry of function.' Discuss.	(24 marks)
Critically consider the lateralisation of function of the cerebral cortex, including the organisation of language in the brain.	(24 marks)

Biological rhythms, sleep and dreaming

2.1 BIOLOGICAL RHYTHMS

Introduction and definitions

Biological functioning and activity occur in cycles that repeat periodically. Examples of types of biological rhythms are as follows:

- *Circadian*. A cycle that lasts about 24 hours, such as human sleep/wakefulness.
- *Infradian*. A cycle that lasts more than 24 hours, such as hibernation, seasonal mating and the menstrual cycle.
- *Ultradian*. A cycle that lasts less than 24 hours, such as respiration and the beating of the heart.

Such rhythms are triggered or controlled by **pacemakers** and/or **zeitgebers**.

- **Pacemakers** are **endogenous** (internal) triggers. They are *biological clocks* that regulate cyclic biological functioning. Rhythms that rely purely on pacemakers and don't depend upon zeitgebers are known as free-running rhythms.
- **Zeitgebers** are **exogenous** (external or environmental) triggers. These are *cues* in the environment that signal time, such as the light–dark cycle and seasonal changes.

Evidence supporting the influence of pacemakers and zeitgebers

- Blind people (who have no input from the light zeitgeber) still have a circadian sleep/waking cycle, though it runs at around 24.9 hours rather than 24 hours (Miles, Raynal and Wilson, 1977). Additionally, participants restricted to a cave for several weeks (again, where zeitgebers are absent) adopted a 25 hour sleep/waking cycle (Aschoff, 1965).
- This research supports the idea that there *is* an internal clock for the sleep/waking cycle that is set above 24 hours, but in normal circumstances this is adjusted by the presence of zeitgebers.

The consequences of disrupting biological rhythms

- 'Normal' rhythms can be disrupted by circumstances, such as with shift work and jet lag.
- Generally, those sleeping during the day obtain less sleep (suggesting that conflicting zeitgebers can **desynchronise** the circadian rhythm); the most negative consequences arise as a result of shift work that involves working nights one week followed by days the next. The body can adjust and **resynchronise** to night shift work, but when there is constant switching of such work patterns from days to nights and back again, total resynchronisation is not possible.

- Such disruption of the circadian rhythm can lead to reduced cognitive functioning (Folkard et al., 1993) and a higher incidence of accidents at work (Novak et al., 1990; Gold et al., 1992).

Describe and evaluate research studies into biological rhythms, such as circadian, infradian and ultradian biological rhythms. (24 marks)

Discuss the insights which psychology has given us into the consequences of disrupting biological rhythms. (24 marks)

2.2 SLEEP

Central theories of sleep

There is no consensus as to what the function of sleep is, but there are two broad theoretical explanations.

- **Recuperation theory** (or **restoration theory**) suggests that being awake disrupts homeostasis or drains bodily resources in some way, and that sleep is therefore required in order to replenish and restore the body (Oswald, 1966). **REM** (rapid eye movement) sleep is thought to replenish the brain, consolidating memories and stimulating protein synthesis. During slow-wave or **NREM** sleep (also called orthodox sleep), bodily restoration occurs, with removal of waste products, stimulation of protein synthesis and increased release of growth hormones and synaptic transmitters.
- **Circadian theory** (or **evolutionary theory**) suggests that sleep is *not* for restoring the body but an **adaptive** response to internal and environmental demands (Meddis, 1975; Horne and Minard, 1985; Horne, 1988). In other words, we have evolved to sleep as we do because in previous populations such behaviour provided an evolutionary advantage. Sleep keeps us still and hidden, so we are less easily detected and less likely to encounter predators. We are protected from mishap by less moving around in the dark, and we also conserve energy.

Evaluation of the theories of sleep and relevant research findings

Infants have rapid growth *and* have much more sleep (especially REM sleep) than adults. This fact provides support to the recuperation theory, which argues that one of the functions of REM sleep is to facilitate release of growth hormones. However, the same fact can be argued to support the circadian theory, in that infants may sleep more as they are more vulnerable to predators and mishap, and their extended sleeping also allows more time for parents to find food.

According to the recuperation theory, we should expect greater activity while we are awake to require greater amounts of sleep, in order to recover energy. Shapiro et al. (1981) found that marathon runners did require more sleep than controls, though similar research by Horne and Minard (1985) found no such link.

From the circadian theory, we would expect animals that need to hunt or forage for food for longer periods to sleep less, and animals that are more likely to be attacked also to sleep less (Lloyd et al., 1984). This appears to be partially borne out. Many vulnerable creatures hibernate, while less vulnerable creatures, such as lions, sleep almost continuously for 2 or 3 days after gorging themselves on a kill (Pinel, 2000). Conversely, cows, which need to eat almost continuously to sustain themselves on their low energy diets, sleep for only 3 hours a day. However, if the evolutionary theory were fully correct, we would expect some animals (such as lions, which have no predators) not to sleep at all.

The fact that certain processes (such as metabolism and release of growth hormones) increase during NREM sleep supports the recuperation theory of sleep. However, during

REM sleep we are extremely active, which is contrary to the function of sleep suggested by the recuperation theory.

Findings from research into sleep deprivation

Some of the most important research to determine the function of sleep has been conducted by looking at the effects of partial and total sleep deprivation. If the recuperation theory is correct, we should expect lack of sleep to be detrimental to functioning.

In terms of partial sleep deprivation (or sleep reduction), the most consistent effect reported is that the desire to sleep increases. This is true of both NREM and REM sleep and is often called the **rebound phenomenon**. Webb and Bonnet (1979) found no major effects of only 2 hours sleep on one night, or of a gradual reduction from 8 to 4 hours sleep. A sudden change of sleep was found to lead to irritability and impaired attention. Many studies of both partial and total sleep deprivation have found no detrimental effects on cognitive performance. Where detriments have been found, they tend to be in terms of attention or reduced performance on more boring and passive tasks that require continuous attention. Such detriments are interpreted not as a negative effect of any bodily or mental exhaustion, but rather as blips that occur due to **microsleeps**. Microsleeps are 2–3 second long periods where people are stationary, have drooping eyelids, and have EEG measurements that are like sleep.

In animals, specifically cats, total deprivation of REM sleep has been observed to have more pronounced effects — Jouvet (1967) reported cats displaying hypersexuality and eventually death after prolonged REM deprivation. Empson (1989) argues that health suffers without sleep. Much of the evidence leans towards minimal effects of sleep deprivation, the main effects being a greater desire to sleep and sleep rebound. This tends to support the circadian, and not the recuperation, theory of sleep.

Discuss one approach to explaining the functions of sleep.	(24 marks)
Compare and contrast two theories of either the functions or evolution of sleep.	(24 marks)
Discuss the implications of findings from studies of sleep deprivation.	(24 marks)

2.3 DREAMING

The content, duration and timing of dreams

Dreams are series of thoughts and images that are experienced mostly during REM sleep, though they can also occur in NREM sleep. When Dement and Kleitman (1957) woke sleepers during REM sleep, 80–90% of them reported dreaming.

Dreams are often fragmented and often contain associations between objects and memories that are unusual or even bizarre.

While a common belief is that dreams last only an instant, evidence suggests that events in dreams run in normal time. Dement and Kleitman (1957) woke sleepers up either 5 or 15 minutes after the recorded onset of REM sleep. Participants were asked to estimate, based on the duration of the events in their dreams, whether they had been dreaming for 5 or 15 minutes. Participants were correct 92 out of 111 times.

Theories of the functions of dreaming

- **The Activation–Synthesis Model** (Hobson and McCarley, 1977; Crick and Mitchison, 1983) — suggests that the brain is activated during sleep by internal stimuli (such as memories) and/or external stimuli (such as the dripping of a tap or a change in room temperature). Our tendency to ascribe meaning to stimuli leads us to impose a story or structure around consequent neural activity. This is partially supported by research by Dement and Wolpert (1958), who sprayed people in REM sleep with water. When they were awakened, around half of them described dreams in which water was involved — the external stimuli had been incorporated into their dream.

- **Cognitive restoration** — Evans (1984) theorised that dreaming is a process that occurs as a by-product of the brain sifting through and updating memory files, rehearsing routines and heuristics, and deleting redundant data.

On similar lines, Ornstein (1986) suggests that dreams are a by-product of the reorganisation of memory schemas to incorporate new data, a process called **memory consolidation**.

- **Dreamwork** or **emotional catharsis** (Freud, 1901) — the traditional view of dreaming proposed by Freud is that during sleep the unconscious mind becomes dominant, and that the **manifest content** of dreams (what we see and hear) represents a **latent content** that is an expression of our unconscious desires and repressed memories. The mind's translation of latent content into manifest content was what he called dreamwork. Freud believed that you could explore a person's latent desires and memories by interpreting their dreams. While interesting, there is no real evidence to support this idea, and the process of interpretation is incredibly subjective and methodologically flawed.

Discuss the implications of research into the nature of dreams.	(24 marks)
Critically consider what insights psychological research has given us into the nature of dreams.	(24 marks)

3 *Motivation and emotion*

3.1 PHYSIOLOGY AND MOTIVATION

Introduction

A motivation can be defined as a drive or 'an inferred underlying state which energises behaviour, causing it to take place' (Stratton and Hayes, 1993, p. 119). Motivation drives us towards satisfying goals that are sometimes related to physiological states (such as hunger and thirst), sometimes cognitive and sometimes socially derived (such as the need for positive regard and social affiliation); motivations are usually experienced in emotional terms. Various theories and researchers suggest that certain brain structures are central to motivational states; some of these are explored in the following section.

Physiology and basic motives

Thirst

Essentially, loss of fluid (which can occur from not drinking enough, dehydration related to extreme temperature, bleeding and various other processes), and imbalances between water and salt, are detected by physiological mechanisms mostly related to the hypothalamus. Water loss from the cellular compartment is detected by osmoreceptors in the brain. Water loss from the extracellular compartment is measured by detectors of blood volume. Either form of water loss or water deficit induces a feeling of thirst and also causes increased release of antidiuretic hormone (ADH) (also known as vasopressin). This increases water retention by the kidneys. A lack of water is detected in the body, and addressed by the hypothalamus, which induces a feeling of thirst and (through the kidneys and ADH) an accompanying increase in water retention.

Hunger

A classic experiment by Cannon (1929) involved testing whether an empty stomach is the stimulus that activates hunger. This feasible idea was tested via the insertion of a balloon into the stomach; changes in the pressure within were measured. Reported hunger correlated with contractions of the stomach induced by the balloon, suggesting an emptier stomach is indeed associated with increased motivation for food. However, later research contradicts this idea — people who have had their stomachs removed still feel hunger.

Glucoreceptors have been found to be located in the hypothalamus and liver (Langhans and Scharrer, 1992). These are neurones that are sensitive to local levels of glucose (a nutrient used to supply energy for cells in the body). When glucose is low in the liver and hypothalamus, feeding motivation is activated. A number of other receptors other than glucoreceptors are proposed to be involved, each type related to a specific nutrient.

How do we stop eating? When there is food in the intestines, a hormone (and neurotransmitter) known as **cholecystokinin (CKK)** is released. CKK is a 'satiety hormone' — it signals that we are full and should not eat any more food. Also, a distended or stretched stomach signals the hypothalamus to cease feeding motivation. While many of the explanations for thirst and hunger motivations appear to fit a simple 'deficit leads to motivation' model, this is certainly not the entire picture. Such a model can't explain, for example, why gross obesity can result when a variety of foods are available (Wirtshafter and Davis, 1977).

Q   **Discuss the role of brain structures in emotional behaviour and experience.**   (24 marks)

3.2 THEORIES OF MOTIVATION

Different theories of motivation emphasise different sources of motivation — some theories emphasise the role of physiology, others the role of psychology, and others the role of social contexts. Some of the theories integrate these different perspectives to offer more complex or multi-faceted models of motivation. The central theories of motivation are summarised below.

Homeostatic drive theories (e.g. Cannon, 1929)

Homeostasis is the physiological process of maintaining a state of balance or equilibrium. Departures from the 'optimal' state of equilibrium are detected and addressed, and the body compensates in order to reach or be as close as possible to the organism's optimal goal state. Homeostatic drive theories argue that behaviour can be explained in these terms; essentially, the body detects an imbalance or a deficit, which leads to a biologically generated need (for example, a drive for food, water or warmth). These drives are then acted upon in behaviours directed to restore homeostatic balance. This is a physiological theory of motivation.

Evaluation

While the principle of homeostasis is a valid one, and is borne out in many instances of biology and basic drives, some behaviours are clearly not motivated in this way. It may be the case that we eat to address a deficit in blood sugar levels, or sweat in order to reduce body temperature, but the theory doesn't explain motivations to meet a vast array of more complicated needs such as aesthetic desires or social identification. There are also many behaviours we indulge in that seem deliberately to move our bodily state *away* from homeostasis. Homeostatic drive theories cannot explain why some people climb mountains, race cars or enjoy parachuting.

Expectancy theory (e.g. Vroom, 1964)

The expectancy theory of motivation was developed with particular focus upon organisational and occupational motivations. Essentially, the model is predicated on the assumption that we as humans are very rational about our decision-making, and our **motivational force** is informed by three perceptual judgements, according to the following formula:

> Motivational force = Expectancy × Instrumentality × Valence

Expectancy refers to the extent to which individuals believe that their effort will result in attaining a performance goal (e.g. 'If I revise harder, will I get a better grade in the exam?'). **Instrumentality** is the extent to which individuals believe that by attaining their performance goal they will be rewarded (e.g. 'If I do better in the exams, will I get a higher paid job?'). **Valence** refers to the value that an individual places upon the reward in question (e.g. 'How much do I want a higher paid job?'). These three appraisals are thought to be at the core of decision making and motivation. This is a psychological theory that is essentially cognitive in nature.

Evaluation

'Expectancy theory is most often used to predict such things as job satisfaction, one's occupational choice, the likelihood of staying in a job, and the effort one might expend at work' (Madden, 2001). As such, while it has applied use, it has been criticised for being too restricted and limited as a theory of motivation. It is reasonable for predicting *some* types of behaviour motivations at work, but is less applicable to a whole range of motivations (such as satisfying simple biological needs or destructive motivations). Additionally, it makes the assumption that motivations are arrived at through calculated deductions, and seems to ignore a lot of motivations that are triggered by emotionality and beyond such rational decision making.

Drive reduction theories (e.g. Hull, 1943)

Drive reduction theories are physiological and psychological. Drive theory still has needs that arise physiologically, such as hunger. The difference is that such theories incorporate an aspect of learning in the tradition of behaviourist psychology. If and when a behaviour satisfies a current physiological need, the resultant satisfaction means that the behaviour is positively reinforced. Thus when faced with such a need again, an individual will be likely to be motivated to repeat that type of behaviour (Thorndike's Law of Effect: 'Behaviours resulting in positive consequences are more likely to be repeated'). For example, an infant is feeling uncomfortably hot and is motivated physiologically to do something about this. After puffing and panting and moaning, he tries moving into the shade. Upon moving into the shade, he feels cooler. Because he has successfully satisfied the motivating need, next time he feels uncomfortably hot in the same environment, he is more likely to repeat this behaviour — he has learned an appropriate and successful behaviour.

Evaluation

Essentially, this theory is the same as homeostatic drive theory, but with a learning aspect 'bolted on'; it shows some incorporation of behaviourist principles such as Thorndike's Law of Effect. As such, it can be criticised in similar ways as the homeostatic drive theories. For example, we are often motivated to behave (e.g. feed) when there is no physiological deficit or need. Also, the motivations explained by this theory are limited to essentially lower-order physiological motivations. And since motivations are argued to arise from physiological deficits, it doesn't address behaviours that increase arousal (such as mountaineering, car racing, etc.). Finally, from its behaviourist angle, it can be criticised for not accounting for the fact that learning can sometimes occur without reinforcement (Tolman and Honzik, 1930).

Psychodynamic theories (e.g. Freud, 1901)

Freud's model of the unconscious mind posits lower motivations as arising in the id, where drives are generated that relate to physiological urges (so this theory incorporates homeostatic drives). While the id drives, the ego and superego regulate the extent to which we actually act on those drives, and also learn and respond to social rules and societal motives. The theory argues that our motivations (some of which we are not conscious of) are directed by and originate in the unconscious mind.

Evaluation

While some practitioners have been very effective in predicting motivations and behaviours from psychodynamic models, the theory is not much supported empirically, is not a scientific and transparent account, and has been criticised as being overly deterministic (free will is not accounted for, since motivations and behaviours are directed by innate and unconscious impulses). The theory does, however, have a wide scope, since it incorporates traditional elements of psychoanalytic theory, physiological theory and psychosocial aspects.

Humanist theories (e.g. Maslow, 1954)

Maslow constructed a 'hierarchy of needs', as shown in Figure 8.1. The theory suggests that the lower needs in the hierarchy must be satisfied before those above can be addressed. The strongest drives are those that are lowest in the hierarchy, since they are driven with physiological urgency and more concerned with survival than any aesthetic or self-actualisation needs.

Figure 8.1
Maslow's hierarchy of needs (1954)

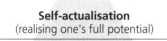

Self-actualisation
(realising one's full potential)

Aesthetic needs
(beauty, order, symmetry)

Cognitive needs
(curiosity, exploration, search for meaning and knowledge)

Esteem needs
(respect from others and self-esteem)

Love and belonging
(receiving and giving love and affection)

Safety needs
(security, protection, shelter)

Physiological needs
(food, water, activity, rest, sex)

Evaluation

While the theory has some logic and offers a useful *description*, its ability to predict motivated behaviours is less impressive. The model has been used in employment settings, but has been proved difficult to test in a scientific fashion. In addition, some motivated behaviours do not fit the model — for example, dangerous sports, such as car racing. Presumably the motivation to engage in such activity can best be attributed to one or more of the following needs: self-actualisation (realising full potential), cognitive (curiosity/exploration) or esteem needs (respect from others). However, since the need for safety is on the second 'tier' of the hierarchy, the satisfaction of this lower need before being free to attend to higher ones would appear to prohibit such motivations.

Compare and contrast two theories of motivation. (24 marks)

3.3 EMOTION

Introduction

Emotion is defined as the 'experience of subjective feelings which have positive or negative value for the individual' (Stratton and Hayes, 1993). The authors of this definition argue that any attempt to clarify the meaning of emotion in a more specific way is not possible without more firmly subscribing to a particular theory of emotion and possibly neglecting others. This is because the emphasis as to what an emotion consists of differs across theories — some popular theories will be detailed in a later section of this topic. Contemporary theories of emotion generally conceptualise emotions as having a physiological component (e.g. elevated galvanic skin response, heart rate, blood pressure, respiration, and other indices of autonomic nervous system arousal/activity, as well as activation of neurological centres — see above) and a subjective cognitive component (e.g. 'I feel depressed'); some also include reference to a behavioural component (e.g. action produced by the emotion).

The role of brain structures in emotional behaviour and experience

Table 8.3 (page 106) summarises some of the functions of various brain structures — note that the functions listed are only those related to emotional experience (certain brain structures listed have other functions, but these are not detailed here as they are not relevant). There is occasional overlap between emotional experience and motivation in these functions. Wherever possible within the space, evidence for the particular function is noted, together with the researcher who studied that function. The list is not exhaustive, but is meant to provide some core material in a concise fashion.

3.4 THEORIES OF EMOTION

The James–Lange theory (1884)

The common understanding of emotion and physiological/behavioural response is that we feel an emotion, and as a consequence respond (e.g. we feel fear on seeing a bear, then run away). The James–Lange theory contradicts this commonsense notion — they argued that we feel fear *because* we are running away. The physiological response occurs initially, *then* an emotional label is attached to it.

Evaluation

The theory is criticised for ignoring cognitive control and learning in shaping emotional experience. It also received a barrage of criticism from Walter Cannon, who along with a colleague proposed the Cannon–Bard theory, detailed below. These criticisms were based on a number of flaws in the James–Lange theory. The theory proposed that an emotional label was attached to the distinctive set of physiological and behavioural indices that resulted from exposure to the stimuli. This assumes that there is a distinctive physiological set of indices associated with each emotion. This has been criticised for the following reasons:

- Many qualitatively different emotions have very similar physiological correlates.
- Some emotions are related to physiological changes which are so minor that the relatively insensitive and inaccurate perceptions we have of them could leave them essentially undetectable.

Brain structures	Suspected functions	Evidence/notes	Researcher
Amygdala and hippocampus	Self preservation (for example, aggression)	Papez-Maclean limbic theory proposes 3 circuits in the limbic system that regulate emotional behaviour	Papez-Maclean (1970)
Amygdala	Aggression/sexual behaviour	Lesions/electrical stimulation variously cause attacks, stop attacks or cause indiscriminate mounting behaviour in some species (e.g. cats)	Aronson and Cooper (1979)
Cingulate gyrus	Pleasure and sexual behaviour	Papez-Maclean limbic theory proposes 3 circuits in the limbic system that regulate emotional behaviour	Papez-Maclean (1970)
Frontal lobes	Aggression	Removal of frontal lobes results in docility; Moniz used such psychosurgery (including frontal lobotomies) to alleviate various affective symptoms	Moniz (1936)
Hypothalamus and thalamus	Sex drive, pleasure and aggression	Papez-Maclean limbic theory proposes 3 circuits in the limbic system that regulate emotional behaviour	Papez-Maclean (1970)
Hypothalamus and cortex	Aggression	Removal of cat's cortex prompted *sham rage*, but this stopped if hypothalamus was also removed — suggests a 'dual role' of the two areas in aggression (cortex directs while hypothalamus expresses)	Bard (1929)
		May be radically different in humans, since stimulation of human hypothalamus has led to no emotional effect	Jacobson (1968)
Right cerebral cortex	Emotional interpretation and expression of negativity	Damage to left hemisphere only allowed emotional evaluation but not understanding of a statement; damage to right hemisphere only allowed understanding but not emotional evaluation	Gainotti (1972)
Serotonin*	Aggression	Evidence tends to be correlational, but there appears to be an association between levels of serotonin and aggression	Valzelli (1973)
	Emotional state	Its involvement in emotionality is also apparent from the fact that many emotional disorders (e.g. anxiety and depression) are treated by drugs regulating serotonin activity	

*Of course, serotonin is *not* a brain structure like the others, but is instead a *neurotransmitter* — it is included since it is associated with brain activity relevant to emotionality.

Table 8.3 Brain structures and emotion

- Some emotions occur with no physiological changes whatsoever.
- Physiological changes often occur with no emotion reported.
- The autonomic nervous system reacts relatively slowly to stimuli, whilst the emotional state may be triggered relatively quickly.

The Cannon–Bard theory (1927)

In line with the criticisms of the James–Lange theory, the Cannon–Bard model suggests that neither the physiological changes nor the subjective labelling of an emotional state precedes the other. Rather, both occur *independently* and *simultaneously* as a direct result of the stimuli.

Evaluation

On a positive note, this theory avoids the long list of criticisms that the James–Lange theory attracted — this was inevitable since it developed from these criticisms and was proposed by its critics. It is also more supported than the James–Lange theory in terms of empirical evidence of emotion occurring without any physiological change (e.g. Valins, 1966). However, some of the assumptions that it is based upon have been disputed. For example, the criticism that all emotional states do not have distinctive physiological patterns has been challenged. It may have been supported by evidence at the time of Cannon, when physiological measurements were certainly not as diverse and accurate as they are today; when multiple and more modern and accurate measures of arousal are employed, however, many emotions (especially primary ones) are more physiologically distinctive than previously thought.

The cognitive labelling theory/two-factor theory (Schachter and Singer, 1962)

This theory shares with the James–Lange theory the notion that physiological changes occur prior to subjective emotional experience. However, it is proposed that a general physiological state (arousal) is *interpreted and labelled* based upon environmental cues and previous experience. So, for example, arousal while seeing a rhino charging would (by most people) be labelled as fear, whilst arousal upon hearing news of a pay-rise would (by most people) be labelled as happiness/pride/excitement, etc. Note the clause 'by most people' — this is because the theory allows for individuals' experience and perceptions to inform how they label arousal. The two factors (hence the alternative title) of arousal and environmental cues interact.

Evaluation

Empirical support for the theory is provided by the classic experiment reported in the research box below. The theory allows for individual differences in terms of differential interpretations of arousal, which are informed by the characteristics and learning history of the person exposed to the arousal, and it allows for situations to be considered in emotional outcomes. However, it assumes that emotion can only be produced with physiological arousal (disputed by Valins, 1966). It also assumes that emotions require cognition, which has been challenged by numerous experiments generating effects through subliminally presented stimuli (Zajonc, 1984; Fulcher, 2000).

> **Research into cognitive labelling**
>
> Schachter and Singer (1962) conducted a classic experiment into how an emotional outcome is shaped by the interaction of arousal and situational cues (the two factors of the two-factor theory). Participants were told they would be injected with some vitamins concerned with enhancing vision, but were actually injected with adrenaline (which Americans call epinephrine). Participants were allocated to four conditions that differed in terms of what they were told about the injection: (1) told the truth about the drug side-effects (arousal); (2) misinformed (told the drug might cause numb feet!); (3) uninformed (told nothing else about the drug); (4) injected with a placebo and told nothing (control). All participants were then exposed to a scenario in a waiting room where a confederate (posing as another participant) behaved in either a jovial or an angry fashion. Condition 1 participants explained their arousal as caused by the drug. Condition 4 participants mostly didn't have arousal to interpret. However, participants in conditions 2 and 3, who had arousal and no explanation of it other than situational ones, attributed their arousal to the confederate, and would report (and often exhibit) emotions in line with the confederate's. This demonstrated the importance of arousal as an emotion 'primer', and the fact that general arousal will be labelled as a particular emotion based on appraisal of the situation.

Cognitive appraisal theories (e.g. Lazarus, 1982; Smith and Ellsworth, 1987)

Essentially, these theories elaborate upon cognitive labelling theory to provide 'decision tree' models to demonstrate how certain conditions lead to specific emotions. For example, Lazarus's theory of primary appraisal has three elements that inform whether emotion is felt, whether that emotion is positive or negative, and what the specific emotion would be. These three elements are goal relevance (is the stimulus relevant to a person's goal?), goal congruence (is the stimulus congruent with the goal or not?) and esteem relevance (is the stimulus relevant to the person's self-esteem?). Answers to these questions inform the resulting emotion; such questions are proposed as examples of how we evaluate or appraise stimuli.

Evaluation

Again, individual differences and learning are accounted for in this model, but it still fails, as do the other cognitive theories, to explain occurrences of emotion without the chance for conscious cognitive appraisals (i.e. in emotion induced through subliminal presentation of stimuli, such as with Zajonc, 1984 and Fulcher, 2000).

Q **Discuss what psychological research has told us about the nature of emotional behaviour and/or experience.** (24 marks)

Attention and pattern recognition

1.1 FOCUSED ATTENTION

The problem of how we focus our attention was best described by Cherry (1953) through his **cocktail party phenomenon**: how is it possible to focus on one person talking when there are several people talking at the same time? Cherry was one of the first psychologists to adopt an **information-processing approach**, which is based on the following assumptions:

- The environment consists of information, which is processed by several systems (visual and auditory sensory systems, central attentional system, etc.).
- Processing systems transform the information in particular ways (e.g. convert two-dimensional retinal images into perception of three-dimensional objects).
- Information processing in computers is a good model of how information is processed in humans.
- Processing systems can be systematically studied through the methods of experimental psychology.

The study of focused auditory attention is a good example of the information-processing approach as the aim is to understand how, using the experimental method, auditory information is selected and transformed.

Cherry (1953) devised the **dichotic listening** task and the **shadowing** technique to study focused auditory attention. The participant is presented with two different messages, one to the left ear and the other to the right, via a set of headphones. The participant is required to listen to the message in one ear; to verify that he or she is doing this; and asked to repeat the message aloud (a practice known as shadowing).

Broadbent devised an alternative method, known as the **split-span** task. In this, the participant is presented with two different messages; sometimes parts of the same message would be presented to the left ear and the other parts of the message would then be switched to the right ear. The participant is required to report what is heard, rather than attend to one ear only.

Cherry found that participants were largely unaware of the contents of the message presented to the unattended ear (the unshadowed message). They could, though, detect basic physical features of the unshadowed message, such as whether the voice was male or female, and whether sounds or voices were presented. Broadbent found that people could recall a set of digits better when they were presented to one ear than when their presentation was switched between the two ears.

Explain what is meant by focused attention. (6 marks)

1.2 EXPLANATIONS OF FOCUSED ATTENTION

Broadbent's filter theory (Broadbent, 1958)

Broadbent's model is based on the idea that we have a **limited capacity** for processing sensory input. He proposed that messages presented at the same time gain access to a sensory buffer. To prevent overloading, the filter selects just one message to be processed further — the one with the more relevant physical characteristics. The theory handles Cherry's basic findings, with unattended messages being rejected by the filter.

Evaluation of Broadbent's theory

Broadbent's theory exaggerates the amount of information that is filtered out, since many studies now show that semantic information (e.g. meaning) in the unattended message can be processed. In addition, this theory cannot account for the fact that attention to the unattended message can be increased through practice (Underwood, 1974).

Treisman's attenuation model (Treisman, 1964)

Treisman proposed a **'leaky' filter** model in which inappropriate information is weakened or attenuated rather than completely blocked by the filter. The first filter would identify stimuli with relevant or irrelevant physical characteristics; the second filter would strengthen significant information and filter out insignificant information.

The model accounts for Cherry's finding that **physical** characteristics of the unattended message can be noticed. Several studies show that the meaning of the unshadowed message is attended to — for example Treisman's (1960) study, in which the message being shadowed was switched to the other ear without the participant being aware of this, yet he continued to shadow the same message. In another study, Treisman (1964) played French and English messages to bilinguals. She found that participants would notice that an English word presented in one ear was the same in meaning to a French word played in the other ear at the same time, even though they were trying to ignore information presented to one ear.

Evaluation of Treisman's theory

Clearly, Treisman's theory can account for more research evidence than can Broadbent's theory, especially the fact that the meaning of the unshadowed message can be processed under certain circumstances. However, the attenuation model denies the possibility of parallel processing: there is some evidence that even more information can be processed in the unshadowed message than is suggested by Treisman's model. Furthermore, filtering might not occur as early as is suggested in this model, as the studies by von Wright et al. (1975) and Corteen and Wood (1972) demonstrate.

Late selection model (Deutsch and Deutsch, 1963)

These authors supposed that all information is processed in parallel, but that selection and filtering occur much later on. Filtering is then based on whether the information is pertinent or not.

Evaluation of Deutsch and Deutsch's theory

The pertinence model appears to be more parsimonious as an explanation of selective attention (it can explain things more simply and elegantly). Few studies have been carried out to help determine which of Treisman's and Deutsch and Deutsch's models is to be favoured.

Key study: Dichotic listening with classically conditioned stimuli

von Wright et al. (1975) presented neutral words accompanied with mild electric shocks, mimicking a classical conditioning procedure. When subsequently presented with the words, participants showed a galvanic skin response, indicating that they responded emotionally to the words. These words were then presented as stimuli to be ignored in a dichotic listening task. Participants showed a galvanic skin response when the words appeared in the unshadowed message, despite participants being unable to report afterwards that they had heard these words. This study demonstrates that the unshadowed message is processed for meaning. In a subsequent study, Corteen and Wood (1972) repeated the procedure, except that they presented synonyms of the words rather than the words themselves. Here, too, participants showed a galvanic skin response to the presentation of the synonyms.

Treisman's account is less convincing at explaining this finding than the account of Deutsch and Deutsch, since the results imply that not only is semantic information in the unshadowed message processed, but so too can semantic associations (synonyms) be activated by unshadowed information. This implies that attentional filtering occurs much later than Triesman had suggested.

Outline and evaluate two theories of focused auditory attention. (24 marks)

Compare and contrast early-selection models (e.g. Treisman) and late-selection models (e.g. Deutsch and Deutsch) of focused attention. (24 marks)

1.3 DIVIDED ATTENTION

Studies of divided attention are concerned with whether we can attend to *more than one task at a time*. One important factor that limits the ability to do so is the degree of task similarity. Allport, Antonis and Reynolds (1972) asked participants to learn a set of words while at the same time shadowing a spoken message. They found that the words could be learned when they were presented visually, but not when presented as spoken words. Another factor is practice. Spelke, Hirst and Neisser (1976) found that with practice, students could learn to read stories while simultaneously writing down a list of words read out to them. Therefore, division of attention is a skill that can be learned.

1.4 EXPLANATIONS OF DIVIDED ATTENTION

Norman and Bobrow (1975) argued that one reason why we find it difficult to attend to more than one task is because **attentional resources** are limited. A second reason is that the information we receive may itself be limited (such as poor reception of a radio channel). Kahneman (1973) suggested that the amount of resources given to a task is flexible. He also proposed that there is an **upper limit** to the amount of resources available, which is determined by several factors. Firstly, a central processor allocates mental resources to the task at hand. How resources are then allocated depends on its allocation policy, which is governed by three things:
- *Physiological state*. If we are tired, we have fewer resources to allocate.
- *Enduring dispositions*. Our personality, habits and long-term goals determine how much attention we allocate a particular task.
- *Momentary intentions*. The immediate relevance of the stimulus, our mood and the context in which the stimulus is perceived all influence attention allocation.

Capacity theory is based on the notion that there is a general-purpose limited capacity central processor. However, the assumption of limited capacity has been challenged by Allport et al. (1972). If capacity is limited, how is it that attention can successfully be divided under certain conditions and can be improved with practice? They argue that the allocation of attention is a cognitive skill (just as doing crosswords or playing video games involve cognitive skills) and can be improved with practice.

1.5 CONTROLLED VERSUS AUTOMATIC PROCESSING

Shiffrin and Schneider (1972) argued that the amount of attention given to a task depends on how **accomplished** we are at the tasks. When learning a new skill, a lot of attention or controlled processing is required, but when we are well practised at the task we can do it without much attention at all. During skill acquisition, the behaviours required to carry out the task well become automatised — performed so well that they do not require much attention and can be performed automatically.

Automatic processes:
- are fast
- make no demands on attention
- are not available to consciousness
- are unavoidable

Controlled processes:
- are slow
- make heavy demands on attention
- are completely conscious

Norman and Shallice (1980) extended the notion that different tasks require different levels of attention based on skill level. They included a third distinct level, which is an intermediate between the automatic level and the conscious, controlled level.

- *Fully automatic processing*. Little conscious awareness is required to carry out the task. There are few attempts to monitor the information.
- *Partially automatic processing*. Information is still being processed without much conscious awareness, but there is competition between incoming stimuli (such as in the cocktail party phenomenon). Attention switches fairly automatically between two messages.
- *Deliberate control*. Conscious attention is allocated to a stimulus, with all other signals or information sources being ignored. Processing becomes conscious and deliberate when the situation is unfamiliar or unpredictable.

Key study: The Stroop effect

Stroop (1935) noticed an interesting effect when naming colour words — people could name a patch of colour more quickly than they could read aloud a colour word. It was later found that if the word to be named was printed in the same colour as its meaning (e.g. the word BLACK printed in black ink), it could be read more quickly than if it was printed in a different colour (e.g. the word BLACK printed in blue ink). This effect shows that when there are conflicting signals, such as the actual ink colour of a word and the meaning of the word, interference is produced and one signal interrupts the processing of the other signal. Controlled processing (of the ink colour) can thus be hampered by automatic processing (reading a colour word, which is almost unavoidable). The effect also highlights the difficulty in attending to one task and ignoring another, when two tasks are semantically related.

Evaluation

The Stroop effect has been replicated in hundreds of studies and is therefore a pretty reliable result. It has been used to explore a range of attentional phenomena, including the influence of anxiety and depression in selective visual attention. For example, Gotlib and McCann (1984) found that depressed people were slower to name the colour of words that have a depressed content (such as worthless, inadequate) than the colour of neutral words. People who were not depressed did not show this difference in response times. So theoretically important is the Stroop effect that several researchers have developed a computational model of the processes thought to underlie the effect (e.g. Cohen, Dunbar and McClelland, 1990).

Describe one explanation of divided attention. To what extent has psychological research supported this explanation?   (12+12 marks)

1.6 ACTION SLIPS

The everyday notion of 'absent-mindedness' involves behavioural mistakes or action slips.

Attention failures are *usually* associated with action slips and they may emerge from the interplay between controlled and automatic processes.

Sellen and Norman (1992) argued that action slips arise when:
- There are errors in the formation of an intention.
- Two tasks require different schemas; the incorrect schema is activated.
- One schema is triggered in a way that is faulty.

Hay and Jacoby's (1996) theory of action slips is that they occur when:
- The correct response is not the most habitual one.
- Attention is not allocated sufficiently to selecting the correct response.

This theory is based on their laboratory studies in which action slips were induced in a word completion task.

Key study: Diary study of action slips

In Reason (1979), 35 people kept diaries over two weeks and recorded their action slips. Reason identified several different types of slips:
- Storage failures (40%) — intentions and actions are forgotten or recalled incorrectly (for example, attempting to refill an already full teapot).
- Test failures (20%) — failing to monitor a series of planned actions (for example, going to the garage and putting on wellington boots instead of getting the car out).
- Subroutine failures (18%) — insertions, omissions or reordering of stages in an action sequence (for example, attempting to take off one's glasses when they are not being worn).
- Discrimination failures (11%) — failing to discriminate between objects (for example, mistaking shaving cream for toothpaste).
- Programme assembly failures (5%) — inappropriate combinations of actions (for example, throwing a sweet into the bin and eating the wrapper).

Evaluation
Reason's work is useful in highlighting types of everyday action slips. However, the method used can be criticised on the grounds that participants were likely only to have recorded slips which they detected — many other kinds of slips may have gone unnoticed. A further problem, identified by Grudin (1983), is how an action slip is categorised, as a single slip (e.g. a typing error) may involve more than one process.

1.7 PATTERN RECOGNITION

Although we recognise objects effortlessly, it is a very complex process. Key research questions concern:
- how we recognise objects that are partially hidden
- how we recognise the same object at different distances and in different orientations
- how we categorise a diverse range of stimuli as the same object

Template-matching theory

According to this theory (e.g. Ullman, 1989), we have internalised 'templates' stored in memory for every pattern or object. Recognising an object means **matching** a visual stimulus with the most similar template. Through experience we acquire a large library of templates.

The main problem for this theory is that recognition of even the most simple object (such as the letter A) requires us to store a template for every possible A we might come across. Given the number of different fonts and differences in handwriting that exist, this theory seems implausible. Furthermore, the theory predicts that the more templates that are stored, the longer it should take to find a matching template. Yet we know that, generally, the more knowledge people have the quicker they respond.

Feature detection theories

According to this theory, each object will have **critical features** that enable it to be recognised. Other features that are less critical may or may not be present. For example, the letter A has two diagonal lines and a connecting cross-bar as its critical features. If we read a handwritten A with the cross-bar projected beyond one or both of the diagonals, then this would be a non-critical feature that could be ignored.

Neisser (1964) obtained evidence to support feature theory by comparing the time taken to recognise a straight lined letter (Z) among other straight lined letters (W, V) or among letters consisting of curved lines (O, G). Performance was faster when both the target and the other letters were straight lined letters.

Key study: Recordings of individual neurones in the visual cortex (Hubel and Wiesel, 1979)

If a visual stimulus is processed according to its features, it should be possible to find individual neurones that only respond to specific features. Hubel and Wiesel (1968) identified three types of cell that appeared to be specialised for the detection of different visual stimuli:

- simple cells that respond to a dot in one part of the visual field or to a line at one particular angle and no other. Large numbers of these cells cover all of the visual field, collecting simple information about dots and lines
- complex cells that receive information from many simple cells and combine the information about lines at particular angles in the visual field
- hypercomplex cells that receive information from complex cells, and appear to respond to simple figures and shapes

Evaluation

The discovery of these cells appears to offer neurophysiological support for the feature detection theory. However, more recent research suggests that spatial frequency is more important than individual features in pattern recognition (Sekular and Blake, 1994). Spatial frequency concerns the amount of light–dark contrast between the lines of a particular pattern. Harvey et al. (1983) found that, while many letters having features in common (e.g. K and N) do not get confused when presented very briefly, letters with similar spatial frequencies do.

The role of context in pattern recognition

Psychologists distinguish between types of processes in pattern recognition: **bottom-up processing** and **top-down processing**.

- Bottom-up processing is also known as data-driven processing, because perception begins with the stimulus itself. Processing is carried out in one direction from the retina to the visual cortex, with each successive stage in the visual pathway carrying out ever more complex analysis of the input.
- Top-down processing refers to the use of contextual information in pattern recognition. For example, understanding difficult handwriting is easier when reading complete sentences than when reading single and isolated words. This is because the meaning of the surrounding words provides a context to aid understanding. There are many experimental examples of the influence of top-down processing, such as Palmer (1975), who found higher recognition accuracy scores of cartoon facial features when they were presented together rather than in isolation. Another example is given in McClelland, Rumelhart and Hinton (1986), who pointed out how easy it would be to read a word if one or two of its letters became partially obscured by an ink blob.

Discuss the role of biological mechanisms and of context in pattern recognition. (24 marks)

Face recognition

We often see the same face in various guises (different emotional expressions, different distances and lighting, different angles, and even the same face several years later when it has changed with age), yet our ability to recognise it often appears to be effortless and automatic. According to Haig (1984), this ability arises not just from the recognition of particular facial features, but also from the detection of the way the facial features are combined (for example, the spaces between individual features).

Bruce and Young (1986) developed a model of face recognition based on experimental evidence, as well as evidence from individuals with clinical disorders that leave them with an impaired ability to recognise faces. The model makes several key assumptions:

- It is assumed that faces we know are stored as recognition units. When we see a known face, its corresponding recognition unit is activated automatically, bypassing any need to analyse facial features. However, unknown faces do not have corresponding recognition units; therefore, in recognising them their facial features need to be analysed.

- Facial recognition units are associated with information we know about a person (semantic information), but not his or her name. In the model, person names are stored separately from both recognition units and associated semantic information. Furthermore, it is claimed that there is no direct link between a name and a face in memory, and that in putting a name to a face we have to draw on semantic information.

Experimental evidence that supports the model comes from Bruce and Valentine (1985), who showed that names are not very good aids for priming the recognition of faces. People can recognise that a presented face is one that has been presented previously, but associating a name with each face neither helped nor hindered the recognition process.

Clinical evidence for the model comes from the disorder known as **prosopagnosia**. In one study by Bruyer et al. (1983), an individual with prosopagnosia could learn to recognise new faces, but could not recognise faces of people he knew. Another patient studied by Malone et al. (1982) could identify familiar faces, but had great difficulty in matching up photographs of unfamiliar ones taken at different angles or with different expressions. The evidence suggests that the difficulties experienced by prosopagnosic patients occur because of brain damage to specific face-processing mechanisms, rather than a general inability to discriminate precisely.

Discuss what psychological research has shown us about the nature of face recognition. (24 marks)

2 *Perceptual processes and development*

2.1 THE VISUAL SYSTEM

The eye

The wavelength of visible light ranges from 380 to 760 nanometres (nm). Different wavelengths are perceived as different colours (e.g. 380 nm looks violet and 760 nm looks red). All other wavelengths are invisible to the eye, such as those corresponding to ultraviolet radiation, X-rays, gamma rays, and TV and radio waves. The cornea is a

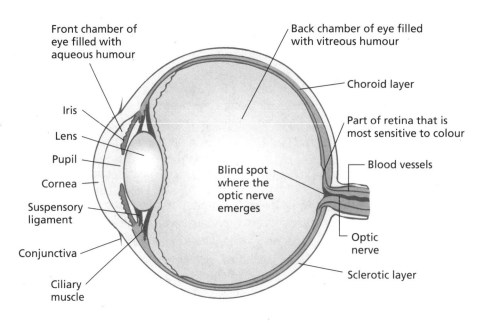

transparent bulge located at the front of the eye that admits light. The iris consists of two bands of muscles that are controlled by the brain to regulate the size of the pupil and hence the amount of light entering the eye. The space behind the cornea is filled with aqueous humour (a watery fluid), which nourishes the cornea and other areas of the eye. The lens lies behind the iris and causes images to be focused on the inner surface of the eye, known as the retina. The shape of the lens is altered by muscles to obtain a focused image of either nearby or distant objects (a process known as accommodation).

The retina

The retina performs the **sensory** functions of the eye; it consists of over 130 million photoreceptors (specialised neurones that convert light into neural activity). Information from photoreceptors is transmitted along the optic nerve, which travels to the brain. The retina consists of two general types of photoreceptors: 125 million rods and 6 million cones. Rods function mainly in dim light; cones function in clear light and respond to colour. The fovea, a small pit in the back of the retina, about 1mm in diameter, contains only cones and is responsible for our most detailed vision (the point at which we are looking). Farther away from the fovea, the number of cones decreases and the number of rods increases.

Visual pathways

The optic nerve projects to the lateral geniculate nucleus, a structure that is involved in early processing of movement, colour, fine texture and objects. Damage to this structure impairs such processing (Schiller et al., 1990). Neurones project to the primary visual cortex or V1, which appears to carry out further processing of motion, colour, location and orientation of objects. In terms of the function of the remainder of the visual cortex, the most popular theory is that different parts have become specialised for different visual functions (Zeki, 1992).

2.2 RESEARCH INTO THE NATURE OF VISUAL INFORMATION PROCESSING

Sensory adaptation

The phenomenon of sensory adaptation can be illustrated by the observation of how difficult it is to find your seat in a darkened cinema and how overly bright it appears to be when you leave the cinema (during a daytime showing). It is caused by the action of photopigments, which are two molecules that exist in the photoreceptors on the retina. They react to light by becoming bleached; this action stimulates the photoreceptors. As photopigments become bleached they need to be regenerated before they can respond again to light. When high levels of light strike the retina, the rate of regeneration falls behind the rate of bleaching. With only a small percentage of the photopigments available to respond to light, the rods become insensitive to light. If you enter a dark room after being in a brightly lit room, there are too few photopigments ready to be stimulated by dim light. However, after a while the regeneration of photopigments overcomes the rate of bleaching, and at this point the eye becomes adapted to darkness.

Perception of colour

Any colour can be produced by varying the amounts of **red**, **blue** and **green**. This observation inspired the first theory of colour perception, the Young–Helmholtz theory, which proposed that the retina consists of three different types of colour-detecting cells, sensitive to either red, blue or green wavelengths of light. Different rates of firing of these cells give rise to the perception of different colours. However, there are two phenomena that this theory cannot explain easily:

- Colour blindness occurs when a person is unable to distinguish between certain wavelengths of light (e.g. shades of red from shades of green). In some cases there is no perception of colour at all. It is difficult to see how a theory based on different types of cone cells for red, blue and green could account for colour blindness.
- Negative after-effects occur after staring at a red patch for a couple of minutes or so, and then looking at a white sheet of paper. An after-effect will appear in the form of a green patch of colour. After-effects reflect the opposite of the stimulus to which they have been exposed (the opposite of the pairs red/green, blue/yellow or light/dark). The Young–Helmholtz theory cannot explain after-effects.

Opponent-process theory

Hering (1878) developed an alternative theory of colour perception in an attempt to explain colour blindness and negative after-effects. It is based on the idea that there are three types of cells in the retina, which respond to pairs of opposite colours: red/green, blue/yellow and light/dark. In its anabolic phase, a cell processes one colour of the pair it is responsive to and processes the opposite colour in its catabolic phase. Negative after-effects can be explained by assuming that cells become fatigued by prolonged stimulation of the same colour, and that they will work in the opposite way as they recover.

Support for the opponent-process theory was obtained by De Valois, Abramov and Jacobs (1966), who found bipolar cells in the second layer of the retina and also in the thalamus. However, MacNichol (1964) found three different types of cells in the retina that respond maximally to one of the three different wavelengths of light as predicted by the Young–Helmholtz theory. It therefore seems that processes described by both theories are evident in the visual system.

Q **Describe and evaluate research into the nature of visual information processing.** (24 marks)

2.3 PERCEPTUAL ORGANISATION — THEORIES OF VISUAL PERCEPTION

Gibson's direct theory of perception

Gibson (1972, 1980) argued that perception was direct and did not require cognitive processes to bring together fragmented data. He argued that perception is a bottom-up process, which means that sensory information is analysed in one direction: from simple analysis of raw sensory data to ever-increasing complexity of analysis through the visual system. Gibson attempted to give pilots training in depth perception during the Second

World War, and this work led him to the view that our perception of surfaces is more important than depth/space perception. Surfaces contain features sufficient to distinguish different objects from each other. In addition, perception involves identifying the function of the object: whether it is throwable or graspable; whether it can be sat on — in other words, what the object affords us, what its meaning is (what Gibson referred to as the object's affordance). This approach has been known as the ecological approach because it recognises that stimuli mean something to the perceiver. In this sense, perception is said to be a direct decoding of information.

Gregory's top-down theory of perception

In contrast to Gibson's theory, Gregory argued that perception is a constructive process which relies on top-down processing. For Gregory, perception involves making inferences about what we see and trying to make a best guess. He considered that prior knowledge and past experience are crucial in perception. As we perceive something, we develop a perceptual hypothesis which is an explanation of what we are seeing and this is based on our knowledge. The hypotheses we develop are nearly always correct; however, on rare occasions, perceptual hypotheses can be challenged by the data we perceive.

Evidence for direct and constructivist theories

Perception of movement

Gibson (1979) argued that our nervous system is perfectly attuned for detecting necessary information in the environment. For example, he understood movement and action to be an integral aspect of perception. In real environments people move their bodies and heads in order to understand their visual environment better. Movement of the perceiver or of the objects helps to clarify the boundaries and textures of objects. In addition, the optic array gives important information about movement, such that we can detect whether an object is moving or whether we are moving. The perception of movement, Gibson argued, is not dependent upon developing a perceptual hypothesis, since there is enough information in the optic array. The **waterfall effect** illustrates Gibson's position. If you were to look at a waterfall for some time and then look away, it seems as though the objects we see are moving in the opposite direction. The same occurs when a train stops and you have been looking out of the window for some time. This effect arises from the way that sensory mechanisms adapt to the stimulation they receive.

Another illusion, known as the **phi phenomenon**, supports Gibson's view. Two alternatively flashing lights are seen as having continuous movement between them. This effect is used in illuminated advertisement signs that can be found in city centres, such as Piccadilly Circus in London. It is explained by the fact that our perceptual system makes allowances for breaks in tracking a visual target. For example, if we follow a bird flying through trees, we will only see it as a complete object intermittently. In these examples of the perception of movement, the visual system does not appear to require perceptual hypotheses, since there may be sufficient sensory information to perceive directly.

Depth perception

The distances of objects are detected in two main ways.

- **Monocular cues** are cues that operate equally with one or two eyes. These cues are used by artists, who try to indicate distance in a painting. One cue is **relative size** and is simply the fact that the same object has a smaller retinal image the further away from the viewer it is. Another cue is **shadowing**, which gives rise to an awareness that one object is in front of another object. A third cue is **superposition**, which occurs when a close object obscures parts of a more distant object. Another important cue is **texture gradient**, which can be observed by comparing the texture details of near and distant objects: objects at a distance appear to be smoother in appearance and more grey in colour, while near objects have clear, sharp colour and are more detailed. **Motion parallax** is a further key cue to depth and can be observed when looking out of the window of a moving vehicle: objects in the distance appear to move more slowly than do near objects.

- **Binocular cues** are those that arise from the two retinal images obtained with two eyes. The difference between the two retinal images, known as **binocular disparity**, can give rise to distance (this difference can be directly experienced by holding a pencil at arms length and closing one eye and then the other). Another binocular cue is **convergence**, which is the movement of the eye muscles as we focus on near and distant objects.

Such visual cues to depth could be taken as evidence of direct perception, since they are not dependent upon top-down processes. However, Gregory argued that certain visual illusions arise because depth cues are misinterpreted. The Müller–Lyer illusion consists of two equal length parallel lines, which appear to be different in length — one line has inwardly pointing fins and the other has outwardly pointing fins. Gregory (1963) argued that the illusion occurs because it brings in depth cues. For example, one line can appear to represent the outside corner of a room, and the other the inside corner. In using depth cues, incorrect perceptual hypotheses are created, and in this case the hypothesis is a mismatch between past experience of depth and the raw sensory information.

Object constancy and visual illusions

Although the retinal image of the same object can appear quite different depending upon the viewing conditions, we perceive it as the same object. For example, in **shape constancy**, the retinal image of a cup being viewed from above and the retinal image of it being viewed on its side are quite different, yet it is perceived as the same object. Other constancies concern the object's **size** (which varies with distance from the perceiver) and the object's **colour** (which appears to remain constant even in different lighting conditions). According to Gregory (1963), many visual illusions occur due to misapplied constancy scaling. One example is the **Ponzo illusion**, in which two horizontal lines appear to be of unequal length when enclosed between two converging lines. Another example is the **Necker cube**, which is a line drawing of a hollow cube that appears to change its orientation as it is viewed. Gregory argued that this object appears to flip between orientations because the brain develops two equally plausible hypotheses and is unable to decide between them. Another type of illusion is the **paradoxical illusion**, which consists of figures that seem plausible initially but are physically impossible. Examples are the 'impossible triangle' and the paintings by M.C. Escher, of which *Waterfall* is probably the best known. Gregory argues that in these illusions the brain develops more than one hypothesis and that they contradict one another. This results in a paradox and gives rise to the illusion.

Gibson argued strongly against the idea that perception involves top-down processing and criticised Gregory's discussion of visual illusions on the grounds that they are **artificial** examples and not images found in our normal visual environments.

Key study: Interactions between top-down and bottom-up processing

Tulving, Mandler and Baumal (1964) presented participants with words that had to be identified as quickly and as accurately as possible. Sometimes the words were presented quite briefly and at other times they were presented for longer durations. Also, in some trials a word appeared after a semantically related sentence (a sentence that related to the meaning of the word) had been shown; in other trials the word followed a semantically unrelated sentence. If the word was presented very briefly, the sentence helped participants to recognise the word accurately. This demonstrates the importance of contextual or top-down influences in perception. However, when the word was presented for a longer duration, the sentence neither helped not hindered recognition accuracy of the word. This implies that when viewing conditions are clear, top-down processing is not required and visual processing can proceed in a bottom-up manner.

Q Compare and contrast constructivist theories and direct theories of perceptual organisation.

(24 marks)

2.4 Perceptual development

Explanations of perceptual development

Piaget's enrichment theory

According to Piaget (1952), perception develops as an infant interacts with the world by performing **operations** and noticing the **results** of its actions. The sophistication of these operations is said to develop over several stages. The sensorimotor stage is the most critical period of perceptual development. In this first stage, infants under the age of 2 years learn to coordinate their sensory and motor skills. An infant relies on innate sensorimotor schemas, such as mouthing, grasping and touching objects. These innate schemas develop through experience, by comparing new sensory information with the existing schema. Piaget emphasised the influence of the infant's action in its perceptual development; however, this influence may be overestimated since, in one study, infants who had the most crawling experience showed no more depth perception than other infants (Arterberry et al., 1989). In addition, 5 month old infants who have limited ability and experience with independent mobility, do not tend to reach for objects that are out of reach (Meadows, 1986).

Shaffer's three stage theory

Shaffer (1990) argued that there are three stages of perceptual development during the first year. The first stage, 0–2 months, is described as a stimulus seeking stage in which the infant develops the ability to make general visual discriminations between stimuli. In the second stage, 2–6 months, which is described as a form constructing stage, infants can perceive numerous forms and shapes. In the third stage, 6–12 months, which is described as a form interpretation stage, infants begin to make sense of what they perceive. Findings from the visual cliff studies (see p. 121) tend to lend support to the notion of the existence of these stages.

The nature–nurture debate

Many studies discussed above suggest that aspects of perception appear to be innate, although the evidence can be difficult to interpret when using infants. Other methods for answering the question of whether perception is innate or whether it is nurtured by the environment include depth perception, distortion studies, readjustment studies, deprived environment studies and cross-cultural studies.

Depth perception

Bower et al. (1970) presented infants with one object just out of reach and another object at twice the distance but twice the size. This resulted in the infant perceiving the two different objects with the same retinal image size. Infants were found to be significantly more likely to reach for the nearer object of the two, suggesting that there may be some **innate** aspects to depth perception. However, this method can only be tested on infants who are able to reach out with their arms, and hence the possibility that depth perception may begin to develop about the time the infant is able to do this cannot be ruled out.

Key study: Depth perception and the visual cliff

Gibson and Walk (1960) placed infants on a 'visual cliff', which is a transparent platform placed over a checkerboard pattern. Babies between 6 and 12 months of age were reluctant to crawl over the 'cliff' edge, even when called by their mothers. This suggests that the infants perceived the drop and that depth perception is innate. However, since the infants were 6 months old, depth perception may have developed in this time. Other evidence of innate depth perception is from studies that show that newly born kittens, as well as small ducklings, refuse to go over the visual cliff. Later studies on infants revealed that depth perception may not be innate for humans. The heart rate of 2 month old infants placed on the edge of the visual cliff tends to decrease (Campos et al., 1970); this implies that the infant is interested in the visual aspects of the apparatus. If the infant were afraid of the visual cliff (and hence perceived depth), it would have shown an increase in its heart rate. This study was replicated by Schwartz et al. (1973), who also showed that increases in heart rate in response to the visual cliff occur at the time when the infant develops mobility. Thus, before this point the infant merely perceives a difference, which stimulates interest, but does not perceive depth.

Defending against approaching objects

An interesting method of testing for infants' abilities in depth perception is to monitor their responses to approaching objects, especially those on a collision course. Two week old infants were found to move their arms and head as if to defend themselves against the object, suggesting that some depth perception is innate (Bower et al., 1970). Other studies have found that infants can even discriminate between approaching objects that will hit them and approaching objects that will miss them (Ball and Tronick, 1971). However, since small head and arm movements can be interpreted as either under-developed defending actions or as random movements, this evidence for innate perception of depth is inconclusive.

Distortion studies

G.M. Stratton, in the late 19th century, developed a method of dramatically altering his visual world by wearing a lens on one eye that turned the world upside down (with the other eye covered). Within five days he reported that he could walk around and write comfortably. In total, he wore the lens for eight days, after which the world he saw was immediately recognised. This shows that the visual system is **highly flexible** and **adaptable**. Hess (1956) applied a similar prism lens to chickens, with the result that they never completely learned to adapt, showing that the visual system of animals may be less adaptive than that of humans.

Readjustment studies

Gregory and Wallace (1963) discuss the case history of SB, who gained sight at the age of 52, having been blind from birth. Within only a few days he began to understand his visual sensations. However, aspects such as depth perception and understanding of visual forms were only partially acquired, and his visual sensations were at times more of a hindrance than a help, and he often preferred to sit in darkness in the evenings. The implication is that visual abilities are either **innate** (and degenerate without use) or that they require **experience** to develop. von Senden (1932) presented a summary of 66 such cases and concluded that some aspects of vision appear to be innate (identifying a figure from the background, and visually tracking an object), while others are learned (depth perception and identification of more complex visual forms).

Deprived environments

Several studies have deprived an animal of vision until a certain age to determine the sorts of visual abilities that remain unimpaired. This might give an indication of which abilities are innate and which are learned. Riesen (1950) raised chimpanzees in total darkness until the age of 16 months and found that their perception of simple forms was severely impaired. Wiesel (1982) sewed one eye of a kitten shut and found that if it is done early enough the eye remains blind. Blakemoore and Cooper (1970) found that by restricting a cat's visual environment from birth, it found the perception of certain visual forms extremely difficult.

> **Key study: Blakemoore and Cooper's restricted visual environment study**
>
> Blakemoore and Cooper (1970) attempted to understand how the visual system develops by restricting the visual environment of cats from birth. As soon as their eyes opened, kittens were placed in a drum that had only vertical or only horizontal lines. After 5 months the kittens were placed in a normal environment and behaved normally, except that they were virtually blind for lines that were at right angles to those of their earlier restricted environment. For example, kittens kept in drums that contained only vertical lines, tripped up over ropes stretched out in front of them. The cells in the visual cortex of kittens kept in vertically-lined drums were later found to be unresponsive to horizontal lines (similarly for kittens kept in horizontally-lined drums, cells were unresponsive to vertical lines). The study suggests the importance of the environment in perceptual development, especially during the early critical phase of development.

Cross-cultural studies

Several studies have made use of visual illusions to determine whether they exist cross-culturally. Segall et al. (1963) found that people from Zulu tribes were unable to perceive the Müller–Lyer illusion. This might imply that because their visual environment contains few rectangles, straight lines and regular corners, they were unaffected by top-down processing (and hence implying the importance of environmental influences in perception). Annis and Frost (1973) found that Canadian Cree Indians who lived in the countryside were very good at determining whether two lines were parallel, regardless of whether they were presented diagonally, vertically or horizontally, yet Cree Indians who lived in the city performed poorly when the lines were presented diagonally. The explanation offered is that exposure to the vertical and horizontal lines of the city makes perception of diagonal lines more difficult. Other studies, such as Gregor and McPherson (1965), found no differences between rural and urban dwelling Aborigines on a number of visual illusions. Hudson (1960) found that black children and adults in South Africa with little experience of drawings found it difficult to perceive depth in two-dimensional drawings of three-dimensional objects.

One problem with cross-cultural studies is that they rely on self-report measures and their verbal responses may be difficult to interpret accurately. Another is the fact that they have been based mainly on two-dimensional visual illusions and may tell us little about visual perception in the natural visual world.

Discuss psychological research into whether perceptual development is a matter of nature or nurture. (24 marks)

Outline and evaluate two studies of the development of perceptual abilities. (24 marks)

---

3 *Language and thought*

3.1 LANGUAGE AND CULTURE

Language serves the functions of social interaction and the acquisition of knowledge.

According to Sternberg (1995), language can be defined as 'an organised means of combining words in order to communicate'.

The **behaviourists** equated thinking with inner speech. To test this hypothesis, Smith allowed himself to be given a curare derivative that prevented any sub-vocal speech through paralysis (Smith et al., 1947). If thinking was nothing more than inner speech, then if speech were prevented, thinking should cease. However, despite almost total paralysis, he reported still being able to think. Other studies reveal that thinking can occur without language, such as the study by Humphrey (1951). Participants shown a repeating sequence of cards could identify the next card long before being able to articulate how they arrived at their decision. Therefore, cognitive processes can occur independently of language.

The Whorfian hypothesis

Whorf (1956) developed his linguistic relativity hypothesis, in which it is argued that the linguistic system is 'not merely a reproducing instrument for viewing ideas but rather is itself the shaper of ideas, the program and guide for the individual's mental activity…We dissect nature along lines laid down by our native language' (pp. 212–13).

In other words, **language determines thinking**. In regard to the question of the relationship between language and thought, there are three hypotheses (Miller and McNeill, 1969):
- the strong hypothesis, which is that language determines thinking
- the weak hypothesis, which is that language affects perception
- the weakest hypothesis, which is that language influences memory

The strong hypothesis. If there is no word for a concept in a particular language, then according to the strong hypothesis, that concept will not be available to the speakers of that language. In this view translations of words between languages can only ever be accurate if both languages use the concept that the word refers to in the same way. Supporting evidence comes from Boas (1911), who pointed out that one Eskimo language has 27 different words for snow. Individual snow words are used to refer to whether the snow is falling or has settled, whether it is lightly falling or is heavy, where the snow has fallen, and so on. Clearly, the large number of concepts Eskimos have about snow influences their language. However, it could just as easily be argued that since snow is an important aspect of their environment, it is the environment that has influenced both their language and their thinking.

The weak hypothesis. Farb (1974) showed how language could influence thinking, by studying Japanese women living in America. They were interviewed in both English and Japanese. Different attitudes were revealed, depending upon the language the question was asked in. When asked to complete the sentence: 'When my wishes conflict with my family's…', in Japanese, they responded with '…it is a time of great unhappiness', but in English they said '…I do what I want'. According to Farb, language expresses cultural ideas and attitudes, and these women responded with attitudes appropriate to the language they spoke.

Inferring cognitive patterns and mental concepts from language can be misleading. For example, Hopi Indians use the same word for 'insect', 'air-pilot' and 'aeroplane'. However, this does not mean that they categorise these as being the same kind of object, just as English speakers do not categorise motor vehicles, playing a golf stroke, and a wide pathway leading to a house as the same when using the word 'drive' (Greene, 1975).

Evidence that language can influence perception comes from Miyawaki et al. (1975), who found that while Japanese babies are able to distinguish between pure /l/ and pure /r/

sounds, Japanese adults are unable to. This distinction is unlearned because in Japanese, both sounds can be used in production of the same word.

The verbal deprivation hypothesis

According to Bernstein (1961), sophisticated forms of thinking are dependent upon language. He distinguished between **universalistic** meanings that refer to knowledge which exists independently of specific contexts (general understanding of concepts) and **particularistic** meanings that refer to immediate, specific ideas or examples, which are often tightly dependent on the context in which they occur. Universalistic meanings were considered to involve more sophisticated forms of thinking than particularistic meanings. Based on this distinction, Bernstein defined two different linguistic codes: elaborated code, which invites use of universalistic meanings; and restricted code, which invites particularistic meanings.

Bernstein argued that the class system, through socialisation, exposes individuals to either code: the working class predominantly use restricted code and the middle class use elaborated code. Because of socialisation practices, middle class children begin school with a distinct advantage, and working class children are verbally deprived.

Criticisms of verbal deprivation theory

The main critic of this approach is Labov (1970), who argued that although **working class** children are exposed to a certain dialect rather than a standard form, they are nonetheless exposed to a linguistically rich environment. He argued that the differences between elaborated and restricted codes were less significant and more superficial than Bernstein thought. Labov (1972) studied black children's use of language and concluded that black English was of comparable complexity and sophistication to standard English.

The developmental view

Piaget's view was that language is only one of several ways in which knowledge can be represented and that knowledge is the **precursor** to language. The child experiences the world and then uses language to represent the experience, both in terms of knowledge and in terms of social interaction. For Piaget then, thinking influences language development much more than language development influences thinking.

Vygotsky's view: language and thought are separate

Vygotsky, a Russian psychologist, argued that language and thought have different origins. Thinking, he argued, is a cognitive activity that occurs as the child experiences its environment. It needs to store memories about the world in order to understand it and adapt to it. Language, on the other hand, is a social activity that arises from hearing it from others. Much of everyday language is **affiliative** (involved in acting socially and developing social relations) — it commonly exists as 'small talk'. Language is not all cognitive, that is to say, it is not always about transmitting knowledge in an elaborate way.

The cognitive functions of language are served by inner speech, which acts as a way of monitoring and structuring mental activity. Young children often produce egocentric speech in which the child's speech reflects what is in its own mind without reference to any listener. This is because the child is unable to separate the two main functions of language, which are cognitive and social.

Q Language is 'not merely a reproducing instrument...but rather itself the shaper of ideas, the program and guide for the individual's mental activity' (Whorf, 1956). Discuss the extent to which it is accurate to say that language determines thought. (24 marks)

3.2 LANGUAGE ACQUISITION

Research into the process of language development

Shaffer (1993) identified four kinds of **knowledge** that children learn about language:

- *phonology*: the sounds produced in a language
- *semantics*: the meanings of words and utterances
- *syntax*: the rules that govern how words may be combined to make sentences (grammar)
- *pragmatics*: the ways in which language use is modified according to the context (e.g. talking to a child versus talking to a college tutor)

It is thought that children learn a language in the order listed below.

Early vocalisations

At 3 weeks the infant makes 'fake cries', which occur in the absence of any distress and probably reflect the infant's enjoyment at making sounds. Between 3 and 5 weeks the infant begins to coo, and by 4 to 6 weeks it begins to babble, which sounds like random combinations of vowel and consonant sounds. After a while the infant shows echolalia, which is a repetitive sound, such as 'mamama'. Up to 8 months, babbling sounds are universal in the sense that they sound the same, regardless of the language of the infant's environment. After 8 months, babbling begins to reflect the language heard.

By 18 months, the child has entered the one word stage, and begins to utter single meaningful words, such as 'mine'. From 18 months onwards the infant is in the telegraphic period, where words begin to be combined in a way that is reminiscent of the way telegrams were written, such as 'daddy chair'. Brown (1973) identified early rules that the infant uses in this stage, such as the basic order rule: a sentence consists of agent + action + object + location (e.g. 'Daddy eats lunch at home'). Two-word utterances tend to be of the form agent–action (e.g. 'Daddy walk') rather than action–agent ('walk Daddy').

Grammatical morphemes

As language develops, the child acquires the use of grammatical morphemes, such as prepositions, prefixes and suffixes ('in', 'on', the use of 's' to denote the plural, 'the', etc.). All children learn grammatical morphemes in the **same order** (de Villiers and de Villiers, 1973), starting with simple ones followed by more complex ones (e.g. 'they are').

Over-regularisation

Children's acquisition of linguistic rules can be evidenced by the mistakes they make, such as over-regularisation. The child notices that the past tense of a verb can be created by adding the suffix 'ed', but over-uses the rule for irregular verbs (e.g. 'The dog runned away').

Pragmatics

Children also begin to alter their use of language according to the context. For example, Shatz and Gelman (1973) observed that 4 year old children used complex sentences when talking to adults about a toy, but simplified their speech when talking to younger children.

Explanations of language development

Nativist theories of child language

Chomsky (1965) presented a theory of language acquisition based on the idea that it is innate and hard-wired into the system. He argued for a **Language Acquisition Device** (LAD) that enables children to acquire language.

Chomsky distinguished between **surface structure**, which is the actual phrases used in a sentence, and **deep structure**, which is the meaning of sentences. Transformational grammar allows us to transform the deep structure of a sentence into the surface structure of the sentence. According to Chomsky, transformational grammar is innate. He further argues that there are linguistic universals, which are features found in every language. Thus we are all born with a universal grammar and this determines the surface structure of sentences. For example, Greenberg (1963) found that in 98% of languages the subject precedes the object.

Critical period hypothesis

Lenneberg (1967) argued that although language is innate, it does depend on biological maturation. For example, it is easier to learn a second language before puberty than after. Support for the critical period hypothesis comes from studies of aphasia. Lenneberg (1967) reported that children who become aphasic before puberty, especially before the age of 5, recover most or all of their lost language functions, whereas after puberty such recovery is slow and only ever partial. However, other evidence refutes this, such as Harley (1995), who found that recovery rates were not predicted by age. Studies of second language learning, such as that of Newport (1994) on Asian immigrants to the USA, show that the younger the individuals were when entering the country the better they learned the language, which supports the critical period hypothesis. Other evidence has been taken from studies of deprived children, such as the case of the 'Wild Boy of Aveyron' and the case of 'Genie'. These studies show that if children are not exposed to language, up to a certain age, they never subsequently acquire it. Other studies are based on deaf children's use of sign language.

Key study: Deaf children in Nicaragua

Pinker (1994) discussed an interesting study of Nicaraguan children of various ages attending a new school for deaf children created by the government in 1979. They were not taught sign language, but spontaneously developed their own system, which later became widely used (known as the Lenguaje de Signos Nicaragüense or LSN). Furthermore, younger children who were subsequently taught the new sign language developed it even further. Because these were younger than the children who developed LSN, the sign language they developed, which became known as the Idioma de Signos Nicaragüense, included grammar. Taken together, these spontaneous developments in the use of sign language support the critical period hypothesis.

Environmental theories

Skinner (1957) argued that language is acquired through operant conditioning. Parents reinforce the required utterances and so these become more likely to be repeated. As the linguistic abilities of the child become progressively more sophisticated, so does the reinforcement become more selective. This process of reinforcement is known as **shaping**. He contended that children also learn through imitation: the child often tries to repeat what the parent says (called the echoic response).

Although children do often learn through imitation, the evidence for learning by reinforcement is generally not supportive. Brown et al. (1969) found that parents tend to reward children's speech on the basis of its truth rather than on the basis of the grammar used. The way parents influence their children's language development is through the way they speak to the children and through expansion. For example, many parents use 'motherese' when talking to very young children. It consists of very short, simple sentences which gradually become longer and more complex as the child's own use of language develops (Shatz and Gelman, 1973). In addition, parents tend to expand the sentences uttered by their children. So, for example, the child might say 'Cat out' and the parent might respond with 'The cat wants to go out'. This expansion instructs the child on the construction of grammatical sentences.

The interactionist approach

Social interactionists suggest that language acquisition depends on **social stimulation**. For example, Sachs et al. (1981) studied a young boy whose parents were both deaf and did not speak. By the time he was 4 his speech was below age level. Although subsequent speech therapy led to quick improvements, his early impoverished speech was due to exposure to an impoverished linguistic environment. Bruner (1983) proposed that instead of a LAD, children have a **LASS** (language acquisition support system), whose maturation depends on social and verbal interaction, especially with adults.

Compare and contrast environmental and nativist theories of language acquisition.   (24 marks)

3.3 PROBLEM-SOLVING AND DECISION-MAKING

Early research: the Gestalt school

Gestalt psychologists such as Wolfgang Kohler argued that reproductive problem-solving involves the **reuse** of previous experience. Our previous knowledge and understanding of the world can be used to solve new problems we encounter.

Productive problem-solving is characterised by insight into the structure of the problem and by productive restructuring of the problem. Insight occurs suddenly, when a solution to a problem is identified. Kohler (1925) claimed to have observed insight in apes, when they appeared to realise suddenly that two sticks could be joined together to bring an out-of-reach banana within their grasp. Sometimes problem-solving is achieved through restructuring the problem (seeing it in a different way).

Key study: The two-string problem

Maier (1931) devised the 'two string' or 'pendulum' problem in order to understand insight and restructuring. In the problem, a person is standing in a room that has two strings hanging from the ceiling and several objects, such as pliers, poles and extension cords. The task is to tie the two strings together. However, the simplest solution, to hold one of the strings and walk to the other string, will not work since the other string is out of reach. The solution that best represents insight is to appreciate that the pliers, when attached to the end of one string, can form a pendulum. By swinging one of the ropes, holding the second rope, and walking back to the swinging rope, the ends of the string can be tied together. Restructuring was demonstrated by giving the participants a clue to the fact that the ropes can be swung. They then quickly produced the pendulum solution.

Key study: Functional fixedness

Although knowledge can often help problem-solving, it can also hamper it. This is often due to what is called functional fixedness: we often perceive an object as serving only the particular function it was designed for rather than seeing it as useful for solving other problems. Duncker (1926) devised the 'candle problem'. Participants were presented with a candle, a box of nails, a book of matches and numerous other objects. The task set was to attach the candle to the wall so that it did not drip onto the table below. Most participants focused on the main function of the objects, and nailed or melted the candle to the wall. Few thought of nailing the nail box to the wall and placing the candle inside the nail box. Most participants were fixated on the normal function of the objects.

Evaluation of the Gestalt approach

The attraction of the Gestalt approach is that it suggests that problem-solving is more than just applying existing knowledge to a problem, and more than just trial-and-error (as the Behaviourists argued). However, concepts such as functional fixedness and insight require explanations above a mere description of them, since they are not easy to test.

Information-processing theories

Perhaps the approach with the biggest impact on theories of problem-solving is that of information-processing theory and, in particular, **problem–space theory** first introduced by Newell and Simon (1972). The theory is based on the analogy of finding one's way around a maze. A problem can be characterised as a set of **states** (the alleys of the maze), beginning from an initial state and ending with a goal state (the maze's exit). Actions are performed or 'operators applied' (such as 'turn left' or 'turn right' in the maze analogy) and the problem moves from one state into another (one moves from one alley to the next). Some actions will lead one away from the solution (towards 'dead ends') whereas other actions will facilitate movement towards the goal state. According to Newell and Simon (1972), for each problem a problem–space of all possible states and paths exists.

An example of how the problem–space approach is applied is in the Tower of Hanoi problem. There are three vertical pegs and three different disks that can be placed over the pegs. The problem begins (the initial state) with the disks placed over one peg in order of size, with the largest at the bottom. The task (the end state) is to reproduce the pattern of disks onto another peg with the two constraints that (a) only one disk can be moved at a time, and (b) a larger disk cannot be placed onto a smaller disk. The movements of disks are referred to as **mental operations**. The strategies that people use to solve the problem are known as **heuristics**. A correct solution is known as an **algorithm**. Means–ends analysis is a heuristic that involves comparing the current state with the goal state, creating a sub-goal to reduce the difference (e.g. move to a state in which there is one disk per peg) and selecting an operator that will solve the sub-goal (move two disks onto empty pegs).

Q **Discuss means of translating representation research (e.g. Gestalt approaches; means-end analysis) into problem-solving.** (24 marks)

Decision-making

On what grounds do people base their decisions?

- *Utility theory*. Many decisions we make involve an element of risk. Risk-taking behaviour in decision-making can be considered as being based on evaluating positive outcomes against possible negative outcomes. Utility theory is based on this idea and says that the **expected utility** (or expected outcome of an action) is determined by how likely a certain outcome is and the known benefit or harm of the outcome. However, this account assumes that people are **entirely rational** in their decision-making and does not explain why, in making decisions, individuals tend to give too much weight to negative outcomes. An example of this is the 'loss aversion' study by Kahneman and Tversky (1984), who asked participants whether they would accept a bet that involved winning £20 if a coin came up heads, but paying £10 if it came up tails. Despite the fact that the odds were in their favour, most people refused the bet.
- *Elimination by aspects*. Tversky (1972), using the example of buying a house, argued that people formulate a list of attributes that they see as important before making a decision (such as distance from school, the size of the master bedroom), and that they then eliminate each option that does not meet the aspects listed.
- *Satisficing*. Simon (1978), using the example of deciding who to marry, argued that people identify an acceptable or satisfactory level, which is then adjusted upwards or downwards, depending upon what is both desirable and realistic.

- *Reasonableness*. Tversky and Shafir (1992), using the example of buying a holiday in Hawaii, argued that people make decisions they feel they can justify. Students who passed an exam see a holiday as a reward; students who failed an exam see it as compensation; while students whose exam results are unknown are less likely to consider the holiday in the first place.

Using knowledge of probability in making decisions

- *Representativeness*. Kahneman and Tversky (1973) argued that people make poor use of knowledge of probability when making decisions. One way in which people make bad decisions is through a poor understanding of what they termed 'representativeness'. If you toss a coin six times, the outcome HHHTTT is just as likely, statistically, as HHTTTH. Yet most people report the second one as more likely (Kahneman and Tversky, 1972).

- *Availability heuristic*. This error occurs when one outcome is thought to be *more likely* than another outcome, merely because one can recall a particular example from memory of the one outcome, but not the other. For example, in Kahneman and Tversky (1974), most participants estimated that there are more English words that have 'r' as the first letter than have 'r' as the third letter, when the reverse is the case. Their responses were based on the fact that it is easier to think of words that begin with 'r' than have 'r' as the third letter.

Evaluation

- *Strengths of the approach*. Several simple heuristics (such as representativeness and the availability heuristic) can account for many judgements in a variety of different contexts. These ideas have inspired a great number of research studies.

- *Weaknesses*. According to Gigerenzer (1996), such explanations do not account for the mental processes that give rise to them (why they occur). In addition, although statistics provides a likely solution, other correct solutions exist that do not involve simple statistics. (For example, try telling a lottery winner that she should not have wasted her money on such an improbable event!) Finally, the way that statistical information is presented in many of these kinds of studies differs from the way it is understood in the *everyday setting*. For example, in the key study below, different responses are likely if the 70% and 30% figures are replaced by actual numbers of people (such as 420 people became engineers, while 180 became lawyers). Thus, although some people are extremely familiar with fractions and percentages, most people use relative frequencies, which involve one-step mental arithmetic.

Key study: Conjunction fallacy

Kahneman and Tversky (1973) also argued that people often assess the relevance of qualitative aspects of information and ignore its statistical aspects. In their study, participants were asked to predict the careers of individuals based on personal descriptions and on statistical information about career choice. Consider one example:

Of a sample of students, 70% of them became engineers and 30% of them became lawyers. John is one student from this sample. He is a 30 year-old married man with two children. He has high ability and motivation, and promises to be quite successful in his field. He is well liked by his colleagues. Did John become an engineer or a lawyer?

If participants attended to statistical information, they should conclude that John became an engineer, since this is more likely given the information that 70% of the sample became engineers. However, if they attend to qualitative information, such as the perceived attributes of a lawyer, they are likely to conclude that John became a lawyer. Participants were swayed by the qualitative information and in a way that assumes that each job was equally likely. So, participants completely ignored prior information.

---

1 Cognitive development

Cognitive development is important because it is one facet of child development which, from infancy to adolescence, undergoes dramatic **changes**. These changes in cognitive functioning are linked to measured intelligence (how individuals perform on tests of IQ). However, as will be considered later, theorists disagree on how this is measured and how it develops. In particular, the issue of **universalism** will be considered (whether intelligence as conceptualised by major theorists is relevant to a range of cultures). The theory and research on cognitive development in childhood has practical implications for education (e.g. how learning is structured in the classroom).

Cognitive development, as with all other kinds of development, requires the consideration of a variety of factors, which are frequently discussed in terms of **nature or nurture**. Also, some believe that changes are generally **quantitative** and **continuous** — the key difference between cognition in childhood and adulthood is in terms of the quantity of knowledge held by individuals. Others argue that development is more **discontinuous** and **abrupt**, usually in the form of qualitatively distinct changes or **stages** which have a relatively **universal invariant order**.

1.1 DEVELOPMENT OF THINKING

Piaget's theory

Jean Piaget's (1896–1980) theory of cognitive development argues that development is interactive — the child adapts and adjusts to its environment through active discovery learning. Developmental changes are motivated by **disequilibrium** — internal instability caused by a mismatch between what the child expects and what happens or is required by the external world. The child seeks to stabilise — **equilibration** — through two processes: **accommodation**, when cognition is changed in response to the environment (e.g. imitation); and **assimilation**, when events and objects in the environment are responded to using existing cognitive strategies. Cognition is structured into **concepts** (organised properties of the environment) and **schemata** (actions which guide the use of concepts). Piaget's theory makes the following assumptions about cognitive development:

- Development requires the child to move through four stages. These are **universal** (seen across different cultures) and their sequence is **invariant**.
- Development can be inconsistent — children might demonstrate a behaviour indicative of a stage on some occasions, but not on others (known as **horizontal decalage**). For example, Li, Nuttal and Zhao (1999) studied 256 boys and 230 girls in Chinese schools with respect to performance on the Piagetian water conservation task. They found that, as predicted by Piaget, successful completion of the task was greater amongst older children, but also that the children at schools with a reputation for academic achievement performed better at all ages.

The four stages are summarised in Table 10.1. An important feature of this theory is that each stage is defined by the errors made by children on key tasks. These are assumed to reflect **ways of thinking**. Development is characterised by being able to think of objects and situations in different ways:

- During the **sensorimotor stage**, the child learns about the world through acting on the environment. Thinking is defined by action. However, towards the end of this stage, rudimentary symbolic thought is shown. For example, at around 1 year of age, children show **perseverative search**: they will search for an object where they last

Stage	Age	Key features
Sensorimotor development	0–2	Interact with environment (and thus learn) using primitive **reflexive motor actions**. Sensory and motor awareness increases. Generally few distinctions made between self and environment. By 1 year some **rudimentary symbolic thought** (e.g. deferred imitation and perseverative search). Main achievement is **object permanence** (objects continue to exist when out of sight).
Preoperational	2–7	Increased ability to think symbolically, but thought is **thought egocentric** ('my way is the only way') — demonstrated by **realism**, **animism** and **artificialism** in thinking. No conservation. **Language** development **reflects cognitive** development. **2–4** years is period of **preconceptual** thought (difficulty with seriation tasks and showing syncretic thought) – instead show centration. **4–7** is period of **intuitive** thought (**seriation** and **syncretic** thought are easier).
Concrete operations	7–11	**Can conserve** (develops in the order of number and liquid [6/7 years], substance and quantity and length [7/8 years], weight [8/10 years], and finally volume [11/12 year]). Can **categorise and group** (e.g. transitivity) but in the here and now (concrete). **Without abstract** thought (e.g. reversibility is poor).
Formal	11–15	Thought is **abstract** and can be **hypothetical**. Use **operations mathematical** and **logical** reasoning.

Table 10.1 Piaget's theory of cognitive development

found it rather than where it was last seen. However, the children are able to show deferred imitation — they continue to copy an action seen when it is no longer observable. Evidence suggests that Piaget underestimated the symbolic thought of very young children. For example, Meltzoff (1988) found that infants showed deferred imitation when only 24 hours old; and Bower (1982) showed that at 3–4 months, infants showed surprise when an object which was hidden behind a screen had disappeared when the screen was removed.

- During the **preoperational stage**, logical and symbolic thought increases, but thought is **egocentric**. During the **preconceptual substage**, children are unable to show either **seriation** (order objects on the basis of a feature such as length) or **syncretic thought** (the ability to select objects that are alike), because they cannot think about different objects and features simultaneously. Instead, they show **centration** (the tendency to focus on one aspect of a situation). This is demonstrated in their failure on conservation tasks (e.g. being able to judge that an object is the same, despite changing shape, for instance when plasticine shapes are changed). Here, they do not show **reversibility** — they cannot undo what has been done. For example, children will judge two identical balls of clay as the 'same' in amount, but as 'different' when the shape of one is changed.

Three mountains problem

Piaget's three mountains problem illustrates preoperational thought. A child is presented with a three-dimensional display of three mountains. Each mountain is a different height and is distinguished by its colour (e.g. one has a red cross on its peak). The child stands on one side of the model and a doll is positioned at different locations on the model. The child is asked to select a picture which represents the doll's view of the mountains. The child is unable to imagine that her view of the mountains is not held by others, even if they are in a position different from her own.

This **egocentricity** also leads to beliefs that psychological events have a physical reality (**realism**), that physical events and objects have psychological qualities (**animism**), e.g. 'the clouds are angry', and that physical objects and events are made by people (**artificialism**) (e.g. 'mummy makes the sun shine').

However, evidence suggests that Piaget simplified the nature of children's thought at this stage, and that the errors shown by children were not always indicative of their thinking. Instead, they were produced by the nature of the methods and tasks used. In fact, pre-operational children can perform well on tasks Piaget predicted they would fail on if different methods are used.

Hughes (1975) replicated the three mountains study. He argued that children found the task difficult because it was unfamiliar to them. Instead, if intersecting walls were used instead of mountains, and a policeman and a doll were used, 90% of the children studied (aged 3.5–5 years) were successful in the task. For example, nearly all were able to hide the doll so that the policeman could not see him — they did not simply hide the doll so that they could not see it. Also, when a second policeman was introduced and the child was asked to hide him so neither the other policeman nor the doll could see him, most did not simply hide the second policeman so that they could not see him (as predicted by Piaget).

- When children reach the **concrete operational stage**, they can conserve and categorise objects in concrete situations — they cannot conceptualise abstractly.

Conservation of numbers

Evidence suggests that Piaget's methods might have simplified the distinction between preoperational and concrete operational thought. For example, McGarrigle and Donaldson (1974) found that 6 year-olds could conserve number in some circumstances. For example, when shown two sets of counters and asked 'are they the same?', only 16% gave the correct answer 'yes':

Set A   ■ ■ ■ ■
Set B   ■   ■   ■   ■

However, when the children first saw a naughty teddy moving the counters in set B and spreading them apart, 62% answered correctly. McGarrigle argues that in the first instance children believe that the situation has been changed deliberately and therefore answer that the sets are indeed different. However, when the counters are rearranged by the naughty teddy, they believe that the sets are not intended to be different deliberately and so they answer that the sets are in fact the same.

- During the **formal operational stage**, thought is now **abstract** and **logical**, and children can make **hypothetical** judgements (abstract thinking) using mathematical reasoning.

Evaluation

Piaget's theory:
- was the first detailed account of cognitive development
- draws attention to the systematic qualitative differences in cognition throughout childhood
- highlights the importance of the child's activity in development
- has practical implications (e.g. in education)

However:
- As shown, Piaget underestimated the cognitive competence of children by confusing task performance with cognitive competence. For example, Donaldson (1978) suggested that children's competence is underestimated when the task uses disembodied language (language that is not tied to a context meaningful to the child). This suggests that Piaget underestimated the role of language in cognitive development, or at least

cognitive performance. This is illustrated in the study by McGarrigle and Donaldson (1974) described earlier.

- Matusov and Hayes (2000) argued that Piaget exaggerated the universalism of stages and, consistent with the previous point, used methods and interpretations of children's task performance that were at times adultcentric.
- Piaget probably simplified the developmental process by overestimating the invariance of the order of stages.
- Finally, although Piaget identified disequilibrium (conflict between what the child expects to happen and what actually happens) as the motivator of developmental change, this does not explain precisely how and why development occurs as it does.

Vygotsky's theory

Lev Vygotsky's (1896–1934) theory of cognitive development is usually contrasted with that of Piaget, although Rushforth (1999) argued that both are universalist and adult-centric. Vygotsky emphasised the importance of **social interaction**, and in particular the significance of interactional communication between children and older children and adults for development.

Like Piaget, Vygotsky identified four stages of cognitive development. These stages were identified by observing children completing tasks involving wooden blocks labelled with nonsense syllables. These were used to identify consistent patterns in the way children linked labels to certain characteristics of the blocks (e.g. their width). During these tasks children had to identify the meaning of each nonsense syllable. Again, as with Piaget, it could be argued that such a task might have meaning for adults, but might well have less meaning for children (Rushforth, 1999). These stages are summarised in Table 10.2.

Stage	Key features
Vague syncretic	No systematic strategies used. Does not show understanding of concepts used in block tasks.
Complex stage	Strategies used in a non-random manner. Assisted task completion does not help the child find concept features.
Potential concept stage	Strategies used systematically. Focuses on one feature at a time.
Mature concept stage	Strategies used systematically. Can focus on more than one feature at a time, leading to successful concept formation.

Table 10.2 Vygotsky's theory of cognitive development

Vygotsky's theory has certain key concepts:
- Children have capacities that are developing but not fully functional. These can be shown when a child completes tasks in a social context with help from an older child or adult. This is the **zone of proximal development**.
- Wood, Bruner and Ross (1976) refined this idea and described the help provided by knowledgeable adults as **scaffolding**. This decreases as the children's confidence builds. For example, children might be encouraged to complete tasks that they cannot complete by themselves, whilst later an adult will encourage them to continue to use their successful problem-solving strategies, followed by discouragement in the use of inappropriate ones (Moss, 1992). Conner, Knight and Cross (1997) studied the effects of scaffolding on 2 year-olds and found that the better the scaffolding provided by parents, the better the child's performance on both literary and problem-solving tasks; these benefits were maintained at follow-up. Wertsch et al. (1980) examined whether younger children's behaviour is guided by parental behaviour and found that as age increases, this decreases. They studied 2–4 year-olds and their mothers who

were asked to build a model of a truck like the one they were shown. They found that, amongst the youngest children, 90% looked at the model when their mother did, but this behaviour was less frequent amongst older children.

- Unlike Piaget, Vygotsky identified language as important to development, because children use speech to assist problem-solving. Here, speech to others enables **intersubjectivity** — the development of a shared understanding of a task and its completion. This soon becomes private or inner speech (internal). Berk (1994) studied 4–5 and 6–7 year-old children to examine the effects of inner speech. Results showed that inner speech decreased as children's mastery of a brick-building task increased, and that 6–7 year-olds spent around 60% of their time when completing maths tasks engaged in inner speech. Importantly, a year later, those whose inner speech included references to strategies they could use to solve the problem were doing better at maths.

Evaluation

Some of the advantages of Vygotsky's theory include:

- He paid attention to the importance of social factors (overlooked by Piaget).
- There is scope for individual differences in cognitive development, because social contexts are likely to vary both within and between cultures.
- Attention was drawn to the importance of language and interactional communication.
- The theory is positive — it considers the child's potential (zone of proximal development) rather than focusing on the limits of children's thinking.

However:

- Vygotsky failed to consider aspects of the child that might influence development, such as motivation.
- The account is relatively vague compared to Piaget's theory. For example, no clear definition is given of social context and it is unclear how language is involved in the developmental process beyond inner speech.
- The emphasis upon language fails to account for the fact that children with language difficulties (e.g. deafness) frequently experience undisturbed cognitive development.
- The usefulness of social interaction depends on its quality, an issue not considered by Vygotsky. Also, there is evidence that social interaction can help development, not because it provides opportunities for instruction, but because it facilitates motivation. Light et al. (1994) studied the effects of peer tutoring on computer tasks. They found that children working in pairs did better than those working alone, even when the 'instructor' child did no instructing (e.g. remained silent).

Information processing

According to the information-processing account, human cognition comprises an information processing system consisting of small processes (e.g. attention) and structures (e.g. short-term memory) which operate flexibly in response to task demands. The basic sequence of cognition is tripartite: a task (stimulus) functions as input, which is processed, leading to an output (a skilled action). The two main implications for cognitive development are:

- Development results from quantitative changes in basic processes (i.e. the knowledge base expands).
- Automatic processes also increase during development, freeing up processing capacity and increasing the speed of task completion.

These ideas have been developed by neoPiagetian theorists (e.g. Case, 1974; Pascal-Leove, 1984). Pascal-Leove (1984) argued that, due to the maturation of neurological structures, as children grow, the number of cognitive units (schemes) a child can manage simultaneously increases. The capacity is known as 'M'. Overall, development results from four variables:

- the range of schemes available
- 'M' power
- whether the child uses all the 'M' power available
- the importance given to perceptual as opposed to other cues

Evidence to support this account has focused on 'M' power: if younger children's cognitive competence is restricted because of limited 'M', then by reducing the difficulty of tasks, their 'M' power should be maximised, thus improving their performance. Pascal-Leove found this in a study of 7 year-olds. According to Piaget's theory, such children should not be able to conserve number. However, if the demands on 'M' are eased (by children counting the beads), they can conserve number. Case (1992) also supports the centrality of 'M'. Case studied 10–18 year-olds and found that when asked to draw a relatively complex picture, unlike older participants, younger participants drew all the elements but failed to integrate them into a whole picture. Case argued that this was because older participants have greater 'M' power.

Evaluation

Although this approach has greater scope than Piaget's or Vygotsky's theories (i.e. it has relevance across the life span), and its concepts are easier to operationalise (e.g. 'M' power), the account is problematic:

- It is unclear how the number of schemes needed to complete a task (and the number of schemes actually used) is identified.
- It is unclear how to calculate 'M' power.
- It is unclear when performance changes are due to changes in schemes or 'M' power.
- The account is circular — poor performance is due to inadequate 'M' power, and better performance is due to adequate 'M' power. But this is only a description and not an explanation.

Outline and evaluate two theories of cognitive development. (24 marks)

Practical applications

The majority of applications of theories of cognitive development have been to education. The applications of Piaget's, Vygotsky's and the information-processing theories are summarised in Table 10.3.

PIAGET

- His theory was applied to the Plowden Report (1976).
- His theory was applied in the Nuffield Science scheme.
- Capacity to learn depends on readiness (stage of development).
- Discovery learning using assimilation and accommodation.
- Social marking is effective because it initiates disequilibrium (conflict).
- Mathematics is important because schemata are logical and mathematical.

VYGOTSKY

- His theory led to peer tutoring with a more knowledgeable person (zone of proximal development).
- Collaborative learning is effective because it encourages shared meaning.
- Play is effective because it enables the child to operate above the everyday level of functioning.

> **INFORMATION PROCESSING**
> - Ensure tasks are presented in a way that 'fits' the child's processing capacity using task analysis.
> - Do not overload processing capacity.
> - Encourage metacognition.
> - Some tasks are completed using implicit learning and do not require explicit verbal instruction.

Table 10.3 Practical applications of Piagetian, Vygotskyan and information-processing accounts of cognitive development to education

Piaget's theory

The Plowden Report (1967) and the Nuffield Science initiative both acknowledged the usefulness of Piagetian theory for enhancing children's performance in schools. Particular emphasis has been put on the importance of: the child being active; the child being ready to learn, dependent upon its current developmental stage; encouraging children to engage in discovery learning — using assimilation and accommodation to cope with disequilibrium; and using mathematical principles to illustrate fundamental concepts.

Evidence for these applications is mixed. For example, Brainerd's (1983) review of the literature of discovery learning versus traditional tutor-led learning suggested that the latter is more effective. However, Aines and Murray (1982) showed that encouraging disequilibrium can facilitate understanding in 6–7 year-olds. They studied performance on a conservation task and found that the most effective method for improving performance was when the child was paired with another child who failed the task, but whose answer was different from that of the first child. This resulted in better performance than when the child was either given the correct answer or paired with a child who could conserve. According to Piaget's theory, this is because the child needs to experience disequilibrium (conflict) between what it expects and what is experienced to encourage it to accommodate to the demands of the environment (i.e. the task).

Vygotsky's theory

Vygotsky's theory emphasises the importance of the social context and collaborative learning (e.g. peer tutoring) between a child and another individual with greater knowledge. This will enable the child to test out its zone of proximal development. Barnier (1989) studied 6–7 year-olds and found that when completing spatial and perspective tasks, using tutors of 7 and 8 years enabled the younger child of the pair to produce a better performance than when no peer tutor was used.

However, this approach assumes that tutees are motivated to learn and that tutors are effective instructors. For example, Salomon and Globerson (1989) argued that, if the status of the tutor and tutee differ greatly, this can reduce the usefulness of peer tutoring.

Also, it seems that peer tutoring might be more useful for some tasks than others, and for some parts of task completion but not others. For example, Forman and Cazden (1985) studied peer tutoring amongst 9 year-olds completing problems on chemical reactions. They found that collaboration is most useful during the early stages of problem solving, but that conflict (as suggested by Piaget) is more useful during the later stages (e.g. when setting up the experiment).

Information processing

The information-processing approach to cognitive development emphasises the importance of using methods of instruction and tasks which will not overload the child's 'M' capacity. This attention to appropriateness is similar to Piaget's notion of readiness.

However, the difference is that the information-processing approach argues that it is possible to make tasks easier for children by reducing the demands placed on the information-processing system, because the differences between more or less developed cognition are quantitative (not qualitative as argued by Piaget).

For example, Beck and Carpenter (1986) argued that children have difficulty learning to read because they tend to focus on parts of words (the phonic method). However, if they practise this skill (increasing its automaticity and reducing demands on the system), word recognition and comprehension are improved.

This approach also emphasises the usefulness of encouraging children to be aware of their cognitive processes to enhance their strategic (executive) control of lower level processes. This metacognitive activity (i.e. an individual's thoughts about their thinking processing and activity) has been shown to enhance text comprehension, especially if children are encouraged to think about the structure of the text they are reading (Palinscar and Brown, 1984).

The limitations of the approach include:
- difficulty in identifying underlying processes required for a task
- problems assessing an individual's capacity limits
- the inability of the approach to do more than describe task completion — it does not explain how processes and structures develop

Discuss the application of two theories of cognitive development (e.g. to education). (24 marks)

1.2 DEVELOPMENT OF MEASURED INTELLIGENCE

Sternberg (1985) described intelligence as mental activity used to adapt to the real world (e.g. to identify goals, adapt to the environment, select strategies to achieve goals and apply these effectively). Intelligence tests measure basic cognitive abilities and not broader social intelligence encompassed in Sternberg's definition.

Binet and Simon (1905) developed the first formal measure of intelligence to identify the special educational needs of children. Their performance on this, expressed as a numerical score, is their intelligence quotient or IQ. However, individuals will differ in IQ scores because such scales do not measure all 'intelligences' and for reasons other than fundamental differences in intelligence. For example, many intelligence tests are regarded as **culture-specific** (ethnocentric) because they conceptualise intelligence in terms of specific western values. Serpell (1979) found that, whilst English children performed better on drawing tasks, Zambian children performed better on a culturally relevant wire shaping task. The importance of environmental versus inherited factors in determining IQ scores has been investigated by means of: studies of twins; studies of adopted children; and studies of communities that have experienced major social changes.

Twin studies

If **heredity** is important to IQ, identical twins (monozygotic) should have more similar IQ scores than non-identical or dizygotic twins. If the environment is more important, there should be few or no differences between these types of twins. For example, Bouchard and McGue (1981) reviewed 111 studies and found that the average correlation between IQ scores of identical twins *raised together* was 0.86, higher than that for non-identical twins (0.60). However, this comparison confuses heredity with **environment**, because identical twins are also more likely to be treated more similarly than non-identical twins. Nevertheless, when twins reared apart are examined, the correlation is still higher amongst identical twins (0.72).

The Minnesota study of twins reared apart

In this study the twins were separated at birth and were not raised by family members; the correlation for identical twins' IQ scores was 0.75. However, although this research suggests that both heredity and environment are important, it is difficult totally to separate environmental from genetic factors, and it seems that as age increases, the role of heredity increases, possibly because the environmental differences between adults are smaller than those between children.

Adoption studies

If the IQ of adopted children is similar to that of their birth parents, this is used to support the importance of heredity; but if their IQ is similar to that of their adopted parents, this is used to support the role of the environment.

Capron and Duyne (1989) provide a strong test of this method. They tried to eliminate the effect of selective placement — when a child is placed with a family similar to their biological family. They examined high socio-economic status and low socio-economic status biological and adoptive parents. They found that both genes and environment were equally important in predicting IQ scores.

Environment

This research is used to identify whether major environmental changes lead to changes in IQ. If this is the case, the importance of environment on IQ scores is supported.

Ceci (1991) found that IQ scores of children who start school late (after 6 years of age) tend to be lower, and that IQ drops after both missing school because of illness and during the school summer holidays. It is problematic identifying which aspects of the social environment might be important here.

The Home Inventory was developed to classify this environment into six variables that might influence intelligence:
- emotional and verbal responsivity of parents
- parental avoidance of restriction and punishment of children
- how the environment is organised
- provision of appropriate play materials
- level of parental involvement with a child
- the variety of stimulation in the daily environment

Gottfried (1984), in a review of the literature, found the last three factors to be most closely related to IQ.

The Rochester study

Sameroff et al. (1993) studied thousands of children from birth to adolescence. Differences in IQ were related to ten factors, including maternal psychological well-being, education, interactions with the child and attitudes to development, socio-economic status, number of children, absence of the father from the home, ethnic minority status, and the number of stressful events experienced by the children in the first four years of life.

However, all the evidence is correlational — it is not causal. It is possible that genetic inheritance led to some of these events which, in turn, had environmental effects on IQ.

Discuss research into factors associated with the development of intelligence test performance. (24 marks)

Critically consider the role of genetics and cultural differences in the development of intelligence. (24 marks)

Cognitive-developmental approaches

Cognitive-developmental approaches to moral development are illustrated by the theories of Piaget and Kohlberg. These are summarised in Table 10.4.

PIAGET	KOHLBERG
Stage 1 0–5 years *Premoral* Child has no obvious moral rules.	**Level 1** Pre-conventional Stage 1: punishment and obedience orientation — immorality is punished; Stage 2: correct behaviour determined by rewards — moral behaviours are those that are rewarded.
Stage 2 5–10 years *Moral realism* Morality is governed by external rules made by important people and must be applied rigidly. Immorality derived from consequences. Naughtiness determines punishment (expiatory punishment) and will always be punished (immanent justice).	**Level 2** *Conventional morality* Stage 3: good intentions and conformity — moral behaviour is that which gains approval; Stage 4: duty and obey authority — morality involves doing one's duty and obeying authority.
Stage 3 10 years-upwards *Moral relativism* Moral rules derived from relationships with people, rules are flexible, can be broken and vary between people. Naughtiness/immorality based on intentions. People can avoid punishments which now should fit the crime (reciprocal punishment).	**Level 3** Post conventional (principled) Stage 5: morality and legal justice rules can conflict — abstract values of justice can overrule laws; Stage 6: principles of conscience — moral decisions should take into account how decisions will affect others.

Table 10.4 Summary of Piaget's and Kohlberg's theories of moral development

Both theories:

- are stage based
- were developed using hypothetical situations to identify moral principles in children (Piaget used rule-following games of marbles and Kohlberg used moral dilemmas); the moral principles and developmental stage of children were inferred from whether children followed or upheld moral rules
- see moral development as invariant and relatively universal
- conceptualise moral development as an increase in the awareness of the complexity of a child's morality (e.g. increased flexibility, awareness that moral standards vary between individuals and that justice sometimes requires moral rules to be broken).

Piaget's theory

Piaget argued that morality develops significantly as egocentric thought declines and, as children grow, their exposure to views other than those of their parents helps shape their morality. Piaget (1932) provided evidence that in younger children naughtiness is tied to consequences and not actor intentions. When a story about two boys who accidentally broke either one or fifteen cups was read to children, the boy breaking fifteen cups was described as naughtier than the other.

Evaluation

- Shaffer (1993), although finding broad cross-cultural support for the stages, found that younger children follow their parents' rules for some decisions but not others (e.g. friendships and hobbies).
- Overall, Piaget's work has identified how cognitive and moral development are linked; his methods are more rigorous than those used by Freud.

However:

- The theory simplifies the nature of moral dilemmas and assumes that morality is fully developed by 10–11 years of age.
- The methods used only enable statements to be made about children's moral intentions and not how they actually behave.

Kohlberg's theory

Kohlberg's theory attempted to address some of the weaknesses of Piaget. For example, morality is seen as developing throughout early adulthood, and the later stages of Level 3 are seen as *ideals*. Colby et al. (1983) conducted a 20 year longitudinal study of 58 American men and found that at ages 10–16 years there is a reduction in Stage 1 and 2 morality and an increase in Stage 3 and 4; all participants developed through the stages in an invariant order. However, Rubin and Trotter (1977) found that people switch between different levels of morality for different dilemmas. Furthermore, cognitive development (especially abstract thought), whilst necessary for later morality, is not sufficient (Tomlinson-Keasey and Keasey, 1974). Importantly, some cultures will support or impede through different levels, dependent upon that culture's specific values, and *moral intentions are not always linked to behaviour*. However, Kohlberg (1975) studied cheating amongst young adult students and found that those least likely to cheat (an act of immorality) were those at the highest level of morality.

Evaluation

Kohlberg has also been criticised for basing his theory entirely on a sample of males. Gilligan (1977, 1982) interviewed males and females and identified that men tend to value moral justice whilst women value morality of care (e.g. are concerned with upholding principles of human compassion and well-being). However, Kohlberg's theory assumes that the former represents a higher level of moral functioning. However, Walker (1984) reviewed 54 US studies and found that sex differences were only apparent in eight, with no evidence of females showing greater levels of compassion.

Theory of prosocial and moral reasoning and behaviour

Both the theories of Piaget and Kohlberg have influenced more recent theorists. One example of this is Eisenberg, Lennon and Roth's (1983) theory of prosocial and moral reasoning and behaviour.

This theory does appear to be a better **predictor** of moral behaviour because it conceptualises each level of moral development in terms of moral behaviour.

However, there is evidence that children as young as 18–30 months show distress when another child shows distress (Zahn-Waxler, Radke-Yarrow and King, 1979). In such instances, mothers tended to accompany these situations with verbalisations which act as rewards or punishments for behaviour.

Q | **Outline and evaluate two theories of moral understanding.** | (24 marks)

---

2 Social and personality development

2.1 PERSONALITY DEVELOPMENT

According to **social learning** theorists, personality development is an **active process** — individuals are actively involved in the developmental process in which their beliefs about their behaviour and its consequences shape personality development. Bandura's (1973, 1986) theory is one example of social learning theory.

Bandura's theory

- Personality develops through the processes of **direct tuition** or observational learning (the individual learns that certain behaviours are rewarded and some punished) and by observing others (**vicarious learning**).
- Complex behaviours learnt vicariously require more vicarious experiences than simpler behaviour.
- Personality develops out of the individual's **expectancies** (i.e. that certain behaviours follow from other behaviours) and perceptions of the **contingencies** of their behaviour (i.e. that certain behaviours are rewarded or punished).
- Personality development can be described as a process of **reciprocal determinism** — aspects of the individual (*person variables*), the *situation* and behaviours interact to produce personality.
- An individual's beliefs about how successful an action will be in a given situation (**self-efficacy**) will also influence which behaviours are maintained and which are not.

Bandura's research

Much of Bandura's research has examined aggression in children.

Bandura and Huston (1961) found that preschool children who observed an adult being rewarded for knocking a doll down aggressively were likely subsequently to behave in an aggressive manner towards the doll.

Bandura, Ross and Ross (1961) studied whether the sex of the aggressive role model affected imitation. Children observed an adult behaving aggressively to the doll. The children became mildly frustrated and were then left with the doll that had been attacked. Boys were found to be more aggressive than girls and were more likely to imitate the behaviour of a same-sex aggressive model than girls.

Mischel's theory

Mischel (1984) described personality development as dynamic. According to Mischel, cognitive and situational (social learning) factors influence behaviour. For example, one aspect of behaviour is the delay of gratification (when an individual chooses to wait for a later reinforcer rather than accept one which is available immediately). This is influenced by aspects of social learning (e.g. modelling — seeing another person delay gratification) and cognitive factors (e.g. distraction — thinking about other things). Mischel identified five person variables involved in the social learning of personality — these are strategies learned from past experiences which direct future behaviour:

- *competencies* — skills and behaviours, and how these were rewarded in the past to determine future behaviour
- *encoding strategies* (and personal constructs) — individuals' unique information processes which determine how situations are interpreted
- *expectancies* — individuals' anticipations of how a behaviour affects the environment, thus influencing how they behave in future
- *subjective values* — the way individuals value rewards differently
- *self-regulatory systems and plans* — individuals' assessments of how they are performing, and how rewards/punishments are used as feedback to modify future behaviour

The **psychodynamic** approach to personality development is illustrated by Freud's psychosexual theory of personality development. This theory makes certain assumptions about personality development:

- Development is relatively passive — personality is developed through a process driven by instinctual drives which supply psychic energy.

- Personality is both conscious and unconscious.
- Healthy personalities are able to discharge this energy.
- However, strong emotions are actively repressed to protect the individual from unpleasant emotions; consequently aspects of personality are unconscious and are only accessible by accessing the unconscious.
- The personality is made up of different levels of consciousness (or levels of awareness) — the unconscious, the conscious and the preconscious; and three structures — the **id** (instinctually driven, libidinous and requiring immediate gratification), **ego** (the 'self' which controls behaviour, delays gratification and uses a range of defence mechanisms to defend itself from the desires of the id) and **superego** (ego ideal, reflecting social rules and morals).
- Personality develops out of **conflict** — individuals pass through different **psychosexual stages** characterised by different **erogenous zones** (pleasure zones) and move through these stages in sequence to satisfy their libidinous needs.

Freudian theory contains four stages of development:

- The *oral stage* (0–2 years) — the new-born gains gratification from oral stimulation and satisfies its hunger and thirst drives through feeding. However, the child must be weaned, which conflicts with the desire to remain secure (through suckling). Healthy development results in the child finding another outlet for its energy, whilst some get 'stuck' (fixation). Fixation can manifest itself later as dependent behaviour.
- The *anal stage* (2–3 years) — the child gains pleasure from bowel movements (defaecation). However, because parents desire toilet training in children, the child must learn to control this urge. Fixation here can manifest as messy behaviour in adulthood or in extreme tidiness and neatness.
- The *phallic stage* (3–5 years) — the child gains pleasure from stimulating its genitals. It is at this stage that males and females experience the Oedipus and Electra complexes, respectively.
- The final stage is *latency or the genital stage* — here the sex drive is submerged and libido is expressed through heterosexual genital contact. Freud had less to say about this stage than the others — a weakness in the theory.

Q

Compare and contrast the psychodynamic and social learning explanations of personality development. (24 marks)

Critically consider what psychology has shown us about personality development. (24 marks)

2.2 GENDER DEVELOPMENT

Gender refers to organised social beliefs about the sexes, whereas **sex** refers to the biological identity of an individual as male or female. Sex-typed behaviours are culturally approved male and female behaviours.

Cognitive-developmental accounts

An alternative approach is offered by cognitive-developmental accounts of gender development. Kohlberg (1966) argues that gender develops through an active, three-stage process in which individuals interpret and select social experiences (e.g. role models) which reinforce their already developing gender identity.

- First, the child at age 2–3.5 years knows that boys and girls are different, but believes it is possible to change sex (basic gender identity stage).
- Then, at 3.5–4.5 years the child develops an understanding that sex is stable over time but can change in different situations (gender stability stage).

- Finally, at 4.5–7 years of age the child realises that sex is stable over time and in different situations (i.e. conservation) (gender consistency stage).

Evaluation
- This theory assumes that, over time, children pay increasing attention to same-sex behaviours and figures. Slaby and Frey (1975) found that, in children aged 2–5 years of age, those who showed higher levels of gender consistency paid greater attention to the same sex character in a film they were shown than those low on gender consistency. However, sex-typed behaviours appear before the first stage of the theory (prior to 2 years of age), and little consideration is given to the rewards and punishments given for sex-typed behaviour.
- Hutson (1985) argued that even if a child has beliefs about gender appropriate behaviour, this is not linked to the child's own sex-typed behaviour, especially amongst girls.

Gender schema theory
Martin and Halverson's (1987) gender schema theory argues that gender identity develops through *both cognitive and social processes*. Even children as young as 2–3 years of age have organised sets of beliefs about the sexes (or schemata) which influence how they perceive the appropriateness of behaviour and how they behave.

For example, Martin and Halverson (1983) found that 5–6 year-olds tend to have better memories for gender schema consistent pictures than for gender schema inconsistent ones and, after one week, they have distorted their memory of the inconsistent pictures to be more gender consistent.

Masters et al. (1979) found that 4 and 5 year-old boys and girls are more likely to play with toys based on whether they are described as 'a boy's toy' or 'a girl's toy'. The first schemata to develop are beliefs about the toys appropriate for boys and girls, and beliefs about how they should behave.

The process is **active** and much of gender development is complete by middle childhood.

Evaluation
- This theory does not consider social factors that might influence development and it is not always clear whether schemata influence behaviour.
- It is unclear why schemata develop in this way.

Social learning theory
Social learning theory pays greater attention to how social factors influence gender development.

Bandura (1977, 1986) argued that society shapes gender development through both direct tuition and observational learning. Social endorsement (rewards or punishments) is the mechanism by which behaviours are strengthened. For example, Fagot and Leinbach (1989) studied children under 2 years of age and found that, even amongst children this young, parents rewarded sex appropriate, and punished sex inappropriate, behaviour; children whose parents used this style of parenting most frequently were more sex-typed in their behaviour.

There is evidence that mass media images can influence this process. Williams (1986) studied Canadian towns without television, with only one channel, or with four channels. Williams found that more sex-typing was shown amongst the residents in the four-channels towns, and that when access to television was increased (e.g. introduced in the town with no channels), sex-typed behaviours became more frequent.

Evaluation

- There is no *clear evidence* that parents systematically reward/punish sex-typed behaviours and, given that learning involves cognitive processes, the approach does not take into account changes in cognitive development.
- Social learning theory is more suitable for explaining how specific behaviours are learnt rather than how general beliefs develop.

Q

Outline two explanations of gender development. Assess the extent to which research evidence supports these.   (12+12 marks)

2.3 ADOLESCENCE

Major personality theorists agree that, whilst much development takes place in early childhood, the teenage years or adolescence is also a **time of personality change**.

Traditionally, adolescence has been seen as a time of turbulence and trauma. Erikson's theory of development encouraged the view that, during the teenage years, individuals undergo a crisis of identity (role diffusion) and that such a crisis is a normal part of development. However, Erikson's ideas were based on his observations of young people undergoing therapy.

Marcia's theory

Marcia (1966, 1980) challenged the notion of adolescence as a time of crisis. Using semi-structured interviews, Marcia argued that this time is more complex than Erikson suggested. By asking young people about their occupational aspirations, and their religious and political ideology, he identified four possible **identity statuses** of the adolescent:

- The status of individuals is determined by whether they have considered alternatives and are committed to specific goals in terms of their occupational, religious and ideological beliefs.
- Trauma in adolescence results from having to make difficult decisions about one's identity; social pressures motivate the individual to move through four stages:
  - Stage 1: identity diffusion
  - Stage 2: foreclosure (identity has not been considered but commitments have been made)
  - Stage 3: moratorium (alternative goals have been explored but no commitments have been made)
  - Stage 4: identity achievement (alternatives considered and commitments made)

Meilman (1979) provides some supporting evidence for Marcia's theory. He studied males aged 12–24 years and found that all the 12 year-olds and some of the 15 year-olds were at either Stage 1 or 2. Also, whilst 20% of 15 year-olds were at Stage 4, 40% of 21 year-olds and 56% of 24 year-olds were at this stage. However, these data suggest that a large proportion of young adults have still not achieved the highest level of identity (Stage 4) even by their mid-20s.

Evaluation

- Marcia's theory does identify the different pathways that individuals can take to achieve a stable identity, but the theory does not consider the importance that culture might have for dealing with identity crises and establishing identity 'ideals'. For example, Markus and Kitayama (1991) identified two types of culture which are likely to influence the nature of adolescent identity development: (1) some societies, such as the USA, encourage independence and self-containment as an identity ideal; (2) other societies embrace collectivist cultures in which, even as a young adult, individuals have decisions made for them (e.g. a marriage partner is chosen).

- There is evidence that individuals at different stages tend to have parents with different parenting styles. For example, those at Stages 3 and 4 tend to have parents who are affectionate and allow freedom, whilst those at Stage 1 tend to have distant and aloof parents (Waterman, 1982). It might well be that development is influenced by parenting style — and that how individuals develop (or get stuck at a status) depends on their parents' behaviour.
- Archer (1982) found that, amongst 12–18 year-olds studied, only 5% achieved the same stage of identity (status) for occupational, religious and ideological issues. This suggests that identity is more complex than the theory implies and that it is possible for individuals to go back and forth between stages (Marcia, 1976).

Discuss what psychological research has shown us about social development in adolescence.   (24 marks)

Cultural differences in adolescence

As many writers have pointed out, if adolescence was purely a biological process of maturation, the experience would be largely universal. However, many studies have shown considerable variation across different cultures. The 'storm and stress' of 20th century Western adolescence (James Dean's *Rebel Without a Cause* was a role model for a generation in the 1950s) contrasted sharply with Mead's early (1928) study, 'Coming of Age in Samoa', where the period of transition from childhood to adulthood was structured and largely conflict-free.

Even more dramatically, Shaffer (1993) has reported that some cultures, such as the St Lawrence Eskimos, have no adolescence that we would recognise. One day a boy is a boy and the next he is a man; and the same goes for women (as it were!).

Condon (1987) showed that the Inuit people of the Canadian Arctic also have no period we would recognise in our culture as adolescence. Girls were regarded as women as soon as they reached puberty and boys as men as soon as they could build an igloo. Soon afterwards they began to have children. Eysenck and Flanagan (2001) put it thus:

> The difficult living conditions in the Arctic meant that there was no time for teenagers to spend several years thinking about what they were going to do with their lives.

Whether adolescence is a period of storm and stress, or smooth and conflict-free (or even non-existent, as in the two examples above), may well be determined by whether the teenagers live in an individualistic culture (such as the USA and Britain) or a collectivist one (such as may be found in the Far East).

Discuss research into cultural differences in adolescent behaviour.   (24 marks)

Adulthood

3.1 EARLY AND MIDDLE ADULTHOOD

Gould's theory

Gould (1978) examined the life histories of men and women aged 16–60 years of age and found that their world views changed at certain **age phases**. Overall, Gould found that growth in adulthood was typified by the individual challenging childish assumptions (listed below), increased self-acceptance and separation from parental values and beliefs, and that this formed a system of meaning which shaped the individual's behaviour and life choices.

- Ages 16–22 years — the assumption that 'I'll always belong to my parents and believe in their world' is challenged, and individuals' self-doubts begin whilst developing their own identity separate from that of their parents.
- Ages 22–28 years — the assumption that 'Doing things my parents' way with will power and perseverance will bring results...and if I cannot cope they will show me how to' is challenged. Individuals actively attempt to construct their own life and gain self-respect, and in particular begin to focus on achievement at work.
- Ages 28–34 years — the assumption that 'Life is simple and controllable...there are no significant co-existing contradictory forces within me' is challenged. Here, individuals identify their competencies and limits and, whilst some of the goals they considered in their 20s might resurface, overall this stage is typified by a mellowing of attitudes which are enduring.
- Ages 35–40 years — this is the period in which full autonomous adult consciousness develops. This is also a time in which the challenge of mid-life looms (mid-life crisis) and there is an increased desire for security.

Evaluation

- Whilst Gould's theory is relatively detailed, it implies an inflexible linear progression in adult development.
- It fails to consider major and/or unpredictable life events and their effects. Importantly, the sample Gould used was male and the cohort was born in the 1920s and 1930s.

Levinson's theory

Levinson's (1978, 1986) theory of adult development is different from Gould's in the sense that adult development is seen as consisting of **eras** (lasting 20 years each), during which a life structure is constructed which influences and reflects how an individual relates to the outside world. Development is the result of individuals questioning their existing life structure and breaking free from existing structures — they outgrow their current structure. A new structure is developed which enables them to meet the needs of their situation. Approximately, the eras are:

- era of pre-adulthood (0–22 years)
- era of early adulthood (17–45 years) — individuals form a dream or life goals (17–22 years) but then, having constructed an adult lifestyle (22–28 years), reconstruct this at the age 30 transition. Although they realise their aspirations (age 33–40), this era ends with the mid-life crisis (40–45 years) — a time when it is realised that life never matches one's dreams
- era of middle adulthood (40–65 years) — individuals establish a life structure, but experience the age 50 transition (50–55 years), when life plans are reconsidered before they enter the final era
- era of late adulthood (60 years onwards)

Levinson argued that adulthood consists of equal amounts of time in stability and in transitions. Successful development in adulthood results from individuals having dealt with the external world and achieved inner desires.

Evaluation

- Evidence for Levinson's theory is mixed. Roberts and Newton (1987) interviewed 39 women and found that men and women differed in their dreams — men's related to work whilst women's were more complex and included work and interpersonal goals. This is not surprising, as Levinson's original research involved 40 men aged 35–45 years, suggesting that the theory might be sex-biased.

- The method used (intensive interviews over four months) required participants to recall their experiences of earlier adulthood from memory; the interviewer was not 'blind' to the hypotheses being tested. These factors could have caused bias in the data.
- None of the original study participants was an older adult, and Vaillant (1977) found that individuals who experienced mid-life crises tended to have experienced the events associated with this (e.g. divorce) throughout adulthood.

Q **Discuss research into development in early and middle adulthood.** (24 marks)

3.2 FAMILY AND RELATIONSHIPS IN ADULTHOOD

Both Gould's and Levinson's theories tend to see some points in adulthood as times of crisis and stress. There are events that happen in adulthood which are stressful. However, the effects of these events seem to vary between individuals and social groups. For example, there is evidence that becoming a parent for the first time can reduce marital satisfaction (Reibstein and Richard, 1992), especially amongst women who may feel that their expectations of support from their partner are not met (Ruble et al., 1988). Middle class women also tend to experience a greater drop in marital satisfaction than working class women, possibly because becoming a parent is more disruptive for them (e.g. through a career break). Also, it seems that higher levels of marital satisfaction prior to the birth of a child protect a couple from a reduction in satisfaction (Guthrie, 1992); and, unsurprisingly, adequate financial resources are also protective (Bee and Mtchell, 1984).

Another example of this complex pattern of effects is found when considering divorce: Buunk (1996) found that the divorced were more likely to report mental health and physical health problems than those married, single or bereaved. This suggests that the effects of divorce are likely to be attributable to factors other than the loss of a partner. For example, Rutter and Rutter (1992) found that the adverse effects of divorce for women were related to financial problems and increased parental responsibilities.

3.3 COGNITIVE CHANGES IN LATE ADULTHOOD

Continued human development

Late adulthood is also a time of continued human development. However, whilst early and middle adulthood have tended to be conceptualised as a time of identity formation or crises whilst moving through stages, later adulthood is often conceptualised as a period of *adjustment* to diminishing roles and increased personal and social loss. Cumming and Henry (1961) described these changes in their disengagement theory: in late adulthood individuals become less involved in society, both voluntarily and because of social factors beyond their control (e.g. retirement). Furthermore, social expectations of the elderly facilitate disengagement and this process can be a way of coping with age-associated changes (e.g. physical health problems).

Good adjustment to these changes results from progressive adaptation. Cumming and Henry examined 50–90 year-olds over five years and found increased disengagement over the years. Similarly, Folkman et al. (1987) found that older people were more likely to use passive coping styles when faced with problems compared to younger people, who used more action-oriented problem-solving behaviours.

Evaluation

- Havighurst et al.'s (1968) follow-up suggests that disengagement in late adulthood is more complex than first thought. For example, although many participants had disengaged from some social roles, most were satisfied with their lives, remained socially active (in fact those most satisfied were those most active) and were more likely to report being happy than younger people.

- Those who had made the decision to disengage from some roles were most satisfied.
- Durkin (1995) found that in the UK and Australia, many older people remained active socially.
- It seems likely that cultural differences might be important as well — there is evidence that when previously non-western cultures undergo modernisation, disengagement amongst the elderly increases (Turnbull, 1989). Therefore, it seems reasonable to suggest that disengagement is not the typical way elderly people adjust to later life — not all older people are the same; some characteristics related to social isolation are stable across adulthood (Maddox, 1970), and the pattern varies between cultures.

Retirement

The evidence suggests that the *adverse* effects of retirement on individuals have been exaggerated and oversimplified. For example, Herzog et al. (1991) found that amongst working and semi-retired older people and those aged 55–64 years, well-being was linked to whether individuals were doing what they wanted to do — control of choice was linked to better well-being.

Swan et al. (1991) support this. They found that in their US sample, those 'forced' to retire reported poorer levels of well-being than those who chose to retire. Furthermore, they reported that certain personality types were more likely to believe that they had been forced to retire.

Ward (1984) reported that white-collar workers adjust better to retirement than blue-collar workers, probably because the former have better pension plans and physical health when entering retirement.

Bereavement

Bereavement is more likely to occur in later life and is linked to changes in life structure and personal identity. In particular, bereavement is likely to affect **social functioning**, such as a loss of social and emotional support and the loss of material and task support (Stroebe et al., 1982).

Once bereaved, an individual is likely to feel shocked and numb, and to feel an intense longing for the person lost, followed by prolonged depression and hopelessness, culminating in a reconstructed life (Parkes, 1986).

However, it seems likely that linear progression through these stages is simplistic (Ramsay and de Groot, 1977). Stroebe and Stroebe (1987) found that, 2.5 years after bereavement, some bereaved individuals were still experiencing unpleasant emotions, but the elderly (and those who lost a loved one through a long-term illness) were not affected as badly. This suggests that the effects of bereavement vary between individuals.

Men appear to have greater problems adjusting to bereavement, because it is likely to result in increased new responsibilities (e.g. housekeeping) (Bury and Holme, 1991). However, according to Lopata (1979), women often benefit from a new-found independence following bereavement and are less likely to remarry than are widowers.

Discuss evidence for the existence of crises and transitions in early and/or middle adulthood.
(24 marks)

Coping with bereavement

The one thing we all know about life is that one day we will not have it. With increasingly ageing populations, the question of how we cope with the prospect of dying has taken on greater significance.

The most influential theory has been put forward by Kubler-Ross (1969). From her clinical interviews with people who were terminally ill, she argued that people go through the following stages of preparation for their own death. She did, however, emphasise that the stages are not universal or invariant and one should allow people to come to terms in their own way.

- *Denial.* A person seeks help from others, such as doctors, complementary medicine or the clergy.
- *Anger.* Here the person asks 'Why me?' and may feel resentful of others.
- *Bargaining.* People may try to strike a bargain with fate or God.
- *Depression.* Denial may no longer be possible and the individual is forced to confront his or her mortality both physically and psychologically.
- *Acceptance.* Here the person may feel emotionless and weak but, perhaps, resolute.

Wadeley (2000) has written about how cultures vary in the ways they deal with death. Contrast the following three, for example.

- The Hopi Indians of Arizona have a fear and dread of the dead and consequently try to break the bonds between the living and dead as soon as possible.
- For the Kota of southern India there are funerals and remembrances for a while, but these come to be replaced by a mood of celebration. As she puts it, 'The sombre mood ends abruptly, to be replaced by an atmosphere of celebration. There are more rituals (including sexual intercourse for the widowed, preferably with a sibling of the dead person), all intended to return the bereaved to normal life'.
- In Japanese Shintoism and Buddhism, those who die become ancestors, and small shrines or altars are erected in homes where gifts can be left for them.

Issues in the classification and diagnosis of psychological abnormality

1.1 CLASSIFICATORY SYSTEMS

Abnormality is one of the most difficult terms in all psychology to define and this makes **classification** problematic. Classification is difficult, mainly because psychologists have different ideas about what causes abnormality and how it manifests itself. Some psychologists believe it is mainly due to 'failures' in a person's basic biology (for example, brain chemistry); others believe that it is due to 'faulty' **learning**; some believe it is caused by 'faulty' **cognitions** (such as perceptions and belief systems); still others believe it is the result of problems of the **mind** and the **personality**.

All these different views of abnormality have enjoyed dominance at different times and their influence varies across cultures. Fernando (1991), amongst others, argued that the model which at any particular time is dominant in the Western world will be the one which exerts most influence.

Considering the biological and psychological models of abnormality, the most *influential* has been the biological or medical model whose essence is diagnosis through classification.

There are two major classification systems: the Diagnostic and Statistical Manual of Mental Disorders (DSM), now in its fourth revision, hence DSM-IV; and the International Classification of Diseases and Health Related Problems (ICD), now in its tenth revision, hence ICD-10.

ICD-10

ICD-10 identifies 11 major categories:
(1) Organic, including symptomatic, mental disorders, e.g. Alzheimer's disease
(2) Mental and behaviour disorders due to psychoactive substance use: e.g. alcohol, cocaine
(3) Schizophrenia
(4) Mood disorders, e.g. depression
(5) Neurotic and stress related disorders, e.g. phobias
(6) Behavioural syndromes associated with physiological disturbances, e.g. eating disorders
(7) Disorders of adult personality and behaviour, e.g. personality disorders and gender identity disorders
(8) Mental retardation
(9) Disorders of psychological development, e.g. dyslexia
(10) Behavioural and emotional disorders in childhood
(11) Unspecified conditions

DSM-IV

In DSM-IV, each of the mental disorders is seen as a clinically significant behavioural or psychological pattern of behaviour that occurs in an individual, bringing with it distress and impairment in one or more important areas of functioning, with an increased risk of suffering, death, pain or disability, or an important loss of freedom. Whatever the original cause, it must currently be considered a manifestation of a behavioural, psychological or biological **dysfunction** in the individual. Neither deviant behaviour (e.g. political, religious or sexual) nor conflicts that are primarily between the individual and society are mental disorders.

In DSM-IV the disorders are organised in **axes**, of which there are five. In Axis I the syndromes are similar to the ICD and include:

(1) Disorders in infancy,
    e.g. autism
(2) Delirium and dementia
(3) Mental disorder due to a medical
    condition
(4) Substance abuse
(5) Schizophrenia
(6) Mood disorders
(7) Anxiety disorders
(8) Somatoform disorders
(9) Factitious disorders
(10) Dissociative disorders
(11) Eating disorders
(12) Sexual disorders
(13) Sleep disorders
(14) Impulse control disorders
(15) Adjustment disorders
(16) Other conditions

Axis I is an extensive list of clinical syndromes which overlap and in some cases are identical to the ICD syndromes.

Diagnosticians must next decide whether a client is displaying Axis II disorders, i.e. mental retardation and personality disorders. The diagnostician must then look for Axis III information, such as general medical conditions. Axis IV information includes psycho-social or environmental problems. Finally, Axis V information is a rating of the overall level of functioning.

Q

Compare and contrast the ICD and DSM as ways of classifying/diagnosing psychological abnormality. (24 marks)

The purpose of classification

The act of classifying enables professionals to communicate more accurately about syndromes and their nature. Knowing how groups of symptoms fare with different treatments enables the clinician to concentrate on the handful of treatments that might be useful in particular circumstances. People's problems are derived from a number of sources, but certain problems may be more reliably associated with particular causes or aetiologies. Finally, there might be a scientific pay-off when collecting data on groups of people with similar symptoms.

The Rosenhan study

For the system to work it must be reliable and valid. To get a feel for the difficulties involved, consider the work of Rosenhan (1973), who reported on what happened when eight psychiatrically normal people from various backgrounds presented themselves at admissions offices of different psychiatric hospitals complaining of hearing bizarre and disembodied voices saying 'empty', 'hollow' and 'thud'.

All of Rosenhan's (1973) *pseudopatients* were admitted to the hospitals, most being diagnosed as schizophrenic. Once admitted, they behaved normally. However, their diagnoses seemed to bias the staff's interpretation of their behaviours. For example, pacing a corridor out of boredom was interpreted as 'anxiety' by the staff. When one pseudopatient began to make notes, it was recorded as 'patient engages in writing behaviour'.

Shortly after admission, the pseudopatients stopped claiming to hear voices, and all were eventually discharged with diagnoses of 'schizophrenia in remission' (a lessening in the degree of schizophrenic symptoms). The only people who were apparently suspicious of them were their 'fellow' patients, one of whom commented, 'You're not crazy, you're a journalist

---

or a professor. You're checking up on the hospital'. It took between 7 and 52 days (the average being 19) for staff to be convinced that the pseudopatients were 'well enough' to be discharged.

Evaluation

- *Reliability*. Here you need to look at reliability as a concept and technique in general. Currently it is too soon to discuss the reliability of the DSM-IV, but there are data on earlier versions. Fleiss (1974), in a study of DSM-II, for example, found that only three categories of behaviour were sufficiently reliable to be clinically useful. Some studies showed reasonable reliability when broad categories were used, but when more specific categories were examined the agreements were low — 32–57%. It must be noted that it is far more important to be reliable with the specific categories.

- *Validity*. Again be aware of the technical meaning of this term in general. Note that if an instrument is not reliable, it cannot be valid, so these concepts are inter-related. Validity is the extent to which a diagnosis reflects an actual disorder. Because there is no absolute standard against which a diagnosis can be compared, for most disorders validity is difficult to assess. One purpose of diagnosis already mentioned is to select appropriate treatment. There is, however, only a 50% chance of correctly predicting what treatment people will receive from a given diagnosis. Bannister (1964) pointed out that in 1,000 cases studied, there was no clear-cut relationship between diagnosis and treatment.

The problem lies with the medical model being **applied** to the psychological. If in a medical diagnosis measles is indicated, the symptoms are the red spots and the underlying cause is a virus. In a psychological diagnosis, for example dyslexia, the diagnosis becomes **circular** in stating its cause. How do you know someone has dyslexia? They can't spell. Why can't they spell? Because they have dyslexia. In this case there is no independent underlying cause, except maybe a hypothetical neurological one.

Q **Discuss research into the reliability and validity of the ICD and DSM.**   (30 marks)

1.2 MULTIPLE PERSONALITY DISORDER (DISSOCIATIVE IDENTITY DISORDER)

People with dissociative disorders are described in the DSM as having an 'alteration in the integrative functions of consciousness, identity or motor behaviour. Dissociation refers to a disruption in memory where a separation of one part of a person's identity from another occurs'. The disruption referred to occurs in the absence of an identifiable physical cause.

DSM-IV distinguishes four major subtypes of dissociative disorders:
- *Dissociative amnesia*. This occurs when people are suddenly unable to recall important information about their lives. The loss of memory is much more extensive than normal forgetting and usually occurs after an upsetting event.
- *Dissociative fugue*. This occurs when people forget their identity and some details of their past life. They usually flee to another location and establish a different identity.
- *Dissociative identity disorder* (*multiple personality disorder*). This occurs when a person displays two or more distinct personalities.
- *Depersonalisation disorder*. This occurs when people have a persistent feeling of being detached from their own mental processes or body.

All of the above, except for the fourth, involve important personal events which cannot be recalled or where one's current identity is lost. This is why, in the DSM, multiple personality disorder is now called dissociative identity disorder, to signal some of the commonalities in the conditions.

Clinical characteristics

A person with multiple personality disorder displays two or more distinct personalities, often called **sub-personalities**, each with a unique set of behaviours, emotions and thoughts. At any given time one of the sub-personalities dominates the person's consciousness and interactions with those around him.

Dissociative identity disorder has existed under a variety of names for a long time, but has been subject to few experimental investigations. As such it has been treated sceptically by some researchers in the field. For example, Spanos (1994) believed that multiple personalities are caused by **role play**. He asserted that patients are influenced by their therapist's goals and expectations, much like an actor who loses all perspective and eventually believes his role to be real. Gleaves (1996) pointed out that, although the disorder does occur in other cultures, it is extremely rare in Europe and Japan, leading some like Mersky (1992) to call it nothing more than a North American diagnostic fad caused by the power of suggestion.

Case study — The Three Faces of Eve

Of all the personalities typical of multiple personality disorder, the most famous must be *The Three Faces of Eve*, described in a book by Thigpen and Cleckey (1957) and made into a film. Eve was a mother in a troubled marriage who sought psychotherapy. During therapy she complained of hearing an imaginary voice. She had blackouts which she was not disturbed by; these bore the elements of fugue listed above. During therapy the authors of the book describe the birth of a new personality: 'After a tense moment of silence her hands dropped, there was a quick reckless smile, and in a bright voice that sparkled, she said 'Hi there, Doc!' A new personality emerged, Eve Black, a happy-go-lucky, flirtatious personality who did not like Eve White, the mother and primary personality. During therapy a third personality, Jane, revealed herself. Hypnosis was used to reconcile the characters. The therapist tried to allow one character, the calmer Jane, to dominate and treatment ended with one character in control. This character was like Jane but she labelled herself Evelyn White. Chris Sizemoore was Eve's real name. Historically psychologists believed that multiple personality disorder usually involved two or three sub-personalities, but according to the American Psychiatric Association the average is nearer 15; although Eve had three faces, she claimed that she had 22 personalities, but they always appeared in groups of three. In a book that she wrote after her therapy was complete, she insisted that her identities were not a result of role play or mood but were separate identities with different appetites, handwriting, skills, IQs, facial expressions and dress codes.

Theoretical explanations of dissociative disorders

The case study of Sybil is described in the box below.

Case study — Sybil

Sybil's mother took delight in suspending her upside down from the ceiling and filling her bladder with cold water through an enema. Sybil's mother was schizophrenic and her father was unable to intervene in the mother's brutality. Day after day, Sybil was systematically sexually tortured and occasionally nearly murdered. Sybil's mother convinced herself that she was preparing her child for sex. Sybil was also given strong laxatives and was prevented from having access to the toilet. Her sexual organs were badly damaged with scar tissue. This abuse took place throughout her childhood.

Outline and evaluate two case studies into multiple personality disorder. (30 marks)

Psychodynamic explanations of dissociative disorders

Repression is a well-known **defence mechanism**, familiar to those who have a basic understanding of Freud's and other psychodynamic theorists' ideas about human motivation. The purpose of the defence mechanism is to prevent the occurrence of anxiety, by preventing painful thoughts from entering consciousness. All of us employ such defences, but in some cases the process results in the application of the defence repression in an extreme way that prevents normal functioning.

Psychodynamic theorists suggest that hurtful experiences, such as a parent's extreme reaction to id impulses, especially unacceptable infantile sexual desires in the oedipal stage, lead to massive repression, resulting in the person unconsciously blocking the memory of emotionally charged situations. Later on in life, however, when internalised values are violated by a person's actions, the resulting anxiety has to be controlled by wiping the event from consciousness. In dissociative identity disorder, individuals are seen by psychodynamic theorists as *using different identities to cope* by escaping elsewhere. Be familiar with the case of Sybil reported by Schreiber (1973).

Theorists have pointed out that extremely traumatic childhood experiences, especially childhood abuse, are central to the development of dissociative identity disorder.

Evaluation

There is some evidence in support of the role of abuse. Kluft (1984) suggested that in 97% of cases there have been instances of physical or sexual abuse.

One problem with this position is that child abuse has an occurrence far greater than the number of multiple personality disorder instances would suggest. Multiple personality disorders are regarded as relatively rare.

Behavioural explanations of multiple personality disorders

In the behaviourist's view, the basis of multiple personality disorder is an acquired response learned through the mechanism of Skinner's **operant conditioning**, the reinforcement being the relief from anxiety that occurs when one's mind drifts to more neutral subjects.

Evaluation

- Proponents of this view have been forced to rely on case histories to support their view. Unfortunately, the case histories also support other views. So, for example, a case that seems to reflect the reinforcement of forgetting, can also be interpreted as an instance of repression.
- The behavioural explanation fails to show how distractions from painful memories can grow into acquired responses.
- It does not explain why more cases do not occur.
- It cannot account for the complicated interrelationship between sub-personalities.

Self-hypnosis

Self-hypnosis enables people to induce themselves to *forget* unpleasant events. Dissociative identity disorder often occurs at 4–6 years of age, when children are most susceptible to hypnotic states.

Evaluation

There is disagreement over whether hypnosis is a special trance-like state or can be explained by normal social, attentional and cognitive processes (Miller and Bowers, 1986). This has implications for whether multiple personality disorder is, in the case of the latter, a less remarkable state than some would claim.

Case study — Kennith Bianchi

During the 1970s Kennith Bianchi brutally raped and killed ten young women in Los Angeles and left their bodies naked in full view on the side of hills. Despite incontrovertible evidence of his guilt as the Hillside Strangler, he continued to assert his innocence, causing some professionals to think he might have dissociative identity disorder. His lawyer brought in a clinical psychologist who hypnotised him and asked whether there was another part of Ken with whom he could speak. Somebody called Steve answered and said he had done all the killing. Steve also said that Ken knew nothing about the murders. A plea of not guilty was entered. A psychologist for the prosecution tried to determine whether Bianchi was simulating dissociative identity disorder. He suggested that most multiple personality patients had at least three personalities, and low and behold a third emerged! However, none of these three personalities had shown themselves prior to the case, so no independent corroboration was established. The different personalities failed to show up as different on personality tests, which is usually the case with genuine instances of the disorder. Bianchi had psychology textbooks in his room. The jury concluded that he was faking it and he was convicted.

Some people do not believe that multiple personalities actually exist.

Iatrogenesis

The theoretical explanations already described are not particularly convincing, and little research has been done in studying multiple personality disorder.

When multiple personality disorder is described as iatrogenic, it means that it has been **induced unintentionally by therapeutic practice**. The therapists create multiple personalities by suggesting their existence during therapy or eliciting them via hypnotic suggestion. The therapist, in looking for such personalities, reinforces certain patterns of behaviour by becoming more interested when their clients exhibit symptoms of dissociation.

In the 1980s Sybil (discussed above) became a well-known example of multiple personality disorder. It was clear to most observers that Sybil was troubled and eager for help. She was not, however, aware of her personalities until her therapist, Dr Wilbus, introduced her to the personalities. In a recent (1999) *Horizon* programme on the BBC, clips of the film 'Sybil' showed that the therapist tried quite hard to convince her that the personalities existed. *Horizon* then interviewed Professor Hubert Spiegel, who explained his doubts about the authenticity of multiple personality disorder as a genuine disorder. He claimed that when Dr Wilbur needed to be out of town, she asked Professor Spiegel to act as a locum. In therapy Sybil was reported to have asked Professor Spiegel 'Do you want me to be Helen?' He replied that it was not necessary but if she wanted to, she should feel free to do so. Sybil replied that if it was not necessary, she would prefer not to. He got the impression that she was being **cued** to live experiences as she recalled them, but as if she was someone else. With Professor Spiegel, however, she did not experience alter egos. As mentioned above, Sybil was troubled and eager for help and was willing to do anything. Dr Wilbur, the *Horizon* programme makers suggested, was the answer to Sybil's willingness to please. At the time the multiple personality disorder condition was almost unknown, yet almost overnight most therapists had clients with multiple personality disorder on their couches. Professor Spiegel called the clinics 'training schools' where therapists learned to uncover multiple personality disorders. This would fit rather well with a behavioural reinforcement view of multiple personality disorder. It must be said, however, that the programme also interviewed Professor Spiegel's son, a therapist who was talking about a client. He seemed totally convinced that his client, whom he knew well and for a substantial period of time, was a genuine case of multiple personality disorder and not a case of an **iatrogenic phenomenon**.

Q   Critically consider whether MPD is iatrogenic or spontaneous.   (30 marks)

1.3 CULTURE BOUND SYNDROMES

Definition

Cultural universality is the assumption behind classification systems such as the DSM and ICD. In DSM-IV some attempt was made to take into account cultural factors which they refer to as culture bound syndromes. For example, ghost sickness is the tendency to focus one's attention on death and on those who have died. This disorder is relatively common among American tribes. Another example, *latah*, is a disorder found in Malaya among uneducated middle-aged women. Certain circumstances seem to trigger a fright reaction in the person concerned, which then leads to behaviour such as repeating the words of others, uttering obscenities and doing the opposite of what other people ask.

Case studies of culture bound syndromes

> **Case study — Red Bear**
>
> Red Bear sits up wild eyed, his body drenched in sweat and every muscle tensed. He had just experienced a horrible dream and he is filled with fear and staring at his wife lying asleep. He had returned from a hunt in which he had failed to catch anything. His behaviour signalled the signs of windigo: deep depression and fear. He had dreamed of the ice monster entering his body to possess him. The form of his sleeping wife changed to a deer. With a fixed stare he takes his knife and with saliva dripping from his mouth and a strong desire to eat raw flesh he uses his knife to kill the deer (his wife). Red Bear's kinsmen rush into the wigwam; horrified at the sight they drag him out and kill him.

Red Bear was suffering from windigo, common among Algonquin hunters. Examples such as these were cited as proof of the existence of culture bound syndromes.

> **Case study — Brain fag in Tanzania**
>
> An African student, while studying for exams, had difficulty concentrating because of the feeling of pressure around his head. He was convinced that print caused the constriction in his pupils and made his brain tired. He could not remember anything of his reading. The onset was sudden and he beat his chest and could not sit still. In an agitated state he sang hymns and complained that objects around him were too bright and things often changed colour. He caused disturbances in the street and was arrested.

Some other examples of culture bound syndromes are as follows:

- *Dhat* is a syndrome found in India. It is characterised by severe anxiety and hyperchondriacal concerns with the discharge of semen; its origins lie in the Hindu belief that semen originates in blood and its loss produces mental and physical impairment.
- *Koro* is a belief amongst the Chinese that the penis is shrinking and will disappear into the abdomen, resulting in death.
- *Kuru* is a progressive psychosis and dementia, indigenous to cannibalistic tribes in New Guinea. It results from an aberrant protein which replicates itself in the brain, rather like Creutzfeldt-Jacob disease.

Be very clear on the strength of claims, because some culture bound syndromes could easily fit into **Western classification systems**, for example, *kuru*, *susto*, *latah*, *matiruku*.

Other conditions seem to be more clearly culture bound, for example *amok*, which occurs in South East Asia and only very rarely is seen outside this location.

Hall (1998) lists a total of 36 culture bound syndromes which have been identified across the globe.

Do culture bound syndromes really exist?

Are they merely **'exotic variations'** of ICD/DSM categorisations or are they really unique to certain cultures?

The central debate is between the **universalist** position espoused by Pow-Meng Yap (1974) and the **culturally-relativist** one of Wolfgang Pfeiffer (1982). Hall (1999) argued that it is difficult to draw a clear conclusion, but perhaps the case of eating disorders (such as anorexia nervosa) illustrates the debate. There are recorded cases of starving and purging going back to medieval times in the Western world, and newspaper articles about an anorexic gene appear frequently. However, food-restriction disorders and pre-occupations are rarely found outside the Western and westernising worlds (at least certainly not in the epidemic proportions currently found in much of the USA and Western Europe).

It might be advisable to recall that in dissociative identity disorder there was a sudden explosion of cases being treated in the USA, whilst the syndrome was almost unknown in Europe. Some people therefore regard it as nothing more than a North American diagnostic fad.

Q

What is meant by Culture Bound Syndromes? Discuss the arguments for and against their existence. (5+25 marks)

'CBSs are merely exotic versions of mental illnesses which are already perfectly well understood in the West. The ICD and DSM are perfectly adequate to explain their nature and possible treatment.' Discuss issues relating to CBSs such as those raised in the quotation above. (30 marks)

---

2 *Psychopathology*

2.1 SCHIZOPHRENIA

Introduction

Schizophrenia is a category of mental disorders known as the **psychotic** disorders. A psychotic disorder is defined by the effects of altering perception, thoughts or consciousness. These alterations are called hallucinations or delusions. Someone who makes an incorrect inference about reality on the basis of these alterations and believes that the inferences are real has a psychotic disorder. Symptoms of psychotic disorder also include disorganised speech and behaviour. These behaviours were formerly referred to as madness, lunacy or insanity.

Clinical characteristics

Schizophrenia is a condition characterised by the *loss of contact with reality*. Often a sufferer's capacity to perceive, process and respond to environmental stimuli becomes so impaired and distorted that he may be unable to achieve even marginal adaptive functioning.

According to DSM-IV there are five types of schizophrenia:
- *Disorganised schizophrenia*. This involves delusions, hallucinations, incoherent speech and changes in mood.
- *Catatonic schizophrenia*. Here the patient remains immobile and stares into space for hours on end.
- *Paranoid schizophrenia*. This involves a variety of delusions.
- *Undifferentiated schizophrenia*. This is a broad category, which includes patients that do not fit the regular categories.

- *Residual schizophrenia*. This includes those experiencing mild symptoms. It is a multiple and complex handicap, where a person's thoughts change dramatically. No single symptom or set of symptoms characterise all schizophrenics.

The symptoms can be separated into *three dimensions*: positive symptoms, negative symptoms and disorganisation. Positive symptoms include hallucinations and delusions; negative symptoms include lack of initiative, social withdrawal and absence of emotional responses.

The DSM-IV definition of the condition requires that the symptoms be shown for six months before meeting the diagnostic criteria. Onset usually occurs during adolescence or early adulthood and then follows a variety of patterns. There are three phases:

- *prodromal phase* — when schizophrenic symptoms, particularly the positive symptoms, are not yet prominent, but the person begins to deteriorate from previous levels of functioning
- *active phase* — schizophrenic symptoms become pronounced
- *residual phase* — a marked return to a prodromal level of functioning

Hallucinations

You need to be clear about what hallucinations are. Some studies, using imaging techniques, suggest that Broca's area is involved. This has led to the theory that people who are hallucinating are not hearing other voices but are listening to their own thoughts and cannot recognise them as their own.

Delusions

These are false beliefs, such as believing that you are God or Napoleon, or that the birds on the lawn have been sent by Martians to kill you. Those afflicted defend their beliefs with the utmost conviction, even though evidence is produced to the contrary.

Disorganised speech

Patients speak, but not much of what is said makes sense. An example of this thought disorder in schizophrenia appears in Neale and Oltmanns (1980):

Interviewer:	Have you been nervous or tense lately?
Patient:	No, I got a head of lettuce.
Interviewer:	You have got a head of lettuce? I don't understand.
Patient:	Well it's just a head of lettuce.
Interviewer:	Tell me about lettuce. What do you mean?
Patient:	Well...lettuce is a transformation of a dead cougar that suffered a relapse on the lion's toe...And he swallowed the lion and something happened. Gloria and Tommy, they're two heads and they are not whales, but they escaped with herds of vomit.

Although grammatical, the speech cannot be understood as it is without meaning. There exists a speech disturbance known as alogia. In such cases thinking is impoverished, leading to poverty of speech. Sometimes a patient has his thoughts blocked, thus interrupting speech.

Social withdrawal

Because schizophrenics have extensive **cognitive** and **emotional** difficulties, the knock-on effects in social terms are devastating. Many withdraw from socialising with others and this provides a clue (before hallucinations and delusions actually show themselves) that something is wrong. They attempt to withdraw from social situations, to minimise the stimuli that exacerbate perceptual and cognitive disruption.

Affective and emotional disturbances

Schizophrenic patients often have an absence of non-verbal emotional expressions. They seem flat, neutral, not happy, not sad. Their voices do not signal emotion; they seem autistic. Anhedonia is the name used to describe their inability to show pleasure in any activity.

Motor problems

Schizophrenics exhibit symptoms collectively called **catatonia**. They become unaware and unresponsive to their environment, remaining motionless and silent for long stretches of time. Catatonic rigidity is the term used to describe the adoption of a rigid, upright position for hours. They do this and resist all attempts to be moved. Others show catatonic posturing, by assuming awkward postures for long periods.

Biological explanations

- *Family studies*. Research indicates a **genetic** component; individuals are more at risk if schizophrenia occurs in first degree relatives than second degree relatives. The evidence is not convincing because the studies do not separate genetic and environmental events.
- *Twin studies*. Gottesmann (1999) reported a concordance rate of 47% for monozygotic twins and only 17% for dizygotic twins; some studies suggest a concordance rate of only 4% for dizygotic twins. No study has found concordance rates of 100%, which one might expect if the condition was *entirely* genetic.
- *Brain imaging*. One consistent finding from scans is that some people with schizophrenia have enlarged lateral ventricles. General conclusions from brain scanning indicate that schizophrenia is associated with patterns of neuropathology, but caution is appropriate because the changes do not appear to be unique to schizophrenia. Many patients with other disorders show similar changes. Many authors, such as Meehl (1992), suggest it is unlikely that a complex problem such as schizophrenia will be related to a single site in the brain. The imaging procedures are not even meaningful diagnostic tests.

Evaluation

One example on record illustrates how important it is to be cautious about physical causes. In a pair of twins, one brother was schizophrenic for 20 years and the other was a successful businessman. The healthy twin had ventricles five times the size of his schizophrenic brother.

Neurochemical theories

The dopamine hypothesis suggests a cause related to the dopamine pathways in the limbic areas of the brain. Excessive dopaminergic activity seems to be the culprit. Such a conclusion was derived from the effects of certain drugs on schizophrenic behaviour.

Evaluation

Most researchers in the field now believe the dopamine hypothesis was too simple. Some patients do not respond to dopamine blockers. Furthermore, the drugs take several days to work, but dopamine blockage begins immediately. Current models involve a much broader array of neurotransmitters, including serotonin. The speculation is that schizophrenia results from a complex interaction of dopamine and serotonin pathways.

Social explanations

It isn't clear what kind of non-genetic factors influence the development of schizophrenia. Much evidence has been assembled to suggest that there is a relationship between **social class** and onset of the disease. One hypothesis is that stressful circumstances or poor nutrition may cause the problem to emerge.

Evaluation

The above hypothesis presents certain difficulties. The disease itself may lead to fewer opportunities for success in employment and be responsible for being in a lower class. It is concluded that schizophrenia is to a certain extent influenced by social factors.

Family factors

Disturbed patterns of communication in families (Mischler and Waxler, 1968) have been cited as one cause of schizophrenia.

Evaluation

There is no evidence to suggest that the behaviour of family members contributes to the onset of the disease, but once the disorder is apparent, relapses are more likely in families that are high in expressed emotion.

Psychodynamic explanations

Freud thought that schizophrenia was caused by early trauma, causing the person to regress to an earlier stage of primary Narcissism, occurring in the oral stage.

Evaluation

Be aware of the limitations of the approach. It is speculative. There is not much evidence in support of it. It ignores the genetic component.

Behavioural explanations

Learning is said to play a key role in the development of schizophrenia. In particular, when people behave oddly they get labelled and conform to the label. Conforming is then reinforced with attention.

Evaluation

- There is limited support for the theory. Researchers have found that patients with schizophrenia are often capable of learning more appropriate verbal and social behaviour if hospital workers continually ignore bizarre behaviour and reinforce normal responses with cigarettes, food and attention. Perhaps, then, the bizarre behaviour was acquired through reinforcement.
- Because a treatment works, it does not necessarily explain the cause of the disorder.
- Most psychologists accept the behavioural view as a partial explanation, especially as to why the symptoms are displayed more at some times than others. It is, however, too limited to account for the origins and many symptoms of schizophrenia.

Key study — The complexities of neurotransmitter research

Researchers have come a long way in a short time towards understanding the chemistry of schizophrenia. Although we still have many questions, research technology is becoming quite advanced. Researchers at the Bronx Veterans Affairs Hospital recruited 19 male inpatients with schizophrenia to participate in a study (Kahn et al., 1993). The patients agreed to take a neuroleptic medication called Haldol (haloperidol) to learn whether — and how — it helped them. The researchers wanted to study the way the medication worked to affect dopamine and serotonin levels in the brain. The subjects selected for the study, who had shown symptoms of schizophrenia for at least five years, had not ingested alcohol or non-prescribed drugs for at least six months. The researchers controlled the patients' diets and had them fast for approximately 12 hours before sampling their cerebrospinal fluid, to ensure that their levels of HVA (a metabolite of dopamine) and 5-HIAA (a metabolite of serotonin) would not be affected by food. A sample of cerebrospinal fluid was extracted from each patient by means of a lumbar puncture. The fluid was used to assess HVA and 5-HIAA levels, which gave researchers the baseline of the two metabolites that they would later compare with the metabolite levels after the patients had received neuroleptic medication. Both before and after they were given Haldol, the patients' schizophrenic symptoms were assessed with the

Brief Psychiatric Rating Scale, so that researchers could determine whether changed metabolite levels predicted behavioural improvements.

Two weeks after the symptom assessments (during which they received no neuroleptic medication), the patients were started on a course of Haldol; five weeks later they again had a lumbar puncture and were assessed with the rating scale. HVA and 5-HIAA levels in the cerebrospinal fluid were measured by a machine called a high-performance liquid chromatograph, which uses light to identify certain chemicals. Results showed that Haldol did affect metabolites, increasing HVA concentrations in the cerebrospinal fluid. This means that dopamine was produced, but was prevented by the Haldol from going to the receptors — as if you blocked your letter-box and the postman threw your post directly into the bin. However, researchers found improvements in schizophrenic symptoms only in patients who had more HVA than 5-HIAA. This suggests that blocking dopamine may not itself reduce schizophrenic symptoms. Rather, you may need to block both dopamine and serotonin, but you may need to block more dopamine than serotonin. Although this study does not answer every question about neurotransmitters and schizophrenia, you should now have an idea of how difficult, but ultimately rewarding (many of the patients improved!), research can be in this highly technical area of schizophrenia.

Compare and contrast a biological and a psychological explanation of schizophrenia. (30 marks)

2.2 DEPRESSION

Depression refers to prolonged and fundamental disturbance of **mood** and **emotion**. It is a pervasive and sustained emotional state that colours perceptions, thoughts and behaviour.

The clinical characteristics are:
- a sad, depressed feeling, often on the verge of tears
- poor appetite; not eating well or healthily
- insomnia; not sleeping well and being restless at night
- lethargy; not feeling like doing anything vigorous
- loss of interest in things previously regarded as pleasurable
- a negative self concept; not feeling good about oneself — always seeing the bad side of things you do
- recurrent thoughts of suicide; continually thinking about ending one's life

Although the symptoms described above may be familiar to you, those who meet the DSM-IV criteria experience many symptoms at once and they are extremely severe. These must persist for at least two weeks.

Psychological explanations
- Early in development, because of over and/or under-gratification, the individual **sticks** in the oral phase, thereby developing excessive dependence on others for maintaining self-esteem.
- When an individual loses a loved one, the process of **introjection** occurs. This involves incorporating (in the case of death) the lost loved one into oneself. Because you harbour unconscious angry feelings towards those you love, introjection involves turning anger in on oneself. In the case of no actual death, this can all occur symbolically.
- **Mourning** follows introjection and this involves separating oneself from the bonds that introjection has imposed. This occurs by recalling memories of the departed. If mourning fails to work itself out, the person continues to be angry with him/herself and continues to castigate him/herself for the faults perceived in the loved one. The anger continues to be turned inwards.

Evaluation

- There is not much evidence and the little there is suggests many confounding variables. The problem is that the psychodynamic approach is complex. Theorising is relatively broad based and some predictions that have been investigated by psychologists don't have much support. If we look at dependent personality styles which predispose one to depression, we find a cluster of personality traits that are classified as dependent. However people's dependency rises and falls with levels of depression. This suggests that it is a concomitant of depression and not a cause.
- Beck's analysis of thoughts and dreams of his patients found statements of loss and failure and not hostility. On the other hand, Weisman found that depressed people were often hostile to those close to them.

Behavioural theory

Lewinsohn suggested that depression was a result of reduction in the level of **reinforcement** caused by the loss of an important relationship. He also saw depressed people as being less socially active. This leads to concern from friends, which reinforces depressed behaviour.

Evaluation

There is not much hard evidence and it seems too simple a model. Depressed people report having fewer pleasant experiences. However, while depression might follow a reduction, it could precede a reduction in those experiences, meaning that people who are depressed lower their participation in reinforcing events.

Cognitive explanations

For Beck it isn't unhappy feelings that produce depression — *it is unhappy thoughts which make one feel depressed*. Depressed people distort what happens to them in the direction of self-blame and catastrophe. This continual interpretation of events as negative, or continual recall of unpleasant events, leads to a feeling of depression.

Seligman chose to explain depression in terms of **learned helplessness**. Be familiar with his experiment on dogs who were restrained so that they could not escape shock. Eventually they gave up. People who are depressed seem to have given up on life. Seligman's learned helplessness hypothesis doesn't explain why some people get depressed and others don't. In order to account for this, Seligman argued that different people react differently to situations because of the interpretation they give to events. In some people, failing an exam would be an unmitigated disaster and they would see themselves as stupid. Such people would be more likely to be depressed than those who attributed failure to the fact that the exam was unduly difficult. In this case attributions enter into the picture, i.e. how you think about events. Attributions can be internal (I am thick) or external (the exam was unfair). They can also be stable and unstable as well as global and specific. Attributions that are internal and stable are more likely to lead to depression.

According to Beck, as a result of poor interpersonal experiences, a person acquires a negative schema, which leads to distortions of thought called faulty inferences.

There are two mechanisms that he describes: the cognitive triad and errors in logic.

- The **cognitive triad** consists of negative thoughts about self, ongoing experiences and the future.

> ### Case study — Stella
> Stella believed that her tennis abilities had deteriorated (negative view of self). She misinterpreted praise as an indication of how bad she was (negative experience). She believed that no one would ever want to play with her again (negative view of future).

- **Errors in logic**. According to Beck, people who are depressed make five different logical errors in thinking that darken their experience.
  - (1) *Arbitrary inference*. They draw a conclusion when there is little evidence to prove it. A man walking in the park fails to secure a woman's eye contact. She is admiring the flowers, but he concludes that the woman is avoiding him.
  - (2) *Selective abstraction*. They focus on one negative detail in a situation instead of the larger context.
  - (3) *Overgeneralisation*. They draw a broad conclusion from a single insignificant event.
  - (4) *Personalisation*. They incorrectly view themselves as the cause of negative events.
  - (5) *Automatic thoughts*. A steady flow of unpleasant thoughts repeatedly reminds them of their perceived inadequacies.

In this view, unlike Freud's, we are a victim of our thoughts, not our feelings.

Evaluation

- Some studies suggest that depression leads to negative thoughts.
- Other researchers, like Hoeksema, have found attributional style to be predictive of depression.
- Cognitive therapy seems reasonably effective.

Biological explanations

A key explanation of depression is the **amine hypothesis**, which involves the catecholamines (noradrenaline, adrenaline, dopamine) and indoleamines (serotonin, histamine).

(1) Catecholamine hypothesis

- **Noradrenaline** is a neurotransmitter which is released into the synaptic gap. After the next cell is activated, the excess neurotransmitters in the gap have to be cleared. This is done by enzymes breaking down the excess and by reuptake, where the transmitters are returned to their sites on the cell sending the message.
- **Reuptake**. When reuptake is too efficient, there is too little noradrenaline in the neural environment and people feel depressed.
- Tricylic antidepressants retard reuptake and are used to relieve depression.
- **Breakdown**. When breakdown is too efficient, there is too little noradrenaline in the neural environment and people feel depressed.
- **Monoamine oxidase** inhibitors retard breakdown.

Evidence for catecholamine hypothesis

- Iproniazid was a drug given for tuberculosis. It did not cure tuberculosis but made the patients feel very well. Iproniazid is a monoamine oxidase inhibitor. It stops the breakdown of noradrenaline, thus making more noradrenaline available.
- Reserpine was a drug given for high blood pressure. It made people depressed and suicidal. Imipramine, related to reserpine, is a tricyclic antidepressant which blocks reuptake, thus making more noradrenaline available.
- Be aware that drugs have a number of effects other than on noradrenaline, so interpretation is difficult.

(2) Indoleamine hypothesis

- The claim here is that the unavailability of serotonin is the cause of depression.
- The monoamine oxidase inhibitors and tricyclics that keep noradrenaline available are 'dirty' drugs; they also affect serotonin levels and are therefore non-specific.
- Fluoxetine (Prozac) inhibits reuptake of serotonin without affecting other transmitters.
- Though effective, it can produce nausea, insomnia, nervousness and suicidal thoughts.

Evidence
- Research is in the early stages.
- As Eysenck (1999) points out, 'Aspirin can cure a headache, but that does not mean that an absence of aspirin caused the headache'.

Genetic factors

Gershon claimed that the rate of depression in relatives is three or four times higher than in the general population. Many theorists argue that we inherit a predisposition to depression. Blehar claims that close relatives have a 4–25% chance of developing the same disorder. There are contradictory findings in genetic studies, which raises questions about the validity of the studies.

Be aware of problems associated with twin studies.

Q **'Biological explanations give us a full and complete explanation of depression.' Discuss.**   (30 marks)

2.3 ANXIETY DISORDERS

In DSM-IV, anxiety disorders are broken down into five subdivisions:
- *Phobias*. A phobia is an exaggerated fear of relatively harmless objects, e.g. spiders.
- *General anxiety*. A pervasive feeling of anxiety is best described as 'being stressed out', yet there is no apparent stressor.
- *Panic disorder*. An abrupt surge of intense anxiety occurs spontaneously and unpredictably.
- *Post-traumatic stress disorder*. After having a highly traumatic experience, person feels a sudden intense fear, helplessness or horror; this may occur after a short or long time.
- *Obsessive compulsive disorder*. People with obsessive behaviour are unable to get an idea out of their minds — they are preoccupied. People with compulsive behaviour feel compelled to perform a particular act or series of acts over and over again, e.g. repetitive hand washing.

Anxiety is at the heart of what we used to call **neurosis,** which was heavily investigated by Freud who saw it as a fundamental motivating force. The behaviour resulting from different forms of neurosis varied greatly, from the fear of avoidance in phobias to the urge to perform rituals over and over again as in the obsessive compulsive disorder.

In Freud's view the observed symptoms varied, but they all reflect the same underlying problem of **repressed anxiety**. Therefore the wide variety of symptoms was not a problem to him.

Evaluation

Many psychologists questioned Freud's assumption, and in DSM-III the category neurosis was nearly dropped. In DSM-III R and IV, neurosis is now called anxiety disorder and is subdivided as indicated above.

Phobic disorders

The term phobic comes from the Greek word *Phobos*, the God who put fear into the enemy. The suffix phobia is preceded by a Greek word which describes the fear. For example, **claustrophobia** is the fear of closed places, **agoraphobia** is fear of public places and **acrophobia** is fear of heights. There are literally hundreds of descriptors and the problem arises when one jumps from the **label** to the **aetiology**. Just because you have a name for something does not mean you have a cause, though many people make the mistake of thinking that if you label something, the diagnosis includes shedding light on its cause.

Explanations for phobic disorders include psychodynamic, behavioural and physiological theories.

(1) Psychodynamic theory

Freud believed that phobias are a defence against anxiety when sexual impulses of the id are repressed.

Be familiar with his famous case of little Hans, who became phobic about horses. Freud argued that the features of the horse's face that resembled the father's were symbolic of the father. Hans is supposed to have been frightened of being castrated by the father because of the sexual urges Hans had for his mother (the Oedipal conflict). By being frightened of horses and thereby staying at home, Hans achieves the aim of being with his love object and displacing his anxiety onto horses.

Evaluation

- There is not much evidence in support of the theory. When Hans's mother was changing him, Hans asked his mother to touch him and the mother responded rather punishingly by threatening to cut off his 'widdler'. The fear of castration was meant to come from the father, even though it was the mother who threatened it! In this view phobias are a defence against anxiety that is produced by repressed id impulses. By avoiding the feared object, the person avoids dealing with repressed childhood conflicts.
- Therapy based around the approach has not been successful.

(2) Behavioural theory

Watson and Rayner (1920) demonstrated that through **classical conditioning** one could produce fear of a previously neutral object. They did this with the now famous case of Albert, an 11 month-old boy. Albert showed no signs of fear of a white rat. Whenever he reached for the rat, they introduced a loud noise which caused Albert to take fright and cry. Albert then became very disturbed at the sight of the rat. Make sure you understand what the **unconditioned stimulus** and **conditioned stimulus** are in this experiment, so that you can easily apply the classical conditioning paradigm to this case.

Mowrer explained why phobias are resistant to extinction, claiming that phobias were acquired by classical conditioning and maintained through instrumental conditioning. The reward for avoidance of the feared object is fear reduction. Make sure you understand the difference between classical (Pavlovian) conditioning and instrumental conditioning (Skinnerian).

Evidence

There is evidence for the theory that some fears are developed through conditioning and fear reduction can be achieved through **systematic desensitisation**, a technique derived from behavioural theory.

Evaluation

- Some puzzles remain. People are less likely to be phobic about dangerous cars than harmless spiders. For evolutionary reasons we seem to be predisposed to be fearful of some objects; this violates a fundamental assumption of classical conditioning, i.e. the 'equipotentiality' of stimuli.
- Keuthen (1990) found that half of a sample of phobics could not remember having an upsetting experience with the feared object.

(3) Physiological basis

The term to investigate is autonomic lability and stability. According to Eysenck (1957), our readiness to be aroused is **genetic**.

Genetic studies (Harris, 1983) showed that first degree relatives are more at risk than others. The evidence is equivocal because relatives share genes and situations.

One study of nearly 4,000 pairs of adult twins attempted to evaluate the separate effects of genetic and environmental factors in anxiety. There was strong evidence of a genetic factor, but a weaker family environment factor.

Evaluation

At present there is a lack of solid evidence concerning how genetic factors shape human personality. However, some clues are being uncovered. Lesch (1996) found that there was a modest link between anxiety-related behaviour and a gene that controls the brain's ability to use serotonin, which is involved in anxiety.

Obsessive compulsive disorder

Those with obsessive compulsive disorder have recurrent and unwanted thoughts that cause anxiety and have a need to carry out repetitive actions to reduce anxiety.

According to DSM-IV, a diagnosis of obsessive compulsive disorder is appropriate when obsessions or compulsions feel excessive, or unreasonable, intrusive and inappropriate. These are very time consuming and interfere with normal functioning.

> **Case study — Georgia**
>
> Georgia's obsessive concern with cleanliness forced her to take as many as three showers a day, one in the morning, one before supper, and one before going to bed; on hot days the number would rise dramatically. She was aware of the effect she was having on her family and friends, but when she tried to alter her behaviour she became very nervous and felt she was losing her mind.

Explanations for obsessive compulsive disorder include psychodynamic, behavioural, cognitive and biological theories.

(1) Psychodynamic explanations

According to psychodynamic explanations, three **ego defence mechanisms** are common in obsessive compulsive disorder: isolation, undoing and reaction formation.

- *Isolation*. People isolate, disown undesirable and unwanted thoughts and experience them as foreign intrusions.
- *Undoing*. People engage in undoing, perform acts that cancel out their undesirable impulses — by washing their hands ritually, for example, to symbolically wash out their unacceptable id impulses.
- *Reaction formation*. People who apply reaction formation assume a lifestyle that opposes their unacceptable impulses. A nun may live a life of devotion and kindness to others to counteract unacceptable aggressive impulses.

Evaluation

There is evidence that people with obsessive compulsive disorder have rigid and demanding parents, but most of the studies are poorly designed.

(2) Behavioural explanations

These propose that *initial* compulsions occur randomly. In an anxiety-provoking situation they just happen to wash their hands or dress in a particular way. When the threat lifts it is then reinforced.

Evaluation

- After repeated associations the people believe that their actions brought them luck. The actions become the main way of avoiding anxiety.

- Why don't more people develop obsessive compulsive disorders? Many people have random anxiety circumstance but don't develop obsessive compulsive disorder.
- Rachman has shown that compulsions do appear to be rewarded by a reduction in anxiety, as do rituals; but this does not address the origins of the behaviour.

(3) Biological differences
Genetic influences are indicated by studies such as Comings (1987), who found that people with obsessive compulsive disorder often have **first-degree** relatives with some sort of anxiety disorder.

Biological theorists believe that two factors contribute to the disorder: low activity of the neurotransmitter **serotonin**; and abnormal functioning in the brain's orbital region and caudate nuclei — antidepressant drugs, which *raise serotonin levels*, appear to be effective in this condition.

Evaluation
- In the genetic studies it was found that, in half of the subjects, the family members had developed ritualistic behaviour, indicating that learning may be equally important.
- In the neurochemical studies, the precise roles of the biological factors are not fully understood. This is indicated by the fact that of those having treatment, over half do not show any clinically meaningful improvement.

Q Discuss one or more psychological explanations of anxiety disorders. Assess the extent to which research has supported psychological explanations. (15+15 marks)

---

3 *Treating mental disorders*

3.1 BIOLOGICAL (SOMATIC) THERAPIES

Biological (somatic) approaches are those based on drugs used by psychiatrists favouring the medical model.

Chemotherapy
Three main types of drug are used:
- **Neuroleptics** are **tranquillisers** or **antipsychotics** and are mainly used to control and lessen the effects of schizophrenia. Pay attention to how these operate. Mostly they work by blocking D2 and D3 dopamine receptors. Note that there are also atypical neuroleptics which act on D4 receptors in the brain. Although these can be effective, they do have side-effects, such as neuroleptic malignant syndrome and extrapyramidal symptoms. Return to the section on schizophrenia (Section 2.1) and examine what is meant by negative and positive symptoms; neuroleptics reduce positive symptoms, but are not very effective on negative symptoms. They *do not cure* schizophrenia but they do relieve the symptoms. Note that there may be other conditions in society (e.g. poor housing or nutrition) which exacerbate the symptoms, thus reducing the effectiveness of the drugs and increasing the likelihood of relapses.
- **Antidepressants**. The amine hypothesis suggests that the biogenic amines are involved in depression. Biogenic amines include the catecholamines (noradrenaline (norepinephrine), adrenaline (epinephrine) and dopamine) and the indoleamines (serotonin and histamine). You need to be aware of the process of neural transmission, especially the breakdown of noradrenaline in the synaptic gap and its **reuptake**. Drugs called tricyclics and monoamine oxidase inhibitors affect these two processes

and thus reduce depression. You must be aware of which affects reuptake and which affects **breakdown** of noradrenaline. The drugs have been called dirty drugs, because of their blanket approach (they affect all neurotransmitters, not just noradrenaline); and their consequent side-effects have led to the use of more specific anti-depressants called SSRIs (selective serotonin reuptake inhibitors). The SSRI Prozac (fluoxetine) has a much more specific action on the reuptake of serotonin, with negligible effects on other transmitters. In some cases, it too has some unpleasant side-effects.

- **Anxiolytic drugs** are used in the treatment of anxiety. They work by depressing the nervous system, especially the sympathetic area of the autonomic nervous system.

Evaluation

- Although effective, neuroleptics (major tranquillisers) have many unpleasant side-effects. These include neuroleptic malignant syndrome which produces delirium, coma and sometimes death, and the extrapyramidal syndrome which involves restlessness and uncontrollable shuffling.
- The anxiolytic drugs (minor tranquillisers) also have side-effects, such as rebound anxiety. They are addictive too.
- Antidepressants take time to exert their effects, which is not much help for those who are suicidal.
- Some drug treatment can be remarkably successful (although sometimes only in the short term). For example, Prozac has been shown to be effective in 65–75% of cases when it is used. This would appear strongly to support the case that, where drug treatment is successful, biochemical factors are important in the aetiology of mental illnesses. However, some psychologists argue that the chemical imbalance is an effect of the mental illness rather than its cause (i.e. the mental illness comes before the chemical imbalance). Furthermore, many drug therapies are used in conjunction with other treatments (such as counselling), so it is impossible to identify which one is effective. Drugs can have serious side-effects and there can be acute problems of patient dependence.

Electroconvulsive therapy (ECT)

In ECT a shock is applied for up to one second to either one or both sides of the brain. This produces a general convulsion which lasts for approximately one minute. Typically, treatments are given two or three times per week for three or four weeks. Originally used on schizophrenics, it is sometimes used to treat depression.

Evaluation

In a study by Persad, depression was shown to be lifted in 80–90% of cases, even on individuals who had not responded to antidepressants. It works rapidly and thus has become a first choice for those who are suicidal. There are some drawbacks, such as disruption to recent memories. Nobody knows why it works, but those backing the amine hypothesis suggest that it effects levels of neurotransmitters. The shock has such a pervasive effect that it would be difficult to pinpoint. Davidson and Neale (1994) point out that there is an increase in neurotransmitters, but these return to normal in 7–14 days, just when the depression lifts.

Psychosurgery

This involves operations on the brain which are intended to ameliorate mental states causing distress. Originally used with aggressive schizophrenics. the patients had leucotomy/prefrontal lobotomy operations. Transorbital lobotomy involves the use of an instrument shaped like an ice-pick which is introduced into the brain via the upper eyelid until it reaches the orbital bone; then, with a mallet, small taps are made, destroying tissue in the brain.

Evaluation

- The leucotomy procedure seemed to be successful in reducing aggressive behaviour in unmanageable patients.
- Reasons for abandonment: even today it isn't clear what the function of the frontal lobes is. Outcomes were inconsistent and the procedure was irreversible.
- There were severe side-effects, such as apathy and epilepsy.
- The operations were carried out without consent; the law has now been changed and consent is required.

Outline the use and mode of action of chemotherapy and ECT as treatments for mental disorders. Assess issues surrounding the use of such treatments. (15+15 marks)

3.2 BEHAVIOURAL THERAPIES

Return to the section on anxiety disorders (Section 2.3) and study **phobias**; you will recall that phobias have been described as developing through the process of classical conditioning. This involves a neutral stimulus being paired with a stimulus that ordinarily causes fear and anxiety. Read up the classical case where Watson demonstrated the acquisition of fear in a child by artificially pairing a white rat with a startlingly loud noise, thereby inducing a fear of rats. The whole point about behaviour therapy is the assumption that if you can acquire a fear through learning or conditioning, you can unlearn the fear through the process of extinction.

One of the problems in explaining the acquisition of fear in this way was the problem of **extinction** being difficult or impossible to bring about. Mowrer (1947) came up with his two factor solution, in which he claimed that fears or phobias were acquired by classical conditioning but were maintained by a second factor — instrumental conditioning. A behaviour is acquired in this manner when it is followed by some **reward**. In Mowrer's account, fear reduction is achieved by avoiding the phobic object, and so avoidance is rewarded by diminishing fear.

Therapies based on classical conditioning

(1) Flooding

This involves **sudden confrontation** with the feared object. For example, if you were frightened of spiders, the treatment would involve placing you in a room full of spiders until your fear disappeared (extinction).

Evaluation

Evidence suggests reasonably good success rates; flooding is more ecologically valid and better maintained when the treated patient actually encounters the phobic object. However, there are **ethical questions** surrounding the procedure of so dramatically exposing phobic patients to their fears and inducing such high levels of anxiety, albeit for the long-term benefit of the patient.

(2) Systematic desensitisation

This involves **gradual exposure** to the feared object and also an element of operant conditioning, i.e. reward for facing up to a 'watered down' element of the feared object and attempting to relax while being exposed to such an element. For example, the first exposure might be to a toy spider, then a small dead spider, then a larger dead spider, then a tiny live spider, and so on until total relaxation is achieved while handling the feared object. Each achievement is rewarded with praise from the therapist. Relaxation is an opposite response to fear, so relaxation in this case is described as involving reciprocal inhibition.

Implosion therapy is like systematic desensitisation, but the feared object is **imagined** as vividly as possible.

Evaluation

Wolpe (1958) and many others have reported good success rates using systematic desensitisation. The therapy relies upon the patient's ability to learn the **relaxation techniques** (which rules out a few), and their preparedness to confront their fears (which all but the most phobic tend to be willing to do for the potential release from the debilitating fear). Clearly the range of disorders systematic desensitisation can be applied to is restrictive; it is solely for treatment of phobia (but that itself is not a major problem, since other disorders have other therapies).

(3) Aversion therapy

Here the point is to make someone feel uncomfortable about a behaviour that is pleasant but undesirable. Anti-alcohol tablets count as a common example. They cause the person to vomit when consuming alcohol; the idea is that alcohol will become undesirable via its association with being ill.

This is a treatment for addictions and unwanted dependencies, such as serious drug addictions as well as alcoholism and nicotine dependency. The maladaptive behaviour (taking the drug, drinking alcohol, smoking cigarettes, etc.) is repeatedly paired with an unpleasant stimulus (such as an emetic substance, which induces nausea and vomiting). This creates a negative association with the craved substance and leads to avoidance of it. This can be regarded as **classical conditioning** in that an innate response to the emetic is transferred through association onto the target stimulus (alcohol, etc.). It can also be regarded as having operant conditioning properties, since the vomiting becomes, through association, regarded as a consequence of the target stimulus.

Evaluation

The therapy has been empirically supported as being effective in many cases. For example, Meter and Chesser (1970) found that over half of their patients abstained from the unwanted substance for at least a year after treatment. However, the treatment can be criticised as being particularly distressing and ethically dubious, and drop-out rates can be high.

Therapies based on operant (instrumental) conditioning

In classical conditioning described above, the behaviours of concern were involuntary behaviours under the control of the autonomic nervous system. In operant conditioning the behaviours being changed are **voluntary behaviours** under the control of the somatic nervous system. The assumption in operant conditioning is that, if a behaviour is being carried out frequently, it must be because the behaviour is being reinforced. There are two ways of increasing a behaviour: **positive** reinforcement and **negative** reinforcement (not to be confused with punishment). There are two ways of **decreasing** a behaviour: **punishment** and **extinction**.

The trick is to be very specific about the **target behaviour** to be changed by describing it operationally (if you can count it, it is operational). For example, if a teacher says to a psychologist that a troublesome child is being disruptive, this is not specific because the child may be disruptive in a variety of ways. Specific examples would include: kicking someone else, getting out of his or her seat, talking out of turn. The idea is to assess the frequency of occurrence and try to work out the reinforcer that is maintaining the behaviour, so that this can be manipulated to change the behaviour.

> **Case study — Behaviour modification**
>
> In a classic study with teachers of disruptive pupils, teachers were asked to count the number of times pupils got out of their seats. In this behaviour modification exercise, such counting over three days produced a baseline level of out-of-seat behaviour. The teachers were then told to tell the children to get back into their seats more frequently; what was discovered was that the children's out-of-seat behaviour increased. This illustrated clearly to the teachers that their own behaviour directly influenced the pupils' behaviour. How? What followed when a child got out of his seat was an instruction to sit down. Getting out of their seat therefore attracted attention (positive reinforcement). The attention was the reward for the out-of-seat behaviour. To change the behaviour, teachers were asked to praise in-seat behaviour and ignore out-of-seat behaviour. After a few days the children were much more likely to stay in their seats because they were being rewarded for a behaviour incompatible with out-of-seat behaviour.

Positive reinforcement is therefore something which follows a behaviour that *leads to an increase in that behaviour.* Assume a student is always late on an assignment. Teachers may go out of their way to praise those that are on time. This can be done informally with verbal praise or formally on a token system. Each student with an assignment on time gets a star next to his or her name; after reaching a specified number of stars, these can be exchanged for a treat like a day out at the zoo.

Negative reinforcement also leads to an *increase* of behaviour. This involves the application of an aversive situation which is *withdrawn* when the target behaviour increases. Telling a child he has to stay in his room with no television until his room is tidy is an example. As soon as tidying behaviour increases, the child is free from being restricted to his room and is also positively reinforced by access to television. *Do not mistake this for punishment*, which leads to a decrease in behaviour. This mistake is common, so one more example of negative reinforcement will be given. Nagging is something continuous and aversive. In this example, children nag for a McDonald's burger. As soon as burger-eating behaviour increases, the nagging stops. A child crying is another example of an aversive stimulus. As soon as the adult's picking up behaviour and cuddling behaviour increase, the child stops crying. Remember that negative and positive reinforcers lead to an increase in the target behaviour.

Punishment is an aversive behaviour that leads to a decrease in behaviour (Cowart and Whitley, 1971).

Extinction is also designed to *decrease* the occurrence of behaviour. Tantrums are a clear example. When a child has a tantrum it usually *gains attention* (it is negatively reinforcing you to give it attention, as are other annoyed onlookers). To change this behaviour through extinction, the parent would be instructed to ignore the behaviour — in other words pretend that nothing is happening. Don't even look at the child. When this first occurs the tantrum will get worse, as predicted by extinction schedules of reinforcement that have been studied in the laboratory. However, although this is a lengthy and difficult procedure to carry out, it is effective and long-lasting as long as you can control the reinforcer. If you let up at all you will wind up with worse tantrums than you started with!

General evaluation of the behavioural model

For

- The underlying theory is extensive and widely supported. The therapies have also achieved some high success rates.

- Patients arguably feel less judgementally labelled by being described as having learned maladaptive behaviours as opposed to being 'mentally ill'.
- The model is sensitive to individual differences and social and cultural context, since the individual behavioural history of patients has shaped their maladaptive behaviour.

Against
- Many of the therapies can be challenged as being distressing and unethical.
- Since only behaviour is addressed, it has been argued that only the symptoms are treated, not the underlying problem. Thoughts and feelings are not considered.
- The model focuses on the influences of environment and learning, yet ignores the genetic element of many disorders (e.g. schizophrenia).
- The model and treatment approaches are reductionist and limited in scope.

Much of the supporting evidence and theory is more appropriate to animals than humans.

3.3 ALTERNATIVES TO BIOLOGICAL AND BEHAVIOURAL THERAPIES

Psychoanalysis

In the Freudian view, hurtful social experiences early in one's development lead to **repressing** the memory of such circumstances via defence mechanisms. These early conflicts are pushed into the unconscious, where they operate to drive behaviour. Thus abnormal behaviour is the expression of the conflicts that occurred early in life. It is not just behaviour that needs changing in therapy, but resolution of the *underlying conflicts*. Psychoanalysis is about uncovering unconscious conflicts and bringing them into consciousness, so that a patient can gain insight into the real causes of his behaviour.

Free association

In free association the patient is asked to say anything that comes into his head, no matter how trivial. This is because the ego acts as a censor, preventing long-forgotten painful experiences from reaching consciousness. In free association the censor can be caught off guard. It takes several sessions before anything significant is revealed. During the analysis the therapist tries to remain **neutral** by not judging the attitudes of the patient and by not being emotionally involved. The analyst is a **sounding board**, who clarifies what is said and tries to interpret it in terms of repressed conflicts. The analyst may draw attention to resistance because, as Freud pointed out, what is unsaid is very important.

Transference

When the interpretation is complete, the repressed conflicts are available for manipulation by the therapist. This involves **displacing** the emotion on to the analyst, who now becomes the object of the emotions. Depending on the nature of the conflict, the feeling may be positive and loving or negative and hostile. This exploration of the transference relationship brings the feelings into the open and the conflicts are thus resolved. The feelings associated with transference are the same for men and women. These are attachment to the analyst, overestimation of the analyst's qualities, and jealousy of those in contact with the analyst. Freud believed that psychoanalysis was ineffective with schizophrenia and depression because patients with these disorders could not be induced to transfer.

Insight

Once patients understand the roots of their conflicts, they have insight and must now deal with the conflicts rationally. The conflicts are worked through so that defence mechanisms don't take over and repress the conflict.

Psychoanalysis is expensive and intensive; however, there are alternatives, described as psychoanalytically oriented psychotherapies, which are briefer and more flexible.

They do not concentrate solely on past events, but also deal with **current** interpersonal experiences. There have been changes to modern psychoanalysis, where it is acknowledged that environmental events are as important as inner conflicts.

Evaluation

Eysenck made an attempt to evaluate its effectiveness and came to the conclusion that it is as effective as no therapy at all. But Eysenck counted those dropping out (sample attrition) as being not cured. When the data were reanalysed taking this into account, the success rate climbed from the 40% level to 60%. One of the problems with looking at efficacy of treatment is that traditional experimental designs do not lend themselves to the assessment of effectiveness. Using experimental designs results in treatment that is very different from what actually happens. This has prompted Seligman to suggest that a consumer reporting methodology may be a much more valid way of assessing effectiveness.

Cognitive behaviour therapy

Supporters of this type of therapy believe that the way we think about things can lead to us being anxious or depressed and that a change in thinking can lead to a change in how we feel about ourselves. Modelling is an example. Some phobias are treated by showing a patient that handling the object they fear is easy. The patient then has a turn. What changes is what Bandura calls self-efficacy. Being able to handle the feared object after seeing someone else do it leads to a re-evaluation of the degree to which the patient believed he could cope.

Rational emotive therapy

This was developed in 1950 by Ellis. It attempts to help people find flaws in their thinking. Say that a person invites some people for dinner, but those invited were already doing something on the day in question. Faulty thinking would lead the person doing the inviting to conclude that the refusal meant that those invited did not like him. Ellis concluded that the two most frequently held faulty cognitions were the belief that one is worthless unless one can do everything perfectly and that one must be approved of and loved by everyone. These beliefs place impossible demands on a person holding them and so they lead to anxiety and depression.

Therapy is about helping the people to see their irrational thoughts by questioning them: 'Who says I have to be perfect?', so that eventually, rather than measuring themselves against impossible standards, they come to see that failures are not disasters but are merely unfortunate.

Evaluation

Rational emotive therapy is apparently effective for some disorders, such as social phobia, but with others, such as agoraphobia, it is not effective. It is effective for people who are self-demanding and who feel that they are not living up to their standards.

'The key issue concerning behavioural treatments is that they work. All other considerations are secondary.' Discuss. (30 marks)

Discuss alternatives to biological and behavioural therapies for treating mental disorders. (30 marks)

Issues in psychology

1.1 GENDER AND CULTURE BIAS

Bias in psychology occurs when the ideas or views of some cultures or societies, or parts of those groups, have an **unfair representation**. This can occur *throughout* the process of constructing knowledge. It can affect choice and conduct of research projects and infiltrate the collection of data and the creation and formulation of theories.

There are two major types of bias — **gender** and **cultural**, the most common forms of which are known as **sexism** and **ethnocentrism**. Both forms have significantly infiltrated psychology.

Implications of bias in psychology

The positivist view of science claims that we can make unbiased, neutral observations of reality and create impartial theories about the world. The best known attempt to implement this view in psychology was radical behaviourism, although any attempt to argue that psychology is a science will tend to reflect these ideas.

Max Weber (1904) presented an early and powerful argument for the impossibility of a 'value freedom' in the social and psychological sciences. He argued that all knowledge about human behaviour was shaped by and embedded in cultural values and beliefs. Humanistic psychology closely reflects this view in arguing that the goal of psychology is to enhance understanding within a shared cultural context.

Gender bias

Two major types of argument have come from feminist psychologists such as Gilligan, Kitzinger, Unger and Crawford. They argue the following:

- Women should be studied in their own right — in other words, an explicitly female psychology should be developed. Examples of this might include the development of female approaches to counselling and psychotherapy described by McLeod (1999). This aims to correct a bias of content.
- Psychology should acknowledge and act on its position as an agent of **social change** for women. This links explicitly to the political goals of feminism in relation to the role of women in society. It also explicitly links to arguments about science in general being a male-dominated activity in a male-dominated society. This is a response to an important bias in approach and in the value system.

Alpha and beta bias

Alpha bias is the idea that there are real *differences* in abilities and personality between the genders. Wilson (1994) claimed that these views are substantiated by psychometric testing and the theoretical framework of sociobiology. He writes, 'these differences are deep rooted, based in biology and are not easily dismantled by social engineering'. The evidence for test differences should of course be considered in the light of the difficulties in devising 'fair' tests, described below.

Beta bias occurs in attempts to provide *universal* psychological theories. It occurs when implicitly male theories are indiscriminately applied to both genders. Such theories are often based on all-male samples in research carried out by male psychologists. They include Kohlberg's account of moral development and Erikson's lifespan psychology.

Gender bias in research

Feminist psychology alleges that female oriented research topics have been discriminated against at the stages of **proposal**, **financial** and **resource support and publication**, reflecting male bias. So studies of the menopause, the menstrual cycle and childbirth are not only not chosen but also often not financially supported by male dominated funding agencies and research councils (Denmark, 1988). Feminists also allege that there is a **hidden** male bias in research, with especially the (usually male) gender of the researcher and the research team often going **unreported**.

Gender bias in theory

In abnormal psychology, Tarvis (1993) has argued that the 'normality' and 'sanity' enshrined in psychiatric diagnostic guides such as DSM reflect a male normality — as it is in fact the consensual view of predominately male psychiatrists in a male-dominated society. Thus in a draft of the DSM, the behaviour of someone that stayed at home to care for others and turned down career opportunities was described as self-defeating personality disorder. This in turn was a retreat from the original masochistic personality (Gross and McIlveen, 2001).

Gould's *The Mismeasure of Man* (1981) reports a similar bias against women in definitions of intelligence and selection of items in test construction.

Gilligan's (1982) critique, *In a Different Voice*, cites Erikson's life span psychology (1950), Kohlberg's view of moral development (1969) and Levinson's *Seasons of a Man's Life* as clear and important examples of **beta bias**. In the case of moral development, both Kohlberg and Freud argued that females were morally inferior, not being capable of achieving the male norm.

Classic examples — three psychological studies showing both gender and cultural bias

Freudian theory, paradoxically, was based largely on interviews with young Viennese *women*. However, the theory discusses childhood from a predominately male view, with the Electra complex receiving far less treatment than the original male Oedipal complex. Female analysts, from Anna Freud to Melanie Klein and Karen Horney, have worked since to rectify this bias. Freudian theories also implicitly assume a two-parent nuclear Western family. Early anthropologists such as Margaret Mead were quick to highlight and research the cross-cultural variety of childhood.

Intelligence testing was used in the USA to operate the Immigration Restriction Act of 1924. Those who scored badly were barred from entry. Gould (1981) suggests that the tests seem to have discriminated against millions of Jews and Southern, Central and Eastern Europeans through use of culturally suspect language and test items. In the state of Virginia from 1924 until as late as 1972, 'low IQ' women were sterilised compulsorily as a form of eugenics — an attempt to implement selective breeding to 'improve the human gene pool'. If one has doubts about cultural fairness and potential bias of these tests, these results are truly disturbing.

Diagnostic bias seems endemic in psychiatry. Consistently more women than men are diagnosed with neurotic disorders (Brown and Harris, 1978), while diagnoses of schizophrenia are vastly more common amongst the working class and blacks in the UK. Bias against minorities (Maoris, French Canadians, US Hispanics) is the norm rather than the exception. Logically this can come from three sources: a 'real' biological difference; cultural experience; or bias from the construction and/or application of diagnostic systems. Although the evidence is complex, the possibility of systematic discrimination is clear.

Critically consider whether psychology has been shown to be gender biased. (30 marks)

Cultural bias

What is culture? It is often defined as the human made part of the environment and it is useful to divide it into objective or 'hard' culture (aspects such as machines, transportation, communications, buildings) and subjective or 'soft' culture (values, belief systems, roles, social stratification, educational systems, etc.). The two parts of culture obviously **interact** with each other and humans inevitably interact with culture constantly, both defining it and being defined by it.

The importance of this issue for psychology is that, as with gender bias and the implicit androcentrism that infiltrates the discipline, there is an implicit **ethnocentrism** or 'Westernism' reflecting cultural bias. Concern is sufficient to have created discussion about **three worlds of psychology** (e.g. Moghaddam, 1987; Moghaddam and Studer, 1997):

- *The First World*, the USA, dominates objective culture by controlling dissemination of knowledge through journals, test production, etc. It dominates subjective culture by promulgating research findings and traditions which are based on research carried out by white, middle-class males on similar subjects. Publication in the English language adds influence and accessibility.
- *The Second World* consists of Western Europe and Russia and has less cultural power and influence. This is ironic in that these countries produced (a) the origins and philosophical roots of the discipline and (b) many of its key figures: Germany — Wundt; Russia — Pavlov; Austria — Freud; Switzerland — Piaget; the UK — Darwin, Galton, Spearman, Bartlett.
- *The Third World* of psychology equates largely to third world countries that import psychological knowledge, techniques and traditions from the USA and, to a lesser extent, from Second World countries — often those with previous colonial ties.

It is argued that **cross-cultural psychology** can provide at least a partial remedy for ethnocentrism. Its traditional tasks have been to investigate what is similar and dissimilar about different cultures.

Dimensions of **cultural differences** which have been suggested for such investigation include:

- *Cultural complexity*. An often-used index of this is the importance of time in the management of everyday life. Members of highly industrialised countries have a large number of diverse roles to manage in a time-sensitive manner.
- *Individualism–collectivism*. This refers to the creation of an individual identity through personal and autonomous choices as against an identity which derives from a defined place in a group such as family, religious denomination or means of subsistence.
- *Tight versus loose cultures*. There is variation in the closeness of definition of norms and the tolerance demonstrated towards deviation. Paradoxically, highly developed Japan is an exemplar 'tight' culture.

Historical bias

This refers to a problem endemic in all historical studies, often termed 'presentism'. All historians work within their own particular society and time, and cannot but interpret the past in terms of the present. Just as the history of conflict tends to be written by the victors, the history of psychology has reflected the views of those who dominate its subjective and objective culture.

Gender bias in history

Beta bias has gone long **undetected** and **unremarked** in historical reviews and textbook accounts of hugely influential theories such as those of Freud and Kohlberg. Both claimed to produce **universal** theories, but in fact wrote from an almost entirely male viewpoint. Feminist historians of science have long complained about the writing of the history of science, which emphasises male and dismisses female contributions. It seems unlikely that psychology should escape this bias.

Cultural bias in history

Another form of bias has been towards **American** and **scientific psychology**. The majority of histories of psychology have been published in America and written by Americans (Mackenzie, 1972, Crampton, 1978). For a long time non-scientific and non-behavioural approaches were given little publicity in the written history of the discipline. The most famous example of this is the 'hundred years of silence' (Cohen, 2000) to which studies of everyday memory were subjected until the 1970s. With hindsight it can be seen that the publicity given to comparative ephemera — such as the thousands of rats' brains sacrificed in Lashley's fruitless 'search for the engram', the supposed location of specific conditioned memories — displays clear bias towards scientific and behavioural experimentation.

Emic and etic in cross-cultural research

The imposed **etic** is the export of cultural dominance. Etics refers to the method of looking for general or universal concepts from a standpoint *outside* a culture. **Emics** looks at cultural meanings from *within*, interpreting culturally specific ideas from the standpoint of the culture. The distinction derives from Pike (1954).

Examples of the imposition of etic are the attempts to replicate experiments cross-culturally (Berry, 1969; Smith and Bond, 1998). Classically the studies of Milgram and Ainsworth stand out (largely because of the sheer effort to replicate both across many cultures). From a narrow positivist point of view, these attempts yield data about obedience and childhood attachments across many cultures. However, the problem is that the participants in different cultures may interpret the studies in very different ways. Results may reflect: different reactions to demand characteristics; different views of the status of psychology; and differing interpretations of the meaning of the experiment. Thus any cultural differences observed may be more **apparent** than real.

Similar issues exist in attempts to **measure intelligence** across cultures, including across subcultures of a society. The meaning of testing, the meaning of particular items and tasks, the status and meaning of psychology, and the perception of the tester and the test instrument may all affect the data obtained. The argument is that such data are inevitably culturally embedded (Lonner, 1990; Brislin, 1993).

Advantages of cross-cultural psychology

Despite the arguments above, handled sensitively there are considerable plus points to a cross-cultural approach.

- Implicit assumptions about the researcher's background can be illuminated (not all cultures have similar gender roles, or ideas about the place and status of the old and the young).
- Different types of explanation for behaviour can be revealed (the importance of religion and tradition varies enormously as a rationale for behaviour).
- Different types of behaviour and experience can be uncovered (different types of parenting and attachment in children).
- Different circumstances can be investigated (e.g. the incidence of aggression in cultures with differing levels of access to TV and cinema).
- The universality of concepts can be investigated (e.g. Chomsky's linguistic universals or Piaget's stages).

Discuss examples of culture bias in psychology. (15 marks)

1.2 ETHICAL ISSUES IN PSYCHOLOGICAL INVESTIGATIONS USING HUMAN PARTICIPANTS AND ANIMALS

Overview

It is only relatively recently that both the British Psychological Society and the American Psychological Association have issued definitive ethical codes for the conduct of investigations using humans and animals. The BPS code for humans first appeared in 1978 and was revised in 1990 and 1993. The code for animal research appeared in 1985 and linked with Home Office legal guidelines and the licensing of research.

Psychology shares an interest in experimenting with live animals and humans with other disciplines such as medicine, biology and physiology. Unlike the natural sciences, our subject matter is sentient, and in experiments can be exposed to pain, discomfort, stress and in extreme cases lasting mental or physical harm including, in the case of animals, death.

Attention was focused on the area by a number of notorious cases.

- In *humans*, the studies of Zimbardo et al. (1973) in the Stanford Prison Study (Milgram, 1963, 1974), investigating obedience to authority, and Hofling et al. (1966) on nurse compliance to medical orders, are invariably used as examples of ethically disquieting studies which were likely to cause lasting psychological harm. Each of these studies caused large levels of **stress** during the research and used inadequate medical screening. The long-term side-effects included possible lasting damage to self-esteem and self-concept as participants were encouraged to (and apparently did) behave in ways which damaged others. These studies helped create a perceived need for an ethical code to prevent future harm to innocent participants.
- In *animals*, the studies of Jouvet (1967) on sleep deprivation in cats, Brady (1958) on stress-related ulcers in monkeys, Harlow (1959) on maternal deprivation of rhesus monkeys, and the legion of studies on linguistic primates have all raised extreme concern. The side-effects of these studies included death, disorientation, illness, sexual and parental dysfunction, and more bizarrely the problem of suitable retirement homes for linguistic apes! Again the psychological establishment felt obliged to act.
- A last unusual general feature in this area is the prevalence in psychology of studies we would like to carry out, which are quite easy practically but which cannot be carried out for obvious and overwhelming ethical reasons. Two simple examples might be depriving infants of the chance to attach to a carer and observing the consequence in a controlled longitudinal study. It would also be methodologically highly desirable to forcibly separate identical twins at birth and bring them up in markedly different environments to observe the consequences. The list is endless.

The ethics of using human participants

Look back at the BPS guidelines on page 55 and refresh your memory.

The ethical code in practice

The code of ethics acts as a set of professional guidelines to which all practising psychologists must adhere. Expulsion and stripping of professional status can occur if they are breached. In many research and academic institutions, research proposals are scrutinised for compliance before the study is allowed to proceed.

Far from being cut and dried, many of the guidelines are capable of various interpretations and are permitted to be broken in certain circumstances. Most obviously, many experiments would be totally pointless if a measure of deception was not used. However, the level of the deception should be as mild and harmless as possible and must only be used if essential for the conduct of the experiment. Milgram has also recently (1992) argued that if all discomfort and stress were rigidly outlawed, the experimental study of any form of conflict would be ruled out. He argued that this would produce a diminished literature based only on positive human emotions.

This leads to Aronson's formulation (1992) of how **cost–benefit analysis** can be entered into — if the outcomes of the experiment are liable to be important and or beneficial to society, small costs may be acceptable. Indeed, it can be considered unethical *not* to conduct studies which are of huge benefit to society but which mildly inconvenience or deceive a few participants.

This is sometimes called the ethical *imperative* (Brehm, 1992) — if research will possibly yield findings of high social value or benefit, there is an argument that the greater good is worth the potential harm or distress to individuals.

Socially sensitive research
Interestingly, there are many studies which comply technically with the ethical code but which are viewed by many as entirely unacceptable.

- Historically we have Cyril Burt's dalliance with eugenics (1948). This work promulgated the danger to the gene pool of the negative correlation between IQ and income and birth rates. Burt conjured up the vision of the less able in society taking over through sheer reproductive success. He advocated measures to level birth rates to prevent this.
- Similarly the work on IQ by Jensen and Eysenck is seen by many as *implicitly racist*. The usual defence is that science is an objective quest and that racial or class differences in IQ are a legitimate focus of study. This debate impinges on the nature of positivism and value freedom covered elsewhere.
- Gould (1980) reported on the systematic sexism of much psychometric testing.
- Money's (1980) research into the alleged genetic or physiological causes of homosexuality can be used to demean homosexuals as 'abnormal', being the result of unusual hormonal activity and brain development.
- Work on interpersonal attraction has until recently been ethnocentric by concentrating on white attractiveness (e.g. Bruce, 1994; Walster, 1966). But Perret's work (1994) is an attempt to broaden this research across cultures.
- Other reference to socially sensitive research can be found in the section on gender and culture bias (Section 1.1). So any research which constitutes a de facto discrimination against any group can be defined as socially insensitive. Thus sociobiology can be seen as being riven with social insensitivity and controversial views on the role of women.

The underlying issue here is that the value system of the research should be sound, and the **ethical** and **socio-political** consequences should be considered. Unlike the more technical aspects of the code of practice, these are issues of social and moral responsibility for psychology to confront. A naive belief in the positivistic approach is seldom seem in contemporary psychology as an acceptable rationale for producing research which demeans or discriminates in any way against any group.

Q **'Due to the nature of the work that psychologists do, such as treating mental disorders, for example, their work will be the subject of ethical controversy.' Discuss the issues raised in this quotation.**

(30 marks)

Ethical issues in using animals

The code exists in a set of safeguards for the use of animals. However, all researchers planning to use animals are obliged to liaise with the appropriate Home Office inspector.

There are also some legal bans on, for example, removing any endangered species from its habitat for experimentation. The BPS advises that research should minimise any discomfort, should take advice as to whether the likely contribution justifies the use of animals, and should consider whether the study could proceed in any other way *without the use of animals*.

The safeguards include the following:
- The level of electric shock is limited by the Home Office to the equivalent of 'unpleasant tickling'.
- Any procedure using pain or discomfort needs a Home Office certificate and there must be no other way of performing the study.
- It is illegal to perform any surgery or pharmacological intervention without a licence.
- There must be expertise and knowledge available about the species' needs for caging and social stimulation (this includes field observation, which can also disturb wild animals).

Arguments for and against the use of animals
These can be broken down into three groups.

Practical arguments
For:
- Animals can be cheap to feed and house.
- Many animals are small, and thus large numbers can easily be used — many can be housed and studied in a small space.
- As consent and debriefing are not needed, procedures can be swift and simple.
- Reproductive cycles are far quicker and thus many genetic experiments become possible (e.g. Broadhurst's work on maze bright strains of rats).

Against:
- The stress and artificiality of laboratory housing may produce unnatural or unusual behaviour. Hence responses and reactions may be atypical.

Theoretical arguments
For:
- Evolutionary theory proposes **continuity** in human and animal behaviour.
- Similarity in the fine and gross structures of the nervous system and brain suggests underlying commonality. For example, many neurotransmitters and endocrine hormones are common throughout mammals.
- An example here is the discovery of the basic laws of operant and classical conditioning largely through animal experimentation.

Against:
- What is interesting about human behaviour is that which is different from animal behaviour.
- There are **discontinuities** in brain structure (despite outwardly similar anatomy) — our vastly superior intellect suggests vast inbuilt differences (emphasised by the attempts to teach primates language).
- There are important differences in brain and body chemistry. Morphine stimulates cats, and penicillin is toxic to guinea-pigs.

Ethical arguments
For:
- Gray's argument (1987) advocates a form of **speciesism** in which we are almost obliged to use animals if this can further human well-being. The possibility of cures and greater understanding of forms of psychological disease therefore justifies animal research.

- Many laboratory animals are well housed and fed, and live far more comfortable existences than in the wild.
- Many simpler organisms almost certainly do not feel pain or discomfort in any meaningful way (hence the millions of fruit flies sacrificed for genetic research seems unproblematic to most people).

Against:
- Animal activists violently disagree with Gray (see above). They argue that all species should be regarded as having their *own rights* and reject the idea that one species can exploit another for its own benefit.
- There is uncertainty about the level of pain and discomfort experienced by animals. Despite observing outward signs, there must always be uncertainty about their level of pain because of the lack of direct communication.

Popular confusions

This area raises many strong emotions. Psychological research is often confused with medically based and cosmetic research. It is important to disentangle psychology from these controversies. It is also worth noting that some 700 million animals are reared and killed every year throughout Europe for food, whereas the number of animals used in experiments is declining steadily — halving since the 1970s and now down to three million in the UK, 85% of these being rodents.

Bateson and cost–benefit analysis

An attempt to clarify some of these issues has been introduced by Bateson, who propounds a form of cost–benefit analysis. When judging the validity of animal-based research we should consider the claims:
- the probability of valuable findings being made and an assessment of their potential value
- the probability of pain and discomfort being inflicted upon animals and the likely magnitude of that discomfort

---

Q **Describe and evaluate the case for the use of non-human animals in psychological research.** (30 marks)

---

2 Debates in psychology

2.1 FREE WILL AND DETERMINISM

Definitions

There is much disagreement about the precise nature of these two ideas. Although easy to understand in everyday life, exact definition has proved extraordinarily complex. This is because they are **philosophical** ideas about the nature of the human mind, which connect to our fundamental religious, cultural and political beliefs, as well as being important for psychology.

A generic definition of **free will** is that it occurs (a) when we are not forced or coerced (by circumstance or biological need); (b) when we have to choose between alternatives; or (c) when we are not acting by reflex or learnt response.

Determinism is the idea that human actions are just like **physical** events and thus have **causes** in a similar manner. This implies that the experience of choice is in some way illusory.

Although apparently opposite, the two ideas are not mutually exclusive. This idea was examined in William James's (1890) idea of **soft determinism** — an appealing solution which, however, has some problems of its own (see below). James maintained that, because science had shown that physical matter behaves predictably and rationally, this *physical realm*, including our bodies, should be seen as subject to determinism. On the other hand, because it is fundamental to human consciousness that we have a certain, indubitable experience of exercising choice and because society embodies ideas about choice and responsibility, this other *mental realm* should be seen as subject to *free will*.

It is interesting to examine the relation of two ideas by looking at the extreme cases.

- If free will is assumed to be absent from human conduct, it implies that our actions and thoughts are either **random** or **determined**. The former is normally ruled out, as the evidence of order in the universe and in personal experience is overwhelming. If we are determined, it is probably in the same way that all other events in the world are caused, by chains of physically linked events. Rather like the sequential reaction of a group of snooker balls being struck, so stimuli produce ordered responses in the mind. This determinist view sees mental events as a side-effect of physiologically caused brain events. This view diminishes or even demolishes the idea of choice and responsibility. Theoretically we could no more be held responsible for our actions than a stone or other inanimate object.

- If free will is present in humans, it implies an absence of determinism in both **behaviour** and **conscious experience**. This implies that we see human action as special and perhaps unique; it must be the result of some non-physical intervention in the physical system of the body. Thus when we experience the agonies of choice between alternatives on a restaurant menu, it is a *real* phenomenon. We really could choose one or the other — we are not determined by some underlying brain state which might reflect our conditioning history or physiological need for certain foods. The reality and status of this process of choice is examined in detail in the novels, plays and philosophy of Jean-Paul Sartre and other existential thinkers. This view sees mental events as not necessarily caused by brain events, but capable in some unique way of self-determination. This view is consistent with ideas of freedom, choice and responsibility.

Arguments for and against free will

For:

- 'We know our will is free, and there's an end on't.' This statement was attributed to Dr Johnson by Boswell. It expresses the powerful argument for free will called 'subjective impression' (Valentine, 1992). Another version of this stance appears in William James's work (1890). He maintained that our experience of free will is so strong, it is sufficient to underpin two forms of explanation of human conduct. One, based on **freedom** and **responsibility**, could explain social, legal, moral, religious and political practices. The other, based on **scientific determinism**, could explain the events in the body and the physical world. Despite the enormous appeal of James's view, it cannot explain the connection between these two forms of action.

Against:

- It is difficult to give a coherent definition of free will. There is a major flaw with every so-called solution to the free will debate — it is always unclear how two different realms, the mental and physical, could *connect*. Determinism is logically appealing — it avoids this problem of connection, but is totally against our everyday experience (while the opposite is the case for free will).

- It is easy to argue that it cannot possibly exist, because the brain is the seat of consciousness and the brain is a physical entity. It is difficult to describe how a physical system like the human brain and body could not behave lawfully. Thus any definition seems to contravene the laws of science, which hold for all other matters. To support free will, one has thus to argue that human beings operate in a way that is different from everything else in the known universe.

Arguments for and against determinism

For:

- Success elsewhere in human enquiry has shown that determinism seems to operate almost **universally** and provides the basis for our way of understanding the world. Science provides us with a workable and useful model of the physical world. Furthermore, the whole edifice of science is based on the idea of **prediction** and **predictability** (see Popper in Section 2.3). The whole idea of an indeterminate world belongs to the realm of science fiction — or perhaps science nightmare.

Against:

- The one exception to the above would appear to be at the subatomic level, where Heisenberg's uncertainty principle maintains that our knowledge of events can only be probabilistic. This provides an argument that indeterminism is at the heart of physical matter.

Positions on the free will and determinism debate in psychological theories

Against free will

- Freud — developed the idea of **psychic determinism**. All conscious experience and all behaviour were caused by events in the unconscious. Psychoanalysis offers a means of uncovering these causes.
- **Radical behaviourism** — John Watson and B.F. Skinner both maintained that our behaviour is the **lawful** result of all our life experiences, which build up complex sets of conditioned responses that comprise our behaviour.

For free will

- **Humanistic psychology**. Most importantly, Carl Rogers and Abraham Maslow maintained that humans were self-determining organisms. They argued that free will and its exercise is a crucial part of the human experience and a central part of the organismic process, which is our capacity for growth and achieving our potential.

Mixed position

- **Cognitive psychology**. The contemporary use of the computer metaphor is implicitly determinist in comparing humans to computers. However, it is possible to maintain that humans have an extra capacity for consciousness and choice and that computers and neurology will only ever provide a partial model. This is a position not unlike James's 'soft determinism'.

With reference to psychological research or theory, discuss examples of the free-will/determinism debate.

(30 marks)

2.2 REDUCTIONISM

There are two sorts of reductionism:

- *Type 1 reduction to a lower level.* Garnham (1991) maintained that it is 'the idea that psychological explanations can be replaced by explanations in terms of brain functioning or even in terms of physics and chemistry'. This version places psychology in a **hierarchy of sciences** between the social sciences (least fundamental) and the physical sciences (most fundamental) (see Figure 12.1).

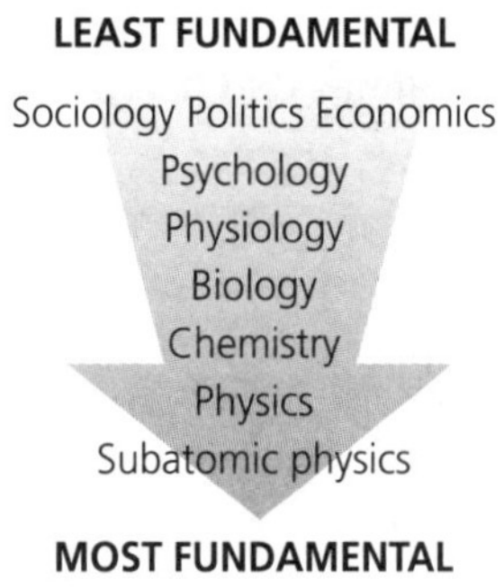

LEAST FUNDAMENTAL

Sociology Politics Economics
Psychology
Physiology
Biology
Chemistry
Physics
Subatomic physics

MOST FUNDAMENTAL

Figure 12.1
Type 1 reduction
to a lower level

- *Type 2 reduction to constituent parts.* This is the idea that something can be explained in terms of the behaviour of all its parts. Thus the behaviour of a motor car can be explained as the result of its assembled components. Society can be seen as the result of the behaviour of all the individuals within it.

Reductionism in psychology

Examples of reductionism in psychological theories include:

- radical behaviourism — which maintains that all the psychological phenomena of behaviour and experience are merely the result of the **physiological** processes of conditioning
- Freud — who maintained that biological **instincts** determine behaviour
- genetic theories of intelligence and personality (Eysenck, Jensen, Burt)
- sociobiology — which maintains that the **evolutionary process** has shaped us, including complex high level behaviours concerned with relationships, attraction and competitiveness
- the medical model of abnormality — which maintains that 'mental illness' has a **physical cause**, and can be physically treated with drugs and electroconvulsive therapy
- computation modelling — the attempt to **simulate** human cognition in terms of computer programs, which theoretically could mimic the behaviour of neurones (so-called machine reductionism)

Two examples of reductionism in psychological research

Studies of the origins of mental illness. An enormous research effort has been made to uncover the cause of mental illness in our genetic make-up (Rose, 1984) and/or in abnormal brain chemistry (Iversen, 1979). The hope of the latter effort is to promote the development of effective psychoactive drugs. Critics argue that this reductionist medical disease model adds nothing to our understanding of the experience of mental illness and fails to lead to compassionate and effective psychotherapy (Lain, Szasz).

Sperry's split-brain research. This research challenges the idea that human consciousness is some sort of unitary, indivisible, soul-like entity. In some patients with rare cases of severe epilepsy, the corpus callosum (the tissue which connects the two halves of the cortex) was surgically severed for medical reasons. Following the operation, they had two cortical hemispheres which could no longer communicate with each other as in the normal intact state. Using tasks which utilised one hemisphere, it was clear that one half of the brain had no knowledge of what the other half was doing. Sperry discovered that patients did indeed have two consciousnesses — in two 'half brains' (Sperry, 1974; Sperry and Gazzaniga, 1976). Such research supports reductionism, as it clearly ties consciousness into specific neurological activity — consciousness itself arises out of neuronal activity.

Arguments for and against reductionism

For:

- Creates the possibility of fully scientific psychology, with all behaviour and experience being ultimately explained by physiology.

- Links psychology to research and theory in related disciplines of biology, genetics, neuroscience, artificial intelligence, physiology and sociobiology.

Against:

- Gestalt psychology argued long ago that the sum of behaviour and experience is more than the parts — by dividing up phenomena we can destroy their character.
- Humanistic psychologists (Rogers, Kelly, Maslow and Bannister) argue for **emergence**. This is the idea that events are only describable and explicable at one level. To reduce them to another level is impossible, because the explanatory terms do not apply (e.g. the feeling of depression is not describable or explicable in terms of the activity of neurotransmitters).
- Applications — emergent explanations may often be more useful and have obvious applications (therapy, behaviour modification and attitude change).
- Understanding — emergent explanations are more likely to spread mutual understanding than more technical reductionist versions, which increasingly may only be intelligible to experts in the field.

'We will never be able fully to understand human behaviour and experience by reductionist explanations.' Discuss.   (30 marks)

2.3 PSYCHOLOGY AS SCIENCE

Definitions/varieties of science

There are three main groups of view.

The inductive empiricist view

This was put forward in the 18th and 19th centuries by the British empiricist school of philosophers (Bacon, Locke, Mill). They maintained that we had **direct access** to reality through observation. The task of science was to observe data accurately and note regularities in the observations, which can be formulated into scientific laws. (Wundt's psychology was modelled on this view.) *Truth* is arrived at by the process of induction from data. Newton' laws of motion and gravitation emerged by the process of attempting to make sense of a vast amount of data regarding the behaviour of earth-bound and cosmological objects.

The hypothetico-deductive model

This was propounded in the 1950s and 1960s by Karl Popper. Contrary to empiricism, it maintains that hypotheses about nature come first and that science should proceed by *testing out predictions*. This allows for the confirmation or change of initial hypotheses. (Freudian theory was used extensively by Popper as an example of bad practice, as its core assumptions and theoretical ideas are almost entirely untestable.) *Truth* exists at an infinite distance — we can always get closer, but the task of science is to test and refine hypotheses, thereby achieving progress towards increasingly accurate and detailed predictions. Science does not progress by chance observation (apples falling on Newton's head) but by testing out hunches or hypotheses. Darwin did not go to the Galápagos Islands by chance! He went to test ideas through observation.

Kuhn's paradigms

Published in 1962, *The Structure of Scientific Revolutions* argues that science can be normal or revolutionary. 'Normal' science progresses within a paradigm — defined as 'a shared set of assumptions about the subject matter of a discipline and the methods appropriate to its study'. From time to time, 'paradigm strain', in the form of refuted hypotheses or inexplicable phenomena, will build up. This creates the conditions for a 'paradigm shift' — the best example of this being the change from Newtonian to

Einsteinian physics. This model needs adaptation to apply to psychology. We have mini- or partial paradigms which co-exist (e.g. Piagetian and Freudian theories of childhood, behaviourist and humanistic views of conduct). *Truth* is **relativistic**, not absolute, being defined within paradigms.

Psychology as science — arguments for and against

Valentine (1982) argued that a mature science should agree on the following criteria. All three relate to the issue of **objectivity**. In essence, science attempts to create an objective account of the world — defined as one based on public and replicable data which can be publicly and unambiguously tested.

Nature of subject matter

For:

- The behaviour of humans can be objectively observed and measured in the same way as the behaviour of animals, other organisms and physical objects.

Against:

- There are fundamental disagreements about this claim. Only radical behaviourists and neuropsychologists can be content with restricting the subject matter of psychology to the observation of behaviour and physiological indices. Others argue for the inclusion of feelings, interpretations and conscious experience.

Nature of theory

For:

- In a Popperian view, theories of behaviour can be formulated and tested in the same way as theories in chemistry or physics.

Against:

- Kuhn would argue that psychology has never approached paradigmatic agreement, spawning instead the development of many competing and incompatible theories. Thus psychology contains many forms of relativistic knowledge.

Nature of methodology

For:

- Psychology uses the *experimental* method and appeals to replication, generalisation and empirical data in the same way as other sciences.

Against:

- More qualitative methods are needed to study the mind. *Understanding* rather than explanation should be the aim of psychology. Unlike objects, people are reflexive and can *react* to being studied or theorised about. This occurs at the macro-level and micro-level. At the macro-level, an example is the way Freudian theory has altered the way people think about themselves and others — perhaps with respect to the role of the unconscious and the pervasive nature of sex, with some terms like 'Freudian slip' entering popular culture. At the micro-level, Orne's (1962) work demonstrates the strength of demand characteristics and the power of the unusual situation which is the experiment. Orne's participants took part in a series of utterly pointless and boring tasks for many hours, simply because it was a psychology experiment. They happily added up strings of randomly generated numbers, writing the answers on pieces of paper which they were instructed to tear up into 32 pieces before starting all over again, and again. Rosenthal's (1966) work confirms a desire to please the experimenter among participants.

Evaluation of the use of experiments in psychology

Plus points:

- allows rigorous tests of hypotheses

- provides public, replicable, objective data
- allows the action of discrete variables in controlled conditions
- increases perception of the scientific status of psychology

Negative points:
- produces an artificial situation
- subject to experimenter effects
- demand characteristics often obvious and sometimes strong (Orne, 1962)
- only suitable for a limited range of behaviour
- prone to ethical problems
- tendency to simplify everyday life behaviour
- participants are usually a biased sample of the population, both demographically and personally (Rosenthal, 1976)

Compare and contrast arguments for and against psychology being considered a science.   (30 marks)

2.4 NATURE–NURTURE

Definitions
Usually this debate is taken to mean a consideration of the respective contribution to human behaviour of genetic or hereditary factors versus environmental or learnt influences. The debate connects to empiricist and nativist views of mind.

Examples in psychology of the nature–nurture debate
Empiricist views

An extreme empiricist view can be found in the work of the **radical behaviourists**. Watson and Skinner maintained that all behaviour was *learnt* through the processes of conditioning. The only genetic component was the biological capacity to learn. It was Watson (1930) who famously said 'I'll take any (child) and train him to become any type of specialist I might select — doctor, artist, merchant — regardless of his talents, penchants, tendencies, vocations and race of his ancestors.'

Humanistic psychology also stresses our capacity for self-determination irrespective of genetic make-up.

Nativist views

Extreme nativist views are found in sociobiology (Wilson, 1978) which stresses the **evolutionary origins** of our behaviour, emphasising the continuity of human and animal behaviour. It claims, for example, that gender differences and male–female romantic relationships are rooted in desires to promulgate and protect our genes.

Piaget and Chomsky suggested that we might have a genetic programme which determines the structure of cognitive capacities and the rate and manner of their development in childhood.

Research on the role of nature and nurture in intelligence
Nurture

Many investigations have demonstrated the effects of *early environment* on later *intelligence*, the rationale being that those 'good' environments should enhance IQ and 'bad' ones should depress it.

Early work included that of Skeels and Dye (1939), followed by Skeels (1966). These studies showed that children institutionalised in orphanages seemed to be adversely affected intellectually, but these effects could be largely eliminated by early fostering.

Later work included **Headstart** and similar programmes of environmental enrichment — largely in the USA. Aimed at culturally disadvantaged pre-school children, Headstart (1965) promoted significant *gains* in intellectual performance. Unfortunately, these gains tended to fall away when the children were assimilated into standard schooling. Similar results occurred in the Milwaukee Project (Heber and Garber, 1975).

Nature

The classic studies are those on **twins** and other related siblings, collectively known as **concordance studies**, the rationale being the simple one that if IQ is genetically linked, sharing genes should mean sharing intelligence.

Bouchard and McGue summarised the findings of 111 such studies. Generally IQ does indeed show greater correlations between those who are highly related than those who are not. Indeed, the correlation gradually decreases as relationship decreases. Starting from identical (monozygotic) twins reared together ($r = 0.86$) or reared apart ($r = 0.72$), the figure precisely follows genetic similarity through siblings reared together ($r = 0.47$), siblings reared apart ($r = 0.24$) to cousins ($r = 0.15$).

There are many **methodological problems** with these studies — including the validity of pooling testing, often across ages and cultures. Also, definitions of *reared separately* includes twins who were actually brought up very similarly, by close-knit families, with the children attending the same school classes (Nielsen, 1965).

Therefore, although the figures look at first sight impressive evidence for genetic influence, they also show a consistent role for environmental factors. Perhaps most of all they illustrate the problems of doing uncontrolled field-based research. The crucial variable of environment is *impossible to control* and in many cases genetic similarity may have influenced carers and parents to rear the children similarly.

Research on the role of nature and nurture on sexual orientation
Nurture

Much work has been done on the role of nurture into **sexual orientation**. Bell et al. (1981) and Bell and Weinberg (1978) investigated the hypotheses, derived distantly from Freudian theory, that homosexual men overly identify with their mothers. Using controlled groups comprising several hundred heterosexual and homosexual men, they did not find support for this theory — but they did find that significantly fewer of the homosexual men wanted to be like their fathers.

Nature

On the nature side, much of the work concerns the role of **hormones** in development — which are of course normally controlled by genetic factors, females and males producing their own cocktails of sex-linked hormones at various stages of development.

One set of studies involved the manipulation of hormones in primates. Goy (1968) and Goy et al. (1968) injected pregnant monkeys with testosterone and observed the results in the female offspring. They showed many primate masculine behavioural traits — more aggression and less fear — and ambiguous genital development. This is consistent with Money's (1988) research, which showed that testosterone changes the structural development of the brains of rats, apparently 'masculinising' the brain.

In humans, studies are limited to *medically available evidence* from rare cases of female fetuses having unusually large exposures of testosterone *in utero*. Money (1980) and Money et al. (1984) reported that girls who experience this often show unusually 'tomboyish' behaviour and a more than average incidence of lesbian fantasies in early adolescence.

Evaluation

The most one can draw from this research at present is that there does appear to be a role for genetic make-up in determining gender-related behaviour. How far this links to eventual sexual orientation is as yet unclear.

Differing views on the genes–environment relationship

The traditional approach was essentially an attempt to weigh up the respective contributions of genes and environment. A typical approach was that of Burt, who infamously (because of the later scandal over faked data) used the rationale of twin studies and complex factor analysis in arriving at the claim that intelligence was *70% innate and 30% learnt*.

The views of Chomsky and Piaget are more **interactionist**. They maintain that the genetic developmental programme, although fixed in type and order, needs environmental stimulation to be successfully accomplished.

A more modern **transactional** view is exemplified by Sameroff (1991), who emphasised that each set of interactions between parents and children is unique and may produce its own unique processes and consequences. For example, a sleepless child may provoke very different responses in the same parents as a good sleeper, and hence have very different experience in technically the same environment as a sibling.

With reference to psychological research or theory, discuss examples of the nature/nurture debate. (30 marks)

---

3 Approaches to psychology

As discussed in the introduction, this is very different from all the rest of the assessment, for both AS and A2. You will be required to answer *one out of two questions*. Each will have different *stimulus material*, but the format of the question will be *identical* for both.

The most important thing to remember is that the question is *future tense*, i.e. it is not concerned with studies which have been carried out, but with ones which could be carried out (in the future). As a bare minimum you need to know the **theoretical assumptions** associated with *two* psychological approaches. By approaches we don't mean a specific theory (e.g. Beck's theory of depression), but a broad approach. Those named in the specification are behaviourism, psychoanalysis, biological/medical and cognitive. In addition, you may focus if you wish upon other psychological approaches, such as evolutionary psychology, humanistic psychology or social constructionism, which are not named in the specification. You can even offer approaches which derive from other, related disciplines such as sociology, biology and philosophy!

We would offer you two pieces of advice in deciding which ones to concentrate on. In the first part of the question you will need to offer *two* approaches. Not all approaches work *equally well* with different stimulus material, so it's wise to cover at least three, even though you will only need to use two in the final analysis. Secondly, choose approaches which are clearly different, e.g. behaviourism and psychoanalysis, which surely none of us could muddle up!

As well as knowing about the theoretical assumptions of the approaches, you need to be familiar with the methods the approaches typically use. Think about how differently psychoanalysts and biopsychologists work!

A good way to think about this is to imagine that you are a professional psychologist — a psychoanalyst, for example. Next, imagine that your university is bidding for a research project, say into eating disorders. When you turn up to the interview representing your university, you will have all of your psychoanalytic approach 'baggage' in your head, all the things you believe in and so on. That's part one of the story. The second part is *how* you would tackle the problem that's up for grabs. In other words, how a psychodynamic psychologist works *in practice*. Be Skinner for a day! Be Freud for a day!

Finally, you need to be evaluative. You will need to not only describe what a particular type of psychologist (behaviourist, biopsychologist or whatever) believes in and what methodologies they use, but know what the *strengths and weaknesses* of these are.

Let's refresh our memories about the format of the question.

(a) Describe how two approaches might try to explain the subject presented in the stimulus material [the question will tell you what it is, so don't worry]. (6+6 marks)

(b) Assess one of these explanations of the subject presented in the stimulus material in terms of its strengths and limitations. (6 marks)

(c) How might one of these approaches given in (a) above investigate the subject presented in the stimulus material? (6 marks)

(d) Evaluate the use of this method of investigating the subject matter presented in the stimulus material. (6 marks)

The task is for you to apply your chosen approaches to the material as we have just discussed. The following are two examples of the type of stimulus material you can expect to encounter in the unit tests:

1 'Rodney loved to flirt with girls. He would spend hours making himself look as attractive as possible, and never missed an opportunity to try to 'chat up' any girl who would listen to him. He enjoyed going out as much as possible and priding himself on being 'a class act'. He rarely stayed with one girfriend for very long, preferring to go out with as many girls as he could.'

The focus would be 'loved to flirt with girls'.

2 'Alison was a shy and rather bashful 14 year-old, but the real passion of her life was her love of animals. In fact she enjoyed the company of her six pets (two cats, two guinea fowl and two goldfish) more than being with the people she knew. She felt ill at ease with people, even her own family, but very secure with her pets.'

The focus here would be on 'her love of animals'.

We will finally consider the key features of the psychological approaches named in the specification, and then work through a mock-up answer to one of the pieces of stimulus material above. The analysis given below is based on that given by Cardwell (2000) and Eysenck and Flanagan (2001).

Behaviourism

Behaviourism was founded by John Watson in 1913. It is an approach which seeks to account for behaviour in terms of **observable events** and without reference to mental concepts such as the mind. We are born **blank slates** upon which experience writes. The prime forces in shaping behaviour are **conditioning** (classical and operant) and **imitation** (according to social learning theory). In the case of classical conditioning already existing, behaviour (initially reflexes) becomes **paired** with new stimuli by association. In operant conditioning, behaviour is **moulded**, as rewarded behaviours are stamped in and punished behaviours are stamped out.

Strengths

- Studies of operant, classical conditioning and social learning theory have given us considerable insights into both human and animal behaviour.
- Many applications, for example therapies, have been derived from behaviourism.
- It is generally seen as a strongly scientific method in psychology (e.g. Broadbent, 1961).

Weaknesses

- The emphasis on learning denies the importance of inheritance in behaviour.
- The fact that results from lower animals are (sometimes uncritically) generalised to humans has led to the accusation of ratomorphism.
- It is reductionist and determinist.
- It denies the influence of all 'internal' factors, such as consciousness and cognitive factors.

Psychoanalysis

Psychoanalysis was founded by Sigmund Freud in 1895. Freud believed that much of our behaviour is under the influence of the **unconscious mind** (with the conscious and the semi-conscious being the other parts of the mind, or psyche). Experiences we live through — especially in the early years of our life — which are too painful to bear, are **repressed** into our unconscious mind until such time as we are strong enough to deal with them. They can, however, **'leak'** through in the form of symbolic dreams, slips of the tongue and so on.

The personality is made up of three dynamic components. (They fight against each other to control our behaviour!) The first is the **id**, which is present at birth and operates under the pleasure principle. (I want it and I want it now!) The **ego**, which is the second to develop, operates on the reality principle. (How can I operate so as to get the best deal I can? It is still after pleasure, but this time is strategic.) Finally, there is the **superego**, which results from a successful resolution of the Oedipus (boys) and Electra (girls) complexes.

According to Freud, we develop through five psychosexual stages, so-called because they are determined by the location of the source of sexual pleasure. These are the **oral** stage (birth to 2 years approximately); the anal stage (2–3); the **phallic** stage (3–6); a **latency** period (6–12); and the **genital** stage (12 onwards). Mature sexuality is only acquired in the final stage. People may 'stick' at an immature stage or regress back to an earlier stage if they are unable to deal with the more mature ones.

Strengths

- Freud's psychodynamic approach has been one of the creative approaches in the history of psychology, and has been very generative (producing ideas and hypotheses for others to test).
- If one is prepared to accept the premises/assumptions made by Freud (e.g. that there is an unconscious mind which exerts an enormous influence over us), the model is very logical and coherent.
- Psychoanalysis made good use of the case study (defined here as the in-depth, longitudinal study of one individual), which gives us a richness of insight and data that broader and arguably more superficial methods may not.

Weaknesses

- Unlike most science, psychoanalysis does not make predictions, but seeks to explain things historically. The difference is similar to that of trying to predict the result of a football match before the game or explaining the outcome after the match has finished. The first is a lot tougher than the second!

- Critics of Freud argue that psychoanalysis is little more than outrageous speculations, with no 'hard' evidence to support them.
- Freud's theories are both determinist and reductionist.

The cognitive approach

This approach came to replace behaviourism as the dominant model in psychology around the late 1950s/early 1960s. It is diametrically opposed to behaviourism as its focus is upon the *processes which occur 'in the head'* (for example, thinking and perception, memory and problem solving). Eysenck and Flanagan (2001) argue that it is based on three assumptions:

- Behaviour can be explained and understood in terms of how the mind or brain works.
- The mind/brain works in many ways similar to how a computer does (in terms of storing information and carrying out analysis). This led to the information-processing model which is a central feature of the cognitive approach.
- Psychology is (or at least should be) a science, mainly using the laboratory experiment as its preferred methodology.

Strengths
- The approach brought the mind/brain back onto the centre of the stage of psychology after years in the wilderness of behaviourism.
- It utilises most of the methods and principles of science (e.g. objective measurement of data and refutability).
- It has provided us with many useful applications — such as how to design vehicles to make them as driver-friendly and safe as possible, how to improve memory, and how people process information under a variety of different situations — which have implications for everyday life and the 'real world'.

Weaknesses
- It can be argued that the scientific approach is an inappropriate one to employ to study humans (see the review of psychology as a science earlier in this topic). Freud and humanist psychologists such as Rogers would take this view.
- It is mechanistic, largely because it is based on comparing human cognitive activity with the way machines such as computers work. As such it is largely an analytical but compassionless approach.
- Much of the work carried out by cognitive psychologists is carried out in the laboratory (as noted above). One disadvantage to this is that the control and manipulation, not to mention the physical setting itself, give the studies questionable ecological validity. This may, however, be compensated for by high experimental validity.

The biological/medical approach

This is based on what has traditionally been called biopsychology, a term given to the scientific investigation of the relationship between biology and behaviour. Biopsychologists normally study the **brain** and **nervous system** in an attempt to establish their impact on behaviour at all levels.

The reference to all levels means that the level of behavioural analysis may be 'large' (**molar**), such as running away from a feared object, or 'small' (**molecular**), such as the action of specific cells in the visual cortex resulting from stimulation by energy in the visual spectrum.

Many biological or physiological factors can influence behaviour (often *interacting* with individual or social factors). Examples include activity of the nervous system, specific brain activity, and the effects of genetic influence across generations. All of these would influence intelligence, for example.

The **medical** component is generally taken to refer to approaches to mental disorders or illnesses. This is consistent with the fact that the other approaches described are also associated with their own particular therapies. You may wish to refresh your memory about the various therapies (see Topic 11, Section 3).

Strengths
- It is objective and enables us to ascertain cause and effect relationships (by seeing how controlled administration of a particular drug may influence behaviour).
- Medical treatment has proved highly effective in controlling or even curing some mental disorders (such as schizophrenia), although there may be side-effects and dependency, as discussed in Topic 11.
- It is arguably the most scientific of all the approaches used in psychology.

Weaknesses
- It is questionable whether psychological phenomena (such as emotion) can be explained purely by biological or physiological processes.
- As well as being reductionist, it is highly determinist.
- It gives little credit to cultural factors (and cross-cultural differences) in influencing behaviour.

Response to stimulus material

Let's finish off by analysing a response to the stimulus material on Alison, on p. 190. Before we do that, however, we need to establish how these answers will be marked. The marking scheme is given below. The AO1 bands relate to part (a) and the AO2 ones to parts (b) to (d).

Assessment Objective 1		
Band	**Mark allocation**	**Marks**
Band 6	Psychological content in relation to the approach which could explain the topic in question is cited, which is **accurate** and **well detailed** at the level of knowledge, description and understanding. The organisation and structure are **presented coherently**. There is substantial evidence of breadth and depth and an **appropriate balance** between these is achieved.	6
Band 5	**Slightly limited** psychological content in relation to the approach which could be used to explain the topic in question is cited, which is **accurate** and **well detailed** at the level of knowledge, description and understanding. The organisation and structure are **presented coherently**. There is evidence of breadth and depth, although a **balance** between these is **not always achieved**.	5
Band 4	**Limited** psychological content is cited in relation to the approach which may explain the topic in question, which is **accurate** and **reasonably detailed** at the level of knowledge, description and understanding. The answer is **reasonably** constructed in its attempt to answer the question. There is **some evidence** of breadth and/or depth.	4
Band 3	**Limited** psychological content is cited in relation to the approach which could be used to explain the topic in question, which is **generally accurate** at the level of knowledge, description and understanding, but lacking in detail. The answer is reasonably constructed in its attempt to answer the question. There is **little evidence** of breadth and depth.	3
Band 2	**Basic** psychological content is cited in relation to the approach which could be used to investigate the topic in question, with **rudimentary and sometimes flawed** description. The answer is **sometimes focused** on the question but may be irrelevant or superficial.	2
Band 1	Psychological content in relation to approach which could be used to explain the topic in question is **just discernible**. Description is **weak** and understanding is **muddled and incomplete**. The answer may be wholly or mainly **irrelevant**.	1–0

Assessment Objective 2		Marks
Band	**Mark allocation**	
Band 6	There is **informed** commentary and assessment of relevant psychological theories, concepts or applications in relation to the strengths and limitations of one of the chosen approaches to explaining the topic in question. Material has been used in a **highly effective** manner and is **coherently elaborated**.	6
Band 5	There is an **informed** commentary and **appropriate** assessment of the relevant psychological theories, concepts or applications in relation to the strengths and limitations of the chosen approach to explaining the topic in question. Material has been used in an **effective** manner and shows evidence of **appropriate selection** and **coherent elaboration**.	5
Band 4	There is **reasonable** commentary, **appropriate but slightly limited** assessment of the relevant psychological theories, concepts or applications in relation to the strengths and limitations of the approach chosen to the topic in question. Material has been used in an **effective** manner and shows evidence of **coherent elaboration**.	4
Band 3	There is **reasonable** commentary, **but** limited assessment of relevant psychological theories, concepts or applications in relation to the strengths and limitations of the chosen approach to explaining the topic in question. Material has been used in a **reasonably effective** manner, and shows **some** evidence of **elaboration**.	3
Band 2	There is **superficial** commentary and **rudimentary** assessment of the psychological theories, concepts or applications in relation to the strengths and limitations of the chosen approach to explaining the topic in question. Material used is of a **restricted** nature and provides **minimal interpretation**.	2
Band 1	Psychological content in relation to the strengths and limitations of the chosen approach to explaining the topic in question is **just discernible**. Assessment is **weak, muddled and incomplete**. The answer may be wholly or mainly **irrelevant**.	1–0

'Alison was a shy and rather bashful 14 year-old, but the real passion of her life was her love of animals. In fact she enjoyed the company of her six pets (two cats, two guinea fowl and two goldfish) more than being with the people she knew. She felt ill at ease with people, even her own family, but very secure with her pets.'

The focus here would be on 'her love of animals'.

(a) Describe how two approaches might try to explain the subject presented in the stimulus material.

One approach to explain Alison's behaviour would be the psychoanalytic one. It might be that at some time in her past she had had a difficult encounter with another person, perhaps a teacher or some other children, which had caused her a lot of anxiety and made her lose faith in dealing with people. Or perhaps she had deep-seated doubts about herself which she projected onto other people.

A second approach could be a behavioural one. Behaviourists believe that all behaviours are learned, so her love of animals would not be something which was inborn or innate. It may have been that she had found the security of her pets comforting in the past and so associated feeling good and comfortable with them. On the other hand, there may have been occasions when she had been punished (even in a very mild form) by some person or persons and this aspect of her behaviour (being with people and feeling good in their company) had been eliminated.

Examiner comment: A good, but imbalanced answer, with the part on behaviourism being fuller, longer and more detailed, and hence better than that on psychoanalysis. The candidate would earn 5 marks out of 6 for the second part and 4 out of 6 for the first.

(b) Assess one of these explanations of the subject presented in the stimulus material in terms of its strengths and limitations.

I will focus on the behaviourist approach. One limitation of the approach is that they aren't interested in how thoughts and feelings (anything inside the head really) influence behaviour. In addition, it tends to reduce things down so they would only focus on aspects of Alison's behaviour rather than looking at her as a whole person, as humanists would do. With regard to helping us understand Alison's love of animals, there wouldn't be any reference to why we might have an innate love of animals (especially furry ones) or an innate need to love and look after things which might be more vulnerable than us. Psychoanalysts might see Alison's behaviour as a rehearsal for parenting and caring behaviour, but again this would not fit with the behaviourists' explanations.

Examiner comment: The big problem here is that the candidate has only answered part of the question as she makes no reference to the advantages of the approach, only weaknesses. This means that her answer would be marked out of 4 rather than 6. The answer is a generally good one, but it could have been more clearly focused on the stimulus material rather than a general evaluation (this is an easy way to lose marks, so beware). The answer certainly earns 3 marks, possibly 4.

(c) Analyse how one of the approaches given in (a) above might be used to investigate the subject presented in the stimulus material.

Psychoanalysts use a variety of different clinical methods. Basically they are aimed at 'making the unconscious conscious'. Part of this is the talking cure. In this case, a therapist would work on a one-to-one basis, but — this is a very important point — a therapist would only work with Alison if she requested it herself or if she was referred by someone such as her doctor or one of her parents. The last point is an interesting one — perhaps the reason she has pairs of pets is because she cannot relate well to or love one of her parents, and this might be a substitute. The therapist would explore this by talking to her and trying to gain access to her 'inner thoughts', perhaps by dream analysis or looking out for Freudian slips of the tongue. It would be essential for the therapist to build a strong sense of trust and confidentiality with Alison, so she regarded his office as a safe place. The essential point is that the therapist would be trying to get underneath the surface to see what made her behave the way she did or make her the person she was.

Examiner comment: This is a very good answer. It is always easy to pick fault and comment on things which were not included which could have been. However, we should bear in mind that there are only 8 minutes available for each of these 6-mark questions. This is a full answer, which addresses the dual requirements of methodology and the stimulus material well. It would earn the maximum mark of 6.

(d) Evaluate the use of the method of investigating the subject matter given in (c) above.

The methods of psychoanalysis are untestable and it has been said that Freud had no real evidence for his theory or methods at all. So, for example, what is there to stop the therapist just seeing what he wants to see or putting ideas into Alison's head (false memory syndrome). The methods are very unscientific. All of these problems would make for difficulties in trying to explain Alison's behaviour.

Examiner comment: Sadly, the candidate lets herself down badly here. The answer is significantly shorter than the others, probably because she ran out of time. The other serious shortcoming is that it rarely engages with the stimulus material (contrast it with the other answers). The candidate would earn 2 marks out of 6 here.

The candidate earns a total of 20 or 21 marks, which would probably just earn a grade A.